EVEN THE
SMALLEST CRAB
HAS TEETH

50 YEARS OF AMAZING
PEACE CORPS STORIES

VOLUME FOUR: ASIA AND THE PACIFIC

Edited by

JANE ALBRITTON

Series Editor
JANE ALBRITTON

Travelers' Tales
An Imprint of Solas House, Inc.
Palo Alto

Travelers' Tales and *Solas House* are trademarks of Solas House, Inc. 853 Alma Street, Palo Alto, California 94301. www.travelerstales.com

Cover Design: Chris Richardson
Interior Layout: Howie Severson
Production Director: Susan Brady

Library of Congress Cataloging-in-Publication Data

Even the smallest crab has teeth : 50 years of amazing Peace Corps stories / Edited by Jane Albritton.
     p. cm. -- (Asia and the Pacific ; v. 4)
  Includes bibliographical references and index.
  ISBN 978-1-60952-002-1 (pbk. : alk. paper)
  1. Peace Corps (U.S.) 2. Volunteers--Asia. 3. Volunteers--Pacific Area. 4. Asia--Description and travel. 5. Pacific Area--Description and travel. I. Albritton, Jane.
  HC60.5.E94 2011
  361.6--dc23

               2011033531

First Edition
Printed in the United States
10 9 8 7 6 5 4 3 2 1

To the memory of

Dr. Maurice "Maury" Albertson
and
Pauline Birky-Kreutzer

Who helped get the Peace Corps off to a good start.
Wish you were here.

Table of Contents

Part One
ON OUR WAY...AND BACK AGAIN

Part Two
WHY ARE WE HERE?

Part Four
CLOSE ENCOUNTERS

Part Five
SUSTAINABLE PEACE

Series Preface

THERE ARE SOME BABY IDEAS THAT SEEM TO FLY IN BY STORK, without incubation between conception and birth. These magical bundles smile and say: "Want me?" And well before the head can weigh the merits of taking in the unsummoned arrival, the heart leaps forward and answers, "Yes!"

The idea for Peace Corps @ 50—the anniversary media project for which this series of books is the centerpiece—arrived on my mental doorstep in just this way in 2007. Four books of stories, divided by regions of the world, written by the Peace Corps Volunteers who have lived and worked there. There was time to solicit the stories, launch the website, and locate editors for each book. By 2011, the 50th anniversary of the founding of the Peace Corps, the books would be released.

The website had no sooner gone live when the stories started rolling in. And now, after four years and with a publisher able to see the promise and value of this project, here we are, ready to share more than 200 stories of our encounters with people and places far from home.

In the beginning, I had no idea what to expect from a call for stories. Now, at the other end of this journey, I have read every story, and I know what makes our big collection such a fitting tribute to the Peace Corps experience.

Peace Corps Volunteers write. We write a lot. Most of us need to, because writing is the only chance we have to say things in our native language. Functioning every day in another language takes work, and it isn't just about grammar. It's everything that isn't taught—like when to say what depending on the context, like the intricate system of body language, and like knowing how to shift your tone depending on the company you are in. These struggles and linguistic mishaps can be frustrating and often provoke laughter, even if people are forgiving and appreciate the effort. It takes a long time to earn a sense of belonging.

And so in our quiet moments—when we slip into a private space away from the worlds where we are guests—we write. And in these moments where we treat ourselves to our own language, thoughts flow freely. We once wrote only journals and letters; today we also text, email, and blog.

Writing helps us work through the frustrations of everyday living in cultures where—at first—we do not know the rules or understand the values. In our own language we write out our loneliness, our fury, our joy, and our revelations. Every volunteer who has ever served writes as a personal exercise in coming to terms with an awakening ignorance. And then we write our way through it, making our new worlds part of ourselves in our own language, in our own words.

The stories in these books are the best contribution we can make to the permanent record of Peace Corps on the occasion of its 50th anniversary. And because a Volunteer's attempt to explain the experience has always contained the hope that folks at home will "get it," these stories are also a gift to anyone eager and curious to learn what we learned about living in places that always exceeded what we imagined them to be.

It has been an honor to receive and read these stories. Taken together, they provide a kaleidoscopic view of world cultures—beautiful and strange—that shift and rattle when held up to the light.

I would like to acknowledge personally the more than 200 Return Volunteers who contributed to these four volumes. Without their voices, this project could not have been possible. Additionally, editors Pat and Bernie Alter, Aaron Barlow, and Jay Chen have been tireless in shepherding their stories through the publishing process and in helping me make my way through some vexing terrain along the way. Special thanks to John Coyne whose introduction sets the stage for each volume. Thanks also to Dennis Cordell for his early work on the project.

There are two people critical to the success of this project who were never Peace Corps volunteers, but who instantly grasped the significance of the project: Chris Richardson and Susan Brady.

Chris and his PushIQ team, created a visually lush, technically elegant website that was up and ready to invite contributors to join the project and to herald both the project and the anniversary itself. He took on the creative challenge of designing four distinct covers for the four volumes in this set. His work first invited our contributors and now invites our readers.

Susan Brady brought it all home. It is one thing to collect, edit, and admire four books' worth of stories; it is another to get them organized, to the typesetter, the printer, and the team of marketers on time and looking good. Susan's good sense, extensive publishing experience, and belief in the worthiness of this project sealed the publishing deal with Travelers' Tales/ Solas House.

Finally, there are the two others, one at each elbow, who kept me upright when the making of books made me weary. My mother—intrepid traveler and keeper of stories—died four months after the project launched, but she has been kind enough to hang around to see me through. My partner, cultural anthropologist Kate Browne, never let me forget that if Americans are ever going to have an honored place in this world, we need to have some clue about how the rest of it works. "So get with it," they said. "The 50th anniversary happens only once."

—JANE ALBRITTON
FORT COLLINS, COLORADO

Thirty Days That Built the Peace Corps

JOHN COYNE

In 1961 John F. Kennedy took two risky and conflicting initiatives in the Third World. One was to send 500 additional military advisers into South Vietnam. The other was to send 500 young Americans to teach in the schools and work in the fields of eight developing countries. These were Peace Corps Volunteers. By 1963 there would be 7,000 of them in forty-four countries.

—*Garard T. Rice,* The Bold Experiment: JFK's Peace Corps

KENNEDY'S SECOND INITIATIVE INSPIRED, AND CONTINUES TO inspire, hope and understanding among Americans and the rest of the world. In a very real sense, the Peace Corps is Kennedy's most affirmative and enduring legacy that belongs to a particularly American yearning: the search for a new frontier.

Two key people in Congress, Henry Reuss (D-Wisconsin) and Hubert Humphrey (D-Minnesota), both proposed the idea of the Peace Corps in the late 1950s.

In January of 1960, Reuss introduced the first Peace Corps-type legislation. It sought a study of "the advisability and practicability to the establishment of a Point Four Youth Corps," which would send young Americans willing to serve their country in public and private technical assistance missions in far-off countries, and at a soldier's pay.

The government contract was won by Maurice (Maury) L. Albertson of Colorado State University who with one extraordinary assistant, Pauline Birky-Kreutzer, did the early groundwork for Congress on the whole idea of young Americans going overseas, not to win wars, but help build societies.

In June of 1960, Hubert Humphrey introduced in the Senate a bill to send "young men to assist the peoples of the underdeveloped areas of the world to combat poverty, disease, illiteracy, and hunger."

Also in 1960, several other people were expressing support for such a concept: General James Gavin; Chester Bowles, former governor of Connecticut, and later ambassador to India; William Douglas, associate justice of the Supreme Count; James Reston of *The New York Times;* Milton Shapp, from Philadelphia; Walt Rostow of MIT; and Senator Jacob Javits of New York, who urged Republican presidential candidate Richard Nixon to adopt the idea. Nixon refused. He saw the Peace Corps as just another form of "draft evasion."

What Nixon could not have foreseen was that a "day of destiny" waited for the world on October 14, 1960. On the steps of the Student Union at the University of Michigan, in the darkness of the night, the Peace Corps became more than a dream. Ten thousand students waited for presidential candidate Kennedy until 2 A.M., and they chanted his name as he climbed those steps.

Kennedy launched into an extemporaneous address. He challenged them, asking how many would be prepared to give years of their lives working in Asia, Africa, and Latin America?

The audience went wild. (I know this, because at the time I was a new graduate student over in Kalamazoo. I was working part-time as a news reporter for WKLZ and had gone to cover the event.)

Six days before the 1960 election, on November 2nd, Kennedy gave a speech at the Cow Palace in San Francisco. He pointed out that 70 percent of all new Foreign Service officers had no foreign language skills whatsoever; only three of the forty-four Americans in the embassy in Belgrade spoke Yugoslavian; not a single American in New Delhi could speak Indian dialects, and only two of the nine ambassadors in the Middle East spoke Arabic. Kennedy also pointed out that there were only twenty-six black officers in the entire Foreign Service corps, less than 1 percent.

Kennedy's confidence in proposing a "peace corps" at the end of his campaign was bolstered by news that students in the Big Ten universities and other colleges throughout Michigan had circulated a petition urging the founding of such an organization. The idea had caught fire in something like spontaneous combustion.

The day after his inauguration, President Kennedy telephoned his brother-in-law Sargent Shriver and asked him to form a presidential task force to report how the Peace Corps should be organized and then to organize it. When he heard from Kennedy, Shriver immediately called Harris Wofford.

At the time, Shriver was 44; Wofford was 34. Initially, the Task Force consisted solely of the two men, sitting in a suite of two rooms that they had rented at the Mayflower Hotel in Washington, D.C. They spent most of their time making calls to personal friends they thought might be helpful.

One name led to another: Gordon Boyce, president of the Experiment in International Living; Albert Sims of the Institute of International Education; Adam Yarmolinsky, a foundation executive; Father Theodore Hesburgh, president of the University of Notre Dame; George Carter, a campaign worker on civil rights issues and former member of the American Society for African Culture; Louis Martin, a newspaper editor; Franklin Williams, an organizer of the campaign for black voter registration, and a student of Africa; and Maury Albertson, out at Colorado State University.

Unbeknownst to Shriver and Wofford, two officials in the Far Eastern division of the International Cooperation Administration (ICA) were working on their own Peace Corps plan. Warren Wiggins, who was the deputy director of Far Eastern operations in ICA, was still in his thirties but had already helped administer the Marshall Plan in Western Europe. He was totally dissatisfied with the manner in which American overseas programs were run; he called them "golden ghettos." With Wiggins was Bill Josephson, just 26, and a lawyer at ICA.

They started developing an idea that would be limited to sending young Americans overseas to teach English. But as they worked on it, their vision broadened. The paper detailing their recommendations was titled "A Towering Task." They sent copies to Wofford, Richard Goodwin at the White House, and to Shriver, who thought it was brilliant and immediately sent a telegram to Wiggins inviting him to attend the Task Force meeting the next morning. It was Wiggins who advocated initiating the Peace Corps with "several thousand Americans participating in the first twelve to eighteen months." A slow and cautious beginning was not an option.

Three times in February, Kennedy would telephone Shriver to ask about progress on the Peace Corps. The final draft of the report was created with Charles Nelson sitting in one room writing basic copy, Josephson sitting in another room rewriting it, Wofford sitting in yet another room doing the final rewrite, and Wiggins running back and forth carrying pieces of paper.

Shriver held the position that Peace—not Development, it might be noted—was the overriding purpose, and the process of promoting it was necessarily complex. So the Peace Corps should learn to live with complexity that could not be summed up in a single proposition. Finally, the Task Force agreed on three.

- Goal One: It can contribute to the development of critical countries and regions.
- Goal Two: It can promote international cooperation and goodwill toward this country.
- Goal Three: It can also contribute to the education of America and to more intelligent American participation in the world.

On the morning of Friday, February 24, 1961, Shriver delivered the report—the Peace Corps Magna Carta—to Kennedy and told him: "If you decide to go ahead, we can be in business Monday morning."

It had taken Shriver, Wofford, Wiggins, Josephson, and the other members of the Mayflower Task Force, less than a month to create what *TIME Magazine* would call that year "the greatest single success the Kennedy administration had produced." On March 1, 1961, President Kennedy issued an Executive Order establishing the Peace Corps.

And today, fifty years later, we are still debating what the Peace Corps is all about. As Sarge Shriver thought all those years ago, "the tension between competing purposes is creative, and it should continue."

Well, it has!

John Coyne, who is considered an authority on the history of the Peace Corps, has written or edited over twenty-five books. In 1987 he started the newsletter RPCV Writers & Readers that is for and about Peace Corps writers. This newsletter, now a website, can be found today at PeaceCorpsWorldwide.org.

Introduction

LET'S BEGIN WITH A QUESTION: HOW IS IT POSSIBLE TO COLLECT stories from countries that fit into a scalene triangle set on a map and marked at its angles by Afghanistan, China, and Samoa and then declare them representative of something called Asia and the Pacific? Quite possible, as it turns out. Drop the boundaries of the triangle and look again. Imagine instead that the "region," with a center somewhere in the South China Sea, is defined by sweeping galactic arms of time and culture, arms that can pick up a spice or an idea and drop it—thousands of miles from home—to rest and root, reformed and new.

Over millennia, the trade routes and trade winds in this region have created a massive, gravitationally bound system that has swept together, mixed and re-sorted both the artifacts and living parts of human societies. This gyre that is Asia and the Pacific—starry with dreams of silk, spices, conquest, and transcendence—has forever pulled merchants, pilgrims, soldiers, and nomads into its embrace and sent them on another spiraling round. Peace Corps Volunteers who for the past 50 years have joined the motion could not and cannot help but be transformed in culturally specific ways.

The 54 individual stories in this volume speak for themselves as they recount the personal experiences of Volunteers in the field. But as I have read and reread them over the past four years, each new story adding another bit of light to this galaxy, I have become aware of three constellations that seem especially bright and clear. There are others, but I will speak for these three: language, memories of war, and freedom to operate outside the norms of an established cultural universe. While these same constellations can be spotted in the other regions where Volunteers have served, the view from Asia and the Pacific is uniquely conditioned by particular kinds of philosophical/religious drift, conflict, and cultural flexibility.

Volunteers learn from the first day of training that learning a local language marks the entry to understanding and acceptance. In Asia and the Pacific, most Volunteers do not study a language imposed on the local population by a colonial power (we already know English), but instead must grapple with Farsi, Hindi, Tamil, Thai, Korean, Tagalog, Malay, a Chinese language, or the creole Bislama among others. Unlike Spanish (in The Americas) or French (in West Africa), none of these languages is part of the typical high school curriculum in the U.S. And even in India where English is one of the sixteen languages printed on a rupee note, English-only in the countryside will just get you lost.

Reilly Ridgell directly addresses the need to learn the local language in "Of Love and Language." Howard Daniel ("Earstaches and a Message from Chang Kai-Shek") notes that a Hindi-speaking foreigner gets special access to big events in Central India, and Michael Schmicker is the Thai-speaking *farang* who gets his language lessons in the "Mosquito Bar" in Bangkok. Words in local languages—italicized to indicate their foreignness—pop up in these and many other stories because they are the translation-defying expressions that Volunteers used (and possibly still use) as they went about their daily work and social lives. As Kristine Alaniz points out in her story "*Sloslo Nomo*," the words *sloslo* and *lego* may sound familiar, tied as they are to English pidgin, but they come to her packed with unexpected cultural information from Vanuatu.

The second constellation tells of armed conflict and the living memory of host country nationals. This region knows something of us by our wars: World War II (Pacific theater), the Korean War, the Vietnam War (aka, the American War).

World War II in the Pacific left a mark on the landscape and in the memories of the local people Volunteers came to know. The Escaler family, Dory Blobner's hosts and friends, lived through the Japanese invasion of the Philippines in Bataan, a last stand of American and Filipino soldiers. The family walked on the edges of the Death March, which killed some 10,000 Filipino and 700 American prisoners of war. In "Families," Dory's *Nanay* rounds out the lore that has been chanted into our own documentaries: "We are the battling bastards of Bataan; no mamma, no papa, no Uncle Sam."

In "Mending Tarawa," Jim Russell recounts his experience of playing a softball game with Japanese construction workers on a makeshift field on the island of Tarawa: Bloody Tarawa, where 1,000 Marines and Sailors and 4,819 Japanese soldiers were killed in just three days. Against a backdrop of rusting Japanese big-gun placements, the former enemies played. Many Americans have visited the battlefields of Europe and our well-groomed cemetery in Normandy, France, but not so many can say "I was there" on the island battlefields of the Pacific.

In "Living in the Land of Morning Calm" Karen Boyle risks being shot by Korean policemen because she must go out after curfew to get to the village's one phone to call a doctor. In that war, the effects of which still linger, two million Korean civilians died. No wonder that Boyle's Korean friends feared for her life.

Volunteers who served in Thailand in the 1960s and '70s got a close-up view of the R&R industry that flourished during the Vietnam War. GI's wearing Aloha shirts strolling through the marketplace hand-in-hand with country girls were a common sight. Volunteers like James Jouppi ("A Spillway for Nong Bua"), assigned to engineering jobs in the countryside, experienced the same wariness as their local counterparts. It was hard to tell the difference between a rabbit snare and an explosive tripwire.

The third constellation that shows up in this collection represents the liberation from cultural expectations Volunteers experienced. A hint of this freedom first appears in the Table of Contents. Readers will notice that about the same number of women and men have told their stories here. That's an interesting detail, one which corresponds to the larger reality of a historical balance between women and men Volunteers generally. But the real point is that in the context of the Peace Corps, gender roles lost their power, and Volunteers found the freedom to serve more fully. Jerr Boschee in "And the Light in Their Eyes Would Begin to Die" writes about the deep satisfaction he felt teaching in India. So does Brent Cromley in "A Letter to Sri Padmanabham." As Volunteers, men were free to become superb teachers without their friends and families wondering when they were going to get real jobs.

Karen Dunne in "Her Fijian Father" describes going spear fishing. In Fiji, women do not spearfish (they get to reach into underwater crevices and pull out octopuses), but far out in the Pacific, her host let her try it all. Nor were female Volunteers "protected" from the hardships associated with their assignments. Afghanistan—with its complex social systems and unforgiving physical environment—tested both Frank Light ("Back to School") and the all-female group of smallpox vaccinators ("Taking Out Smallpox") in exactly the same ways: with exhausting work, no comforts, and vexing human interaction.

The breadth of detail recounted in these stories of the third constellation can be traced directly back to an idea that quickened when JFK and Sargent Shriver set up the Peace Corps as the very first U.S. government-sponsored equal opportunity adventure. They—and the others you will meet in John Coyne's Introduction—created an organization that chose its members for their abilities and desire to serve and declined to use race, gender, sexual preference, and age as winnowing tools. We as Peace Corps Volunteers were set free to experience the worries, intestinal distress, little triumphs, and big understandings conditioned by the forces that have shaped Asia and the Pacific. We came home transformed in unique and enduring ways.

Shanti, shanti, shanti. Enjoy the stories.

—JANE ALBRITTON
FORT COLLINS, COLORADO

PART ONE

ON OUR WAY...
AND BACK AGAIN

STEPHEN WELLS

Bound for the Philippines

*Signing up for the Peace Corps was one thing; getting elected
to serve was quite another—often problematic—matter.*

I WATCHED AS ONE BY ONE THE MEMBERS OF MY PEACE CORPS
group, training for the Phillipines, attempted to swim fifty
meters underwater without surfacing. It was a personal challenge we had known about for twenty-four hours preceding
this moment. The idea was to jump off the edge and somer-
sault in the air so we were going backward when we hit the
water. Then we were to turn around in the water, swim the
length of the pool, then back, the head below the water at all
times. One slip, that's it, you failed this test.

My job was to pull trainees out of the water if they lost
consciousness. I was assigned this job by Freddie LaNue, our
bombastic drown-proofing instructor, former swimming coach
at Georgia Tech. One leg deformed and withered from childhood polio, he referred to himself as "The Ramblin' Wreck
from Georgia Tech."

He took the words right out of our mouths.

Freddie assigned me the job because he knew I had been a
competitive swimmer. It was Freddie's idea, in this final week

of our Outward Bound Peace Corps training in Puerto Rico, to escalate the challenges placed before us, the better to achieve character-building objectives.

It was December 1961; we were part of John F. Kennedy's New Frontier, pioneers in this new idea called the Peace Corps. Few of us knew what to expect when we stumbled off the Pan Am flight from New York to San Juan and were trucked away to a rustic jungle wilderness camp near Arecibo. Freddie was completely in character in the Outward Bound camp. He had invented something called "drown-proofing," a simple method of staying afloat in the water without the usual thrashing of arms and legs, conserving energy and avoiding panic while awaiting rescue.

Down-proofing was easy enough for me to master after a lifetime of swimming and four years of intercollegiate swimming competition. But for those with a lifelong fear of water, learning drown-proofing represented the very kind of self-achievement that Outward Bound was created to foster. The rock climbing, camping, trekking, and the infamous obstacle course were designed to leave each of us with a heightened sense of self-confidence. We would feel prepared to take on any challenge that lay before us, just as the young British merchant seamen must have felt in 1941 when they went through the very first Outward Bound training to prepare them for German U-boat attacks.

Water was one of our challenges. Near the end of our twenty-eight days, Freddie tied legs and arms of each trainee, then pushed them into the water to see if they could stay afloat using the drown-proofing techniques he taught us. They did. So he escalated the challenge several notches.

Freddie talked to all of us the day before about this fearsome challenge. He taught the rest of the group members something he called the keyhole stroke for effective underwater swimming. Then he said we could practice, but were not to swim the length of the pool, just across the width and back. You made it when you touched the end you started on. He reinforced the simple rule: come up for a breath for any reason, and that's it. There was no second chance. Period.

Freddie then did some serious confidence building. He explained to us exactly what to do as we swam: look for the lane lines on the bottom of the pool, come in low at the other end—so we would not mistakenly push our heads out of the water—and graze the bottom of the pool as we pushed off the other end.

He told us how we would feel at critical points: "Your stomach will start to throb," and so on. He said he had a lot of experience with watching people in this situation. When we got close to fainting, he could tell; someone would be right there to "pull you out." So not to worry about drowning.

Then he told us about hyperventilating and how to use it. "When your fingers start to tingle, you are ready."

One of my friends, Chip Salmon, was skeptical. Years later, he recalled, "I knew this was going to be near impossible. I was sure there was no way I could possibly make the length. I couldn't even do the width. Others were of the same mind. Freddie had us snookered."

We were still reeling from the drown-proofing lesson conducted in heavy surf on an isolated beach several days earlier. As waves broke, we were thrust violently into underwater currents that left us with sand burns, bruises, and frightened from the disorienting effect of tumbling over and over underwater. Which way is up? This morning we sat on the edge of the pool, our legs dangling in the water, as we listened disbelievingly to what Freddie wanted us to do. We were quiet, up tight and concerned, but determined, too.

Throughout our training, there was always individual pressure to go further, do more, push the envelope. Each of us fortunate trainees was acutely aware that the Damocles sword of "deselection" constantly hung over us. If any one of us was judged to be somehow unfit, inept, unworthy of Peace Corps' high standards, the staff could simply wash us out and send us home on the next plane. It was that simple. No reasons, just here one day and gone the next, ending forever dreams of serving overseas in the Peace Corps.

So we were all under tremendous self-imposed pressure to excel in anything we did, proving our worthiness, digging deep within ourselves to exhibit impressive levels of motivation, attesting to our commitment to be part of John F. Kennedy's New Frontier.

None of us wanted to fail.

And now it was a test of endurance, swimming without breathing until—what? Until you drowned? Passed out? Came up and got a breath, only to be hustled out on the next flight to the mainland? It had finally come down to this one challenge to individual resolve and commitment. The group couldn't help you anymore. It was self-conflict in its purest form, battling instinct for survival against the will to go beyond endurance, to venture into the unknown.

It was symbolic of all we'd volunteered for.

To build the self-confidence of the group, Freddie planned it so the stronger swimmers, those most likely to succeed, went first. I was picked to be the starting swimmer. I dove in without even the slightest feeling of anxiety. When my group saw me go the required two lengths underwater before I surfaced, it did serve as a confidence-builder for the others: Look how easy it seems!

Chip still remembers seeing me underwater and has to laugh. "Grace itself. I believe you completed the down and back in thirty-seven seconds! Unbelievable, and you were not even breathing hard!"

Then four more went in. All five of us completed the course in under a minute. Then it was the skeptical Chip's turn.

"I found Freddie's predictions exactly on and very comforting, so those disconcerting stomach throbs were O.K. I made it! I was delighted!"

Then others went, with us all cheering each other on. The trouble with the underwater swim was that the people needing encouragement and strength from the others couldn't hear underwater. It was silent down there.

Finally we got to the trainees Freddie knew would have a much harder time. He recruited me to be ready to jump in and help anyone who appeared to be in distress.

"Watch their head and the back of their neck very carefully," he instructed me in a whisper, so the others wouldn't overhear. "Just before they pass out, you'll see this involuntary twitch. For a moment you'll see them raise their head slightly in a jerky way. That's the moment when they lose consciousness. That's your sign to jump in and get them."

I watched. Sure enough, for those who didn't decide to finally surface on their own, there was a slight involuntary twitch just as Freddie said there would be. Then they would go limp, arms floating by their sides, head down in the water. When I saw the twitch, I jumped in and grabbed their jaw and led their face to the surface. They emerged sputtering, blinking and choking, but conscious. And breathing.

And still alive.

What went through the minds of each of the underwater swimmers that morning as they fought instinct to surface and gasp to inhale air? I watched as their arm movements got slower and slower, as they meandered off-course while making their way underwater. I watched them become disoriented, slowing to impossible speeds, strokes becoming feeble and uncoordinated, then still. Finally came that little twitch of the head indicating they'd passed out.

Here it was. January 1962, less a year since John Kennedy gave his famous inaugural address stating "Ask not what your country can do for you, ask what you can do for your country," as he appealed to a new generation of Americans to step forward and accept the challenges offered by the Peace Corps. We had, and now my peers were passing out one by one in the pool.

As a group we almost all made it. We didn't disgrace ourselves. Everyone tried hard. And that, after all, was the whole idea: to muster the courage and wherewithal to try, to reach deep within and haul up heroic levels of performance. It was a moment of accomplishment, a new sense of pride and capability, the very thing Outward Bound attempted to impart in each of us. Still, for each of those who passed out underwater, it must have felt like experiencing a little death that day. Later there was grumbling that Freddie had gone too far, taken the challenge thing over the top. Some who had passed out, inhaling water into their lungs, developed congestion, pulmonary infections and, in one case, pneumonia.

After twenty-eight days in Puerto Rico, we were humbled: not so much by malevolent do-or-die boot-camp schemes and challenges to test us, conjured up by demented Outward Bound staff members like Freddie LaNue, Davey Borden, or Al Ferraro. Humbled instead by coming face-to-face with self-imposed limitations we had unwittingly placed upon ourselves—the result of years of comfortable living and predictable lives. Now, faced with adversity in what seemed to be authentic life-or-death situations, we suddenly became acquainted with our flabby self-resolve and unflattering timidity. Then something special and rare had happened, and we were all a part of it.

Saying good-bye was difficult when our Outward Bound training came to an end and it was time to board a flight back to New York. Then off to Penn State for classroom training. We had a clear sense that the camp staff envied us. They would stay behind while we forged a New Frontier in the Philippines.

Postscript: It's a good thing more Volunteers like me didn't chronicle these tests and send accounts off to our Congressmen or the media. One older female trainee did several months later, and the camp was permanently closed.

Steve Wells was a Group III Volunteer in the Philippines, later supervising Volunteers as a Peace Corps volunteer leader. He became an associate Peace Corps director in the Philippines on 1964, finally returning to the US in 1969. A successful private industry career in training, communication and consulting ended with his retirement in 2005. Steve is an avid sailor, sailing his thirty-foot sloop Cygnet *on lengthy Great Lakes cruises to Lake Huron's North Channel.*

PAMELA COHELAN BENSON

✶

Memories from a Battered Box

Memory comes back not as a single tableau, but as images strung on threads of remembrance, moving lightly in time.

A BATTERED BOX IN ONE CORNER OF MY ATTIC CONTAINS AN assortment of items from another world: jars with rusty lids full of sea shells and white sand, fans woven from *buri* leaves, bamboo clothespins, a small pair of slippers made of wood and plastic, a red-flowered remnant of a curtain—all mementos of my two years in a tiny barrio in the Philippines.

I joined the Peace Corps in the summer of 1963, fresh out of college. For three months of training in Hawaii, I studied the Tagalog language; Philippine culture, politics, and current events; and math, science and English teaching methodology. With my fellow trainees, I dug trenches, cut grass for building traditional *nipa* houses, met with staff psychiatrists, hiked to black sand beaches and the erupting Kilauea volcano. When I arrived in the Philippines, another trainee and I were assigned to the barrio of Inaclagan—six hours by bus from Manila on the island of Luzon—a tiny fishing village on the Lamon Bay, across from the island of Alabat.

Following a six-month stay with a local family, we moved into a house on the edge of the barrio, a place some said was haunted with *aswang* (spirits). Our house stood on low pillars made from the trunks of palm trees, had a roof of thatched palm shingles fastened down with bamboo, and faced the island in the distance. Behind the house was a tangle of banana and papaya trees, flowering creepers, and tall, swaying coconut palms. At night, we lay on our cots and listened to the hollow sounds of paddles against wooden outriggers and low voices as men set out across the water for a night of fishing, their lanterns dotting the bay. In the morning, we awoke to roosters crowing, twig brooms sweeping courtyards, and the bread seller calling, *"pan de sal!"* his warm loaves nestled in a basket lined with paper on the front of his bicycle.

Few people in the barrio spoke English, and we had many opportunities to use our Tagalog. Each morning, I traveled by bus to teach in a school ten kilometers away, while my roommate remained to teach in the school in Inaclagan. At the end of the day, we'd return home, prepare a meal, and try to make sense of our life and work in a place that didn't appear on most maps. In retrospect, we alternated between immersing ourselves in the culture and holding it at bay, afraid, I suppose, of losing our identity.

And throughout, we remained intensely curious about our own country and culture. After all, we had left the summer Dr. Martin Luther King, Jr., made his speech on the steps of the Lincoln Memorial, and we had only been in our barrio a few short months when President Kennedy, our inspiration, was assassinated. Some evenings, we could hear the Beatles singing through static on our battery-powered radio. On the weekends, we sometimes prepared an American recipe from our dog-eared paperback cookbook. When our portable oven got too hot, we lifted it off the kerosene burner and set it on the kitchen floor. In this way, we produced many loaves of banana bread and, once, a miraculous lemon soufflé.

If one of us ventured a solitary walk down the beach, we were soon followed by throngs of village children. We quickly learned that the most difficult things we had given up as young women were our independence and privacy. Each morning as I walked to the bus stop, I would hear these questions: *"Sa'an ka pupunta? Sino ang kasama mo?"* (Where are you going? Who is your companion?)

We slept on metal cots draped with mosquito netting carefully tucked around a thin mattress. If an arm or toe touched the netting during the steamy night, we awoke with itchy welts and hoped that the large pink pills we swallowed every Sunday would suppress the possible malaria. A village carpenter had made us a long table and two benches, as well as a bookcase. A hammock hung across one corner, creating a place to catch a breeze, doze, or read a book. We made pillows and covered them in bright fabric to match our red-flowered curtains.

Our water was stored in an empty oil drum in the corner of our kitchen. Every afternoon, a young boy brought us water from the artesian well near the school. The large square cans hung from wires suspended on either end of a bamboo pole he carried over his shoulders. His wide bare feet took quick steps as he moved carefully under the filled-to-the-brim weight. Water dipped with a tin from a bucket provided a shower; when heated, half a bucket washed our dishes; boiled for ten minutes, it made our tea or coffee; stored in an earthenware crock, it became our cool drinking water. We used it carefully, wasting little.

Most of the villagers lived a subsistence existence. A *tindahan* (small store) in the front of the fish-packer's home sold a stock of commonly needed items. Large wide-mouthed jars held candy, cigarettes, aspirin, and band-aids. Small tins of tomato sauce formed pyramids on the back shelf; under the counter rice and sugar were stored, measured, and sold in paper cones made from old newsprint or student copybooks. Bunches of two and three bananas hung across a string above the counter.

One hot, still Sunday afternoon when the tide had been sucked out and the village dozed, we noticed two figures on the reef, collecting snails and other sea creatures trapped in tidal pools. We made our way across the slippery rocks to where they were—a woman with long gray hair and a young boy. We did not know them. The woman smiled, revealing stained teeth, and gestured to their basket of delicacies. In the evening, the boy appeared at our door holding an enamel cup covered with a cracked saucer. It contained a delicious seafood soup for our supper, made from the afternoon's harvest. The generosity and kindness of our barrio knew no bounds, and this act of kindness from strangers who had so little became a symbol we would not forget.

For two years we lived in Barrio Inaclagan, Quezon, Philippines, sharing the joys as well as the sorrows of the lives of those around us. Together with our counterparts, we planned lessons, attended in-service training sessions, and once demonstrated how to make a model of the solar system using local limes. We talked endlessly about questions of teaching and learning. By far the most important lesson I learned as a young Peace Corps teacher collaborating with a counterpart in a Philippines classroom was that if you're not taking pleasure in your work and your students aren't looking forward to your class, your effectiveness as an educator is questionable.

"The sky is sharply orange...I wonder with what significance I will remember these nights and dawns," I wrote in my journal a few weeks before my departure in the summer of 1965.

My answer is that, like so many others, I was changed forever by my life and work in the Philippines. I married a Volunteer I met in India as I traveled home, and we lived and worked abroad for the next twenty-five years. Our children grew up listening to our Peace Corps stories, and our daughter joined the Peace Corps herself and served in Nepal. She married a returned Peace Corps Volunteer from Romania and traveled with him on assignments to Peace Corps/Ukraine and Albania. More than forty years after my service, I returned to Peace Corps to work in support of programs in the Europe, Mediterranean, and Asia regions.

When our service in the Philippines was at an end, my roommate and I gave away all our possessions—books, clothes, furniture, kitchen utensils—and filled our trunks with mementos that spoke of a much simpler life. She went on to make her life in Sweden, and we do not see each other often. When we do, we easily pick up where we left off. She is an important piece in my life's puzzle, for she knew me when I first tried my wings in a place far from home and family.

I have a wrinkled photo of our house. Several years after we left, it was blown away in a typhoon. Flowering vines must now weave over the old foundation and local children surely tell stories of the *aswang* that inhabit the place.

Pamela Cohelan Benson served in Philippines 10, from 1963-65. She is currently a country desk officer at Peace Corps headquarters and is steeped in Peace Corps lore. Aside from being related to multiple PCVs, she is the daughter of Jeffery Cohelan, a U.S. Congressman from California, who was a vocal supporter of the original authorization of the Peace Corps.

* ★ *

Back to School

There was a time in Afghanistan when bandits were the greatest danger and a friend made a suitable escort through a dark night.

IF YOU WORKED FOR THE U.S. GOVERNMENT IN EASTERN Afghanistan in 2003, any trip in a vehicle required two American soldiers and two Afghan guards. Double that and double the vehicles if you went out of Jalalabad, where we had a small base—some forty soldiers—to deal with three provinces. We couldn't begin to cover it all. So when one of our two four-man Civil Affairs Teams—CATs, the military called them—set out for the Sur Khrod valley south and west of town, it seemed a good idea for me, the State Department's representative and the only unarmed U.S. government employee east of Kabul, to go along for a look-see. True, my motives were more personal that professional. But one can feed the other. Unlike other Americans thereabouts, I had some experience in the area. Admittedly, it happened a long time ago. Not all of it was pleasant. I'd call it mixed, in some ways even premonitory, though I didn't know that at the time.

My first year in the Peace Corps, I taught English as a foreign language at Faqrullah Lycee on the outskirts of Sultan Por village in the Sur Khrod. It was a hard sell. The students could not envision a future in which they would ever use the language, though it was a required subject from seventh through twelfth grade, and the culture permitted, in some ways encouraged, passing courses through cheating if you had a friend (helping the less fortunate), bribery if you had the wherewithal, or threats if you had neither. The merit system was as foreign as the subject. Going to school got you off the farm for the morning. You learned a little. You socialized a lot. Rules to the contrary, most came armed.

I think both the Afghan and U.S. governments just wanted Americans in the provinces. It didn't matter so much what we did. Not really tripwires, we served as reminders of U.S. interest in Afghanistan's nonalignment.

Near the end of the year, a twelfth grader who never got past "hello" in English pointed a pistol at me after class to emphasize his desire to succeed. Any Volunteer worth his salt would see in this an opportunity to help the student reassess his approach to life's challenges. Call it cross-cultural jujitsu. You had to be quick on your feet, and you had to leverage not only guidance received, but also that which was better left unsaid. For example, the subject of guns never occurred in training. We were the *Peace* Corps.

The student looked at me and then at the pistol to accentuate the connection. Around the school he was known as a *badmash,* which translates as *badass.* His mustache added to the effect. It was even bushier than mine. He had on his best black shirt.

"You help me," he said in Pashtu.

Thinking maybe I wasn't cut out for the pedagogical life, let alone two years in the Peace Corps, I grabbed that black shirt and slammed the young man in it against the schoolhouse wall. That surprised him. It surprised me. The students knew I wasn't the impetuous type, nor was I brave or pugnacious.

But in those halcyon days, foreign status provided an invisible shield, and I guess my body just got ahead of my mouth. At a loss for words, I was overcome by the compulsion to communicate in a language he was sure to understand.

His classmates gathered to gawk. All were male, ages twelve to twenty-something. The girls' school went only as far as sixth grade.

My black-shirted charge sneered and strutted away, the pistol back in his trouser pocket. Although he failed English, he had what it took to develop into a hero of the resistance. Or a bandit. Or Taliban. A man with gumption could aspire to all three.

Although the CAT hadn't heard of Faqrullah, I knew the school still existed. The current governor had studied there, and at our first meeting we tried to determine if he had been a student of mine. We thought not. He remembered one of my predecessors, caught in *flagrante delicto* with a Western woman in a cave. Or was that me? he asked with an impish smile.

It's not the same, he warned. The old schoolhouse had been destroyed by the Soviets or in the fighting after the Soviets left, depending on whom you talked to. A German NGO had built a replacement that was already showing its age.

Some things hadn't changed. The brick kilns where our two Toyota Hilux pickups turned off the highway still sent plumes of black smoke over the road, which despite a few gravel patches remained as rough and rutted as ever. Many of the buildings along the route seemed different, or new, though I couldn't say how. Nondescript then, nondescript now. Jouncing along in the Hilux cab, I wished I had kept up with the students and faculty. The new school stood right where the old one had been. It looked flimsy, as though the lesson learned from its predecessor's destruction was "don't bother building anything to last." Indeed, a caretaker sauntered out from the village to show us cracks and misalignments in the foundation and ceiling. In the winter the roof leaked, he complained. They had no heat. I should come out then and see. Then I would see why they needed a bridge.

The governor had mentioned that. It would span Sur Khrod stream, which ran between the school and Black Mountain. The previous CAT had proposed it, and this CAT had been out to take a look. It was doable, they said. They just didn't know if it was worth it. Highway 1 crossed the stream about eight miles north. That was too far, the Governor had argued. Students who lived on the west bank couldn't make it to class when it rained.

I told him I didn't recall that being a problem.

It's dangerous, he insisted. There were no roads to speak of on the far bank. The police couldn't get there. The farmers couldn't sell their crops.

Does it rain that much? I asked. Drought was the problem, then as now. That's why I left teaching to do food-for-work.

It rains in the mountains, he explained. Or snows.

Given that in the valley, anyway, there had been no rain for months, the school smelled surprisingly musty. When I thought about it, however, I remembered the school always smelled like that. The classrooms were empty. As I feared, the students were off that day, the second anniversary of Massoud's assassination.

It felt strange, eerie almost, to stand on ground I'd last trod thirty-two years before. The new, decrepit building looked familiar. *Recognizable* is the word. Same size and layout, with a dim, dusty hallway down the middle. No electricity then, none now, even though the Soviet-built Derunta dam and hydroelectric power plant wasn't ten miles distant. At least a well had been sunk out front.

"Dry," the caretaker said.

In a change for the worse, students no longer had desks as they did when I taught there, though they had to share. Each classroom had a blackboard, no erasers, bring your own chalk. I once brought a film, with projector and generator the Embassy provided to prove Americans had landed on the moon. Few believed it. We hung the sheet in the middle of the one, long hallway. Half saw it from one side, half from the other.

As I recall, the astronauts' movie camera failed, so the film relied on stills and re-creations. The students howled with derision. The hokey presentation confirmed for them this was all propaganda, an empty boast.

Apart from the soldiers who helicoptered in one day to end a student strike, the only government delegation my year there arrived in the guise of a malaria team from the Department of Public Health. I found them on the front steps, where the light was good, pricking each student's finger and putting the blood on glass slides along with the student's name. They were going to take the slides to a lab in Jalalabad and then return with the results.

"Will you give medicine?" I asked.

They smiled. In Afghanistan, they explained, people buy their own.

"Is that your only pricker?" I just realized what they were doing.

The smiles faded.

"Once you get a kid with malaria," I blurted, "you'll give it to everyone who follows."

"It's what we have."

"Same for hepatitis."

"We're not testing for that."

"Please stop."

They shrugged and kept on. "The government has a program," they explained.

The students in earshot didn't know what to think.

I went to the principal, and he sent them away after a long discussion. The team never came back, at least not the year I was around.

So many from that time are gone now, to disease, violence, or a new life in Pakistan. I'm lucky, I know, lucky to have been born American.

"Do they still teach English?" I asked the caretaker.

He looked at me funny.

My Pashtu wasn't what it used to be. Only the CAT's interpreter understood. And his first language was Dari, not Pashtu. He translated.

We should ask the principal, the caretaker replied. In contrast to the old days, nobody joined us. Villagers watched from a distance. I don't think they were scared, or hostile. Wary, perhaps, and wondering if they were welcome.

"Is he around?" I asked.

The caretaker shrugged in a way that meant "no". He stood ready to talk. Stay for tea, a walk by the river, dinner at the khan's place: history and memories would begin to tease out.

But we had to run. The CAT was anxious to get to a nearby village to settle on a site for a well. The previous team had proposed it, and unfinished business kept showing up the wrong color on the spreadsheets at the daily briefing. The recommended site had turned out to be private property. A rich man would get richer. The fallback was at the west end of the village. But men from the east end didn't want their women walking by prying eyes for their water.

Driving through what was left of a former king's winter gardens, we got lost despite our GPS, and then we had to hike for a couple kilometers after the road narrowed to a hard-baked path that led past high and then low walls on through farm fields where not much grew or grazed. Trees were few; I was glad for my sun hat. Finally we came to a leafy shelter, where elders sat on a rope bed as though they had been expecting us. That would have been a breach in our operational security. Anything's possible, the CAT captain conceded; but they were sitting in that same place the last time the team was here.

We chatted while waiting for the tea that facilitated serious discussion. The Karzai government was good, the elders said when I asked, because it brought in donors like us. No donors helped the Taliban, whose leaders came from Kandahar. Or Pakistan. Nobody local.

I brought up Faqrullah.

They looked at me blankly.

An NGO built that, I reminded them. It must have been when the Taliban were here.

The elders dismissed it as a replacement. They were looking for something new. This was their sixth year of drought. Refugees wouldn't return because the springs had dried and the old irrigation systems no longer worked.

Food-for-work taught me the importance of self-help. The CATs believed in it, too. People were more likely to value and maintain a project if they contributed to its construction. Something for nothing never lasted. In practice, however, self-help was management-intensive, and the CATs were spread thin. Headquarters demanded results: wells dug, clinics built, villages assessed. A bureaucracy as large and task-oriented as the Army was always trying to quantify progress.

So we listened to accounts of mice falling into the well despite every effort to keep them out. People were getting sick. Poor and getting poorer. A new well with a tight cover open to all in a central location would solve a lot of problems. Maybe one in the east, another in the west. A sergeant told them two was one too many when other villages had no new wells at all.

Elders and neighbors came by to make their views heard. The eldest of all suggested digging by the mosque. Others noted the existing well there had gone dry. Dig it deeper, the eldest cried. We hit *rocks*, the others cried even louder. *Big* rocks.

Democracy, Afghan-style.

As my mind drifted, it occurred to me that I had gone to a wedding celebration in the hamlet we visited that day. The other English teacher's brother was the groom, and, this being Afghanistan, I never met the bride. I remember we men devouring in a few, furious minutes a meal that must have taken the women all day to prepare. And I remember being advised not to ride my bike back to Jalalabad. It was too late in the day. When I persisted, a teacher named Salim pressed a pistol into my hand.

No need, I said.

The Peace Corps had rules against that. Besides, I didn't know enough of the language or culture to employ it judiciously.

Bandits, he warned.

Who are these bandits? I asked in exasperation. You were always hearing about them. They were like the bogeyman, everywhere and nowhere. Do they come from Pakistan? I gestured toward the White Mountains behind him and Black Mountain at my back. Kabul?

My ignorance amused him. His arms reached wide. "Mr. Light, they are *us*." Two men had been killed on that road in the last year, he added, and an American had been robbed.

"What American?" I asked. "Was it my predecessor?"

He didn't know.

The pistol jammed when he showed me how to use it. He put it on the ground and tried to clear it with the heel of his sandal. The barrel jerked this way and that.

"*No!*" the principal called. He and his coterie hurried over. Eventually they cleared it, trying hard not to point the barrel at their foreign guest and apologizing when they did, all of us laughing with embarrassment and because nothing happened. Maybe it wouldn't fire no matter what. Since I insisted on leaving without it, they decided Salim should take it and ride with me as far as the main road. And they gave me a kerosene lantern to hang from the handlebar. It emitted just enough light to make us a target. I blew it out as soon as we got out of their sight.

Halfway to the main road, gunfire broke out in front of us. We dove into the irrigation ditch beside the road. Fortunately it was dry. More gunfire followed. Although we heard no pings, cracks, or whizzes to indicate it was directed at us, we saw flashes through trees near a building—a house, perhaps—about 100 meters ahead. No lights or other sign of life. The road was deserted. We pulled our bikes into the ditch. After five minutes of nothing happening, we crawled, dragging our bikes with us, then walked in the direction from which we had ridden until we came across two guys working on a broken jeep.

I relit the lantern, and they were grateful for the light. They had heard the shots. Both shrugged when I asked the cause. They and Salim exchanged tolerant smiles. I had a pack of cigarettes to share. After a while two other guys came along on bicycles. Salim and I rode with them as far as the main road. No shots, no lights, nothing happened. Salim went back by himself, with pistol and lantern. Don't worry, Mr. Light, he said, a cheerful lilt to his voice. Everybody knows me.

I was thinking about that evening, not really caring where the well went, when a large explosion boomed from the other side of a nearby knoll. The elders were unfazed, a good sign or a good act—they smiled, they shrugged, they implored us to stay until we talked it out—but the soldiers had orders to evacuate whenever anything like that happened.

We walked back the way we had come, just faster. The elders would have more time to decide on a site. Democracy took time, and tradition required it. We were not able to ascertain the cause of the explosion. Best guess was Afghan deminers. Employed by Western NGOs, they had their work cut out for them.

On the ride out I had this idea that talking to the kids and teachers at Faqrullah, even if I didn't know a soul, would help validate the year I had spent there. That black-shirted student had crossed the line. So had I, from the opposite direction. It was a line in the sand, as things turned out. The winds of change had erased it.

A couple of months after that, the new principal accepted an invitation to my farewell dinner in Jalalabad. Before we sat down, he said some former students remembered me. They wanted me to return for a visit. I secretly hoped one of them might get a chance to say I had made a difference. But that was delusional. The Soviets made a difference.

Frank Light served in Afghanistan from 1970-72, first as an English teacher, then with the food-for-work program. He met his wife on the head of the Buddha that the Taliban later blew up. He and his wife are both retired from careers in the U.S. Department of State.

NOTE: The opinions and characterizations in this story are those of the author and do not necessarily represent official positions of the United States Government.

TINA MARTIN

God, President Kennedy, and Me

Negotiating with God might work. But how? When? God only knows.

I REMEMBER WHAT I WAS DOING ON NOVEMBER 22, 1963, NOT only at the time I heard that President Kennedy had been assassinated, but also in the days *before* it happened. Praying. Not just because I was chairman of Religious Emphasis Week at Columbia High School, but because there was a beauty contest that night and, if it were God's will, I was willing to win it. So I kept checking in with God, letting Him know that He was on my mind, and I sure hoped I was on His. I didn't want Him to fix the contest. That wouldn't be fair. I just wanted Him to help me do justice to whatever God-given beauty I might have so that I could honor the Future Teachers of America Club I was representing and serve as a good example for whoever needed one.

"Dear God," I whispered, "tonight's the night. If it be Thy will for me to wear the crown of Miss Columbian, Thy will be done, and"—I added with special emphasis—"I'll give my first summer paycheck to CARE and the NAACP."

Living in the South in 1964, I was (1) in the habit of praying in and out of school, and (2) in—and out of—beauty
contests. We had them for everything, and at the urging of my
prettier and older sister, Dana, who won the Miss Columbian
Contest when she was only a sophomore, I'd decided to work
on being prettier than me, if not prettier than her, and carrying
on the family tradition of winning, even though it couldn't be
in my sophomore year. I was a senior. Last chance.

People sometimes told me that I looked like Natalie Wood,
but Dana looked like Elizabeth Taylor. She had the same oval
face, perfect nose and teeth, same-shaped eyebrows. Dana's hair
was really medium brown, but she was not about to be medium
anything, so she'd started dying it jet black like Elizabeth Taylor
in *Raintree County* in 1957, the year people started noticing the
similarity. She'd also been dressing pretty much like Elizabeth
Taylor in *Raintree County*. Not that she wore bonnets or anything. But when other girls were wearing matching cashmere
sweaters and straight skirts, she was wearing full skirts and lots
of crinolines more reminiscent of the War Between the States,
as Southerners called the Civil War back then.

In our family, we called the War Between the States the
Civil War because, as my friend Sara cautioned people when
she introduced me, "Tina's not from here." That's why I was
bribing God with my summer wages, promising to give my
first paycheck to CARE and NAACP, which my Southern
friends dismissed as Communist and against State's Rights. I
thought my parents knew better than my peers because they
were much older, closer to God's age.

To help along bribe-induced divine intervention, Dana was
going to come back to Columbia from Winthrop College in
Greenville to help me win the contest. She knew just how to
get my hair to look like Jackie Kennedy's, and I knew I was
lucky that she was doing this for me. But I wasn't counting on

luck or Dana. I was counting on God, which was why I was praying more than usual that day.

"Please, dear God, if it be Thy will." The minimum wage had gone up to $1.15 an hour, and I would give all my first paycheck to these good causes if God would support *my* cause and let me win the crown. Of course, other girls prayed. This was the South, after all. But their prayers were shallow. Mine had depth because *I* had a social conscience. That was one of my advantages in the beauty contest. I had a better idea, I thought, of what God wanted, though it never occurred to me that He would want Negroes in the contest. Of course, there weren't any Negroes at our school.

"It's been a decade since Brown vs. Kansas," my mother would say, "and there's not a face that isn't white at that school."

"Or at any other," I'd say. I knew that Columbia High School was no more prejudiced than any of the others. Most southerners thought the Supreme Court had been infiltrated by communists, and the government was going to take over and destroy our way of life. People in South Carolina were saying that President Kennedy and his brother had already gone to Mississippi and Alabama totally disregarding State's Rights, and they'd probably be coming here, but until they did, it was going to be Separate But Equal. Separate water fountains. Separate parts of the bus. Separate schools and, of course, separate beauty contests for the whites and the coloreds, if they had beauty contests.

I knew even back then that "whites and coloreds" sounded like socks. Black was not yet beautiful. But that night I would try to be. Though I occasionally tried to rise above such petty aspirations, that night, with God's help, I would achieve them. Once I'd gotten being beautiful out of my system, I assured God and myself, I could spend my time praying for the outcast. I knew beauty was but skin deep, but tonight skin deep got crowned. Skin deep got a dozen long-stemmed roses. And most importantly, skin deep got two full pages in our high school yearbook.

I realize now that I didn't really have to win that contest to take up more than my share of space in the high school yearbook. Since entering high school I had excelled. I'd been a dismal failure in junior high school, where I'd gotten a bad reputation for wearing red lipstick the first semester of seventh grade when all the good girls waited till the second semester and started with pink, not red. But Dana had told me that I needed color, so my bad reputation was her fault, and maybe also the fault of Nancy Todd, whose brother I'd let kiss me when I was working on a science project at her house, and she'd told people that *I'd kissed back!* People thought I was fast and cheap, but I never "went all the way" or even half of the way with Greg. We never even went steady. Greg was a local boy, and I was holding out for a foreigner, like Jean-Paul, the French exchange student at Dreher High. Foreigners were my idols. I regarded them as celebrities.

In fact, I had a fantasy of marrying three foreigners—a Chinaman, a Frenchman, and a Mexican—and having a baby with each one. Then the children and I would travel around and spend four months in China learning Chinese and the Chinese culture, four months in France learning French and the French culture, and four months in Mexico, et cetera. That had been my fantasy until President Kennedy introduced the idea of the Peace Corps, a cross-culture dream that could come true.

The point, though, is that I had a bad reputation in junior high, so in high school I'd over-compensated. I'd learned that success consisted of being like everybody else, only *better*, and God willing, *prettier*. I'd learned how not to be weird, not to look too eager. I'd learned how not to dress. I'd learned when to help others and when to help myself. I'd read Dale

Carnegie's *How to Win Friends and Influence People* at Myrtle
Beach the summer before I began high school, and I'd begun
my negotiations with God.

Gradually I'd become socially acceptable—even decent. I
was DAR Girl and Chairman of Religious Emphasis Week. I'd
accumulated awards and been elected to school offices. Now I
was a member of Executive Council and the Editor of the literary yearbook, *The Rebel*. This was a big turn-about for a girl
who'd been nominated for an office only once in junior high
school, and that for Homeroom Coupon Chairman. I'd lost.

But now in my senior year of high school, I was president
of two clubs, including Future Teachers of America, which
was sponsoring me in the beauty contest that night. If I won, it
would be a boon to American education. But I have to admit:
it wasn't just for that that I wanted to win. I wanted to win so
that I'd have a permanent record of how I was before I started
to grow old. Dana always said that from the age of sixteen, we
start to die a little bit every year. I wanted a two-page spread
of how I was before I started to wither and wilt.

Before I left for school that morning, I caught my mom
reading when she was supposed to be working on my dress.

"What's the *Feminine Mystic* about?" I'd asked her.

"It's *Feminine Mystique*," she'd corrected me. "It's all about
the sacred feminine ideal."

I'd nodded. I had a sacred feminine ideal: God willing, I'd
be the prettiest girl of all—please, dear God, just for one night.
If mother ever finished the dress! Mother put down her book
and told me to try on what she'd done so far.

My gown was long and straight—something like the one
Jackie had worn when she'd gone to France with President
Kennedy and he'd introduced himself as "the man who
accompanied Jacqueline Kennedy to Paris." Jackie had spoken
French with DeGaulle. Someday I'd know French, too. I'd

join the Peace Corps right after I finished college, and I'd go to some French-speaking country and learn French while I did good deeds.

"Are you sure this is going to be ready by tonight?" I asked her.

"Don't worry. It'll be ready," Mother said through the pins between her front teeth.

"Please God, please," I prayed silently. "Let it be ready by tonight. Help Mother *focus*."

There were few occasions when I didn't turn to God, and I prayed silently all the way to school. After our classroom prayer during homeroom period, I added my own silent P.S. "If it be Thy will…"

People came by me at my hall monitor post, and a lot of them said, "Good luck tonight." I looked back at them quizzically, as if the beauty contest were the furthest thing from my mind.

"Why don't you get your hair fixed like Laura Petrie on *The Dick Van Dyke Show*?" someone asked. "You already look a little bit like her."

"But it wouldn't be right to *copy* her," I said, and I shrugged. "I just have to be myself."

And my *self* was going to be Jackie Kennedy. Dick Van Dyke was cute, but I wasn't settling for *him*. I was going to be the President's Wife.

I walked by the auditorium where we'd be having the contest in just a few more hours. Tonight we'd hold crescent-shaped cards bearing our numbers, and "Moon River" would play as we walked across the stage—the same stage where Strom Thurmond had stood while getting a standing ovation earlier in my high school career. I had stood and applauded, too, because even though I disagreed with everything Strom Thurmond stood for, I didn't want to stand out by not standing. I knew

I would probably not have made President Kennedy' *Profiles in Courage*, but how many of the men in that book had been rejected for Homeroom Coupon Chairman? I didn't want to alienate my Southern friends, and I knew their fears.

I don't remember any of my morning classes; I assume I prayed my way through them. But I do remember Miss Pearlstine's Problems of American Democracy class after lunch that day because that was when the news came.

Miss Pearlstine was my favorite teacher. She was the sponsor of the International Relations Club, of which I was president. She was one of the few people outside my family who was enthusiastic about my plans to join the Peace Corps as soon as I finished college, culminating a five-year plan that only *began* with tonight's beauty contest.

Miss Pearlstine was the only Jew at our school. As chairman of Religious Emphasis Week, I thought of her and suggested that we drop the "in Jesus Christ we pray" part of our prayers so she wouldn't feel left out. But Miss Webb, the sponsor of Religious Emphasis Week, said, "I'm sure she doesn't mind if we pray our way when there are so many of us and so few of her."

Close to the beginning of our 1:15 class, Mrs. Lindler, a math teacher who had an Algebra by TV class, came to the door.

"You know what?" she said. "They interrupted our Algebra lesson for a news bulletin. There's been some shooting around President Kennedy's motorcade in Dallas."

"Oh, how awful!" Miss Pearlstine said. "I hope nobody's been hurt."

I dropped God a quick line.

"Dear God, let everyone be all right."

But I felt sure that no one had been hurt—not seriously, if at all. I was so certain that President Kennedy was all right that I felt foolish wasting my prayers—prayers that should be directed towars the less certain outcome of the night's beauty pageant.

We went back to our lesson about voting precincts. And then the principal came over the PA system.

"President Kennedy has been shot," he said. "We have not yet received word on whether or not the shot was fatal."

Fatal? Of course the shot hadn't been fatal. Why was Mr. Kirkley being so melodramatic? Presidents didn't get assassinated. Not in our country. Maybe he'd been shot *at*. I could picture him in a Dallas clinic now, charming the staff as nurses bandaged a nicked shoulder.

"I had hoped for a twenty-gun salute," he might say, "but not directed *at* me."

That night I was going to look like his wife. The time he took her to Paris.

A few minutes later Mr. Kirkely came over the PA system again.

"May I have your attention please?"

He had our attention.

"President Kennedy is dead."

There were cries and gasps of disbelief. Jeanne Thigpen began to cry. I turned to her.

"It's not true," I told her. "I know it's not true."

A couple of students cheered.

"He asked for it," Sam Davidson said. "He was practically becoming a dictator."

"I think he was a good president," Miss Pearlstine and I said in unison. *Was?*

"This proves that God didn't want a Catholic president," Sam continued.

"Oh, shut up!" I said. And then I remembered my responsibility as a possible future Miss Columbian, and I added, "Please."

I still couldn't believe that President Kennedy was dead. Reporters made mistakes. They were almost always wrong about the weather.

"Dear God," I prayed silently. "Let President Kennedy really be alive. Make this news a false report, and I will give up being Miss Columbian."

I paused for a moment. I knew I had to go further still.

"I'll even give up being among the finalists," I added silently.

In sync with my prayers, Mr. Kirkley continued.

"There have been some questions about tonight's beauty contest. If this were a frivolous affair, we would cancel it. But it's been planned for a long time, and the publication of the yearbook depends on the money we raise tonight. So the contest will go on as planned."

I convinced myself—sort of—that since I was representing the Future Teachers of America Club, it was my duty to participate in the contest. I decided I would go on, but I wouldn't smile—not unless the news was false and Kennedy was really still alive. Then I would go on and I would smile but, in keeping with my vow to God, I wouldn't win. I wouldn't even be among the finalists.

It was while Dana was teasing my hair to make it look like Jackie's that we received a phone call from the school secretary.

"Some of the judges don't feel like coming," the secretary said. "So the beauty contest will have to be postponed."

Mother stopped working on my dress, and Dana stopped working on my hair, and we all sat down in front of the TV and watched a disheveled Jacqueline Kennedy stand beside Lyndon Johnson as he was sworn in as our next president. She had a dark smear on her dress, and even though we didn't have a colored television, we knew it was blood. She'd taken his head in her lap, and then she'd crawled over the open limousine to get help.

"Now you look more like her than she does," Dana told me.

We spent the weekend right there in the living room, watching all the Kennedys. Caroline, who'd once come to her father's press conference in her mother's high-heeled shoes, was now crying as she held her mother's hand. John John, sometimes photographed romping around in his father's office, was now saluting our dead president's flag-draped coffin. But the biggest change was in what they were saying about Jacqueline Kennedy. No one was talking about her sable underwear or who had designed the dress she was wearing or how much it had cost. All anyone noticed about her dress was that it wasn't the pink suit with the bloodstains on it. It was all black. A black mantilla replaced the pillbox hat. They were using words like courage and dignity. Everything had changed, and I knew I had, too.

As Dana was getting ready to drive back to Winthrop, she said, "I came home for nothing."

"Well, you were here to watch President Kennedy's funeral with us," I said.

"But that's not something only I could do," she replied, as if she were a fairy godmother without a mission. "Well, when they reschedule the beauty contest, let me know the new date, and I'll see if I can come up."

"Thank you, Dana," I said, "But I'm not sure I have my heart in things like beauty contests anymore."

"Oh, that's right. Now all you care about is the Highest Possible Moral Standards Award."

On Monday morning, Mr. Kirkely came over the PA system once again. He gave us the new date for the beauty contest.

"And now, let's have a moment of silent prayer," he said, "for our country and in memory of President Kennedy."

That's when I realized that in spite of what had happened, I still cared about the contest, and even though my silent prayer was all about Kennedy and his family and the nation (I was, after all, DAR Girl), I had to add a little P.S. about the contest. I was too ashamed to ask God to help me win it, with President Kennedy up there within earshot. Still, I had to ask God for something. It was my tradition.

"Dear God," I told Him silently, "I guess, the way we left it, I could ask You to help me win this contest because I only offered not to win if Kennedy didn't die. But, even though we're back where we began, I'd like to move forward and do something to honor Kennedy." I didn't mention anything about meeting foreign men and seeing foreign lands and learning foreign languages. I didn't want God to think I had ulterior motives.

"When the time comes and I've finished Winthrop College and have my B.A. in English, could you and President Kennedy help me get into the Peace Corps?"

When the time came, God and President Kennedy got me in.

Tina Martin (Tonga 1969-71) applied to the Peace Corps, specifying any French- or Spanish-speaking country, and was sent to Tonga, where they speak a Polynesian language in no way related to French or Spanish. She teaches ESL students at City College of San Francisco. Her other writings include 28 Peace Corps journals, three plays, three novels, and numerous short stories which she keeps in a trunk for her son to inherit. Two stories "Crash Course in Spanish: Getting Robbed in Chile" and "An Algerian Wedding" appear in I Should Have Just Stayed Home *and* I Should Have Gone Home.

BONNIE   HARRIS   MCKENNA

*

Far Away Places

A glimpse of adventure on an old black-and-white TV and the words of three popular songs were the start of a lifetime of travel.

WHILE VISITING A FELLOW THAILAND II FRIEND IN OAKLAND, many years after our service, I went to her writer's club. To encourage participation, the group leader gave the members several prompts to focus a story on. We had only twenty-five minutes to think of something and then write a story.

The prompt I chose that afternoon was *song.*

When I was growing up in Southern California and television was a new phenomenon, travelogues kept us all glued to the tiny screen. One was a series of films shot by Martin and Osa Johnson. I cannot recall the title of the series, but I was an avid fan. Martin was a pioneer in filming adventure. Together the Johnsons flew and sailed to the South Pacific and Africa long before it was commonplace. Their adventures exposed this little six-year-old girl to the world, and I knew that I would see that world someday. I was not sure how, but I knew it would happen.

There are songs that also crept into my dreams. I am sure songwriters hope their songs resonate in other people's souls.

One stanza from "You Belong to Me," a pop ballad from the 1950s, and two other songs have found their way into my life and have guided my dreams since I first heard them.

The verse from "You Belong to Me," that always seems to fit, goes like this:

Fly the ocean in a silver plane
See the jungle when it's wet with rain
Just remember till you're home again
You belong to me

For a young child growing up in a children's home, that song took me away and into the sky. That is not to say I had a miserable time, quite the contrary; I believe I succeeded because of the way I grew up.

The song "Far Away Places" has stood by me the longest, and little did I realize that the words had more significance than I could foresee.

Far away places with strange-soundin' names
Far away over the sea
Those far away places with the strange-soundin' names
Are callin', callin' me

The other important song in my life has been "Moon River." The lyrics, *Moon River, wider than a mile*, to me, meant the world's oceans. The meaning of the words, *I'm crossing you in style someday; Oh, dream maker, you heart breaker, wherever you're going, I'm going your way*, did not reveal itself immediately. I had to wait until I was in college.

I was sitting in my German class when the teacher read the daily school bulletin, "The kiddy corps is holding placement exams at the Pasadena City Hall this Saturday." At that moment, in my mind I heard Patti Page singing, *Fly the ocean in a silver plane, see the jungle when it's wet with rain*. I knew I had to go to Pasadena to take the test.

The application asked if I had a country of preference. How could I have a preference? I had never been further out of the country than Tijuana.

Days passed; maybe it was weeks. Then the letter finally arrived inviting me to join a group training to go to Thailand. Destiny was revealing itself. Within six months, I was in that silver plane flying over jungles wet with rain. The pyramids mentioned in that song would come later.

After returning home and trying to readjust from Peace Corps life, I read in the *L.A. Times* that Continental Airlines was hiring flight attendants. I could not get to the interview fast enough, and now years later I can say I have crossed that river "wider than a mile," seen the "pyramids along the Nile," and have done it all "in style."

I will never have a chance to thank Martin and Osa Johnson for the seeds they planted in that six-year old girl all those years ago, but it has been one heck of a ride, and I am ready to do it all again.

Bonnie Harris McKenna served in Thailand II from 1962-64. After Peace Corps, she went to work for Continental Airlines and for thirty-four years stayed underway visiting those far away places with strange sounding names. She would like to thank Marjorie Larney for being a good friend and encouraging her to send her story to Peace Corps at 50.

JAMES C. STEWART

✷

Visits with the Veterans

*Easing into an unfamiliar culture is best done
with a little help from our friends.*

PHILIPPINES FOUR, OUR PEACE CORPS GROUP, TRAINED AT
Penn State University in the spring of 1962. After a brief
home leave, we arrived in Manila June 21. We had two days
of orientation at the University of the Philippines, then were
sent for a week of field visits with volunteers from Group I
who had arrived in October and were considered to be real
veterans by this time.

Four of us were booked on the plane to Legaspi in the Bicol
Region of southeastern Luzon. Ralph Thomas, our Volunteer
leader, came by to roust me out of bed at 3:30 A.M. Then he
did the same for two of the other guys, Jerry Wildman and
Howard Sansbury. We had the earliest flight. Everybody else
in the men's dorm was still sleeping. We washed up and finished packing while Thomas went to get Mara Taub. She was
going with us. When they came back, we piled into the jeep
with them and drove to the domestic airport. Dawn was just
breaking as we got there. The balmy air was stirred by a light
morning breeze. Ground crews were busy around a dozen or

more DC-3s near the terminal. I could hardly believe where we were and what was happening.

We took off and flew over countless miles of rice paddies and coconut groves, then over a low range of forested mountains. Suddenly we began our descent. I looked out to our left. There, grand and unmistakable, was the Mount Mayon volcano. Its gray-green slopes rose gently in the shape of a perfect cone. A wisp of white vapor trailed from the peak. It was truly a magnificent sight. No wonder it was a national symbol.

The plane slowed to a stop on the grassy airstrip. Paul Hare, the regional rep, was standing just inside the fence and greeted us as we walked from the plane. He was the staff member in charge of Volunteers in the area. He was probably in his mid-thirties, a trim and wiry guy, but he looked a little bedraggled. He had his two kids with him, which may have explained part of it. They were bubbling over with rambunctious energy. It was a treat to see American kids in these surroundings.

Because we had too much stuff to fit into Paul's jeep, he hired a cab to follow him. The taxi was in pretty bad shape. The driver couldn't start it on the first try. He reached down and jiggled some wires hanging under the dash. He tried again, and the engine boomed, coughed, sputtered and caught. A cloud of smoke came up through a hole in the floorboard. The driver crossed himself quickly and put it in gear. I turned and looked at Howard in the back seat. It was all we could do to keep from cracking up.

We followed Hare to the bus station. He helped us find the southbound bus for Sorsogon and supervised as some men loaded our luggage in the big open space at the rear. He gave us final instructions about how to get to the places we were going. We boarded the bus, which involved climbing up and in from the open right side. There was no aisle down the middle, just rows of bench seats all the way across. A lot of people liked to sit on the open side where they could get more fresh air. This meant we had to crawl over or around them to get seats of our own. Mara got in among a row of women. We climbed into the seats right behind her and got as close to the windows as we could.

Then we sat and waited. And waited. More cargo was loaded into the space at the back, including two big baskets of chickens. Other cargo was stowed in compartments under the bus on each side. Then they loaded some more on the roof and tied it down. People kept clambering aboard. One man was carrying a small pig trussed up in the bark of some plant. He slid it under the seat like carry-on luggage. A few more passengers climbed into the baggage compartment at the rear. Finally the driver seemed satisfied with the load and started the bus,

We headed due south through lush, beautiful countryside. The air was delightfully fresh and clean. It was quite a contrast after Manila. Everything here seemed more appealing. We gazed out the windows and kept tapping each other to point out one new sight after another. There were marvelous old Spanish-style churches and plazas in the towns just outside of Legaspi, then miles of open fields dotted with houses built on stilts and water buffalo grazing all around. Here and there we could spot the blue sea sparkling in the distance to the east and west of the peninsula. The whole scene was turning out to be everything that I had dreamed about.

We got to a narrower section of the road where there was dense vegetation on both sides. All of a sudden—BLAM!—something hit the side of the bus and a gusher of water spewed in through the window. A little bit spattered on me, but Howard got drenched. There were gales of laughter as all the passengers craned their necks to see what had happened. Then there was a mad scramble to drop the heavy curtains on both sides of the bus. A moment later a big SPLAT! sounded on the partly closed curtains along the right side, and some passengers near the front got sprayed with another torrent of water. There were howls of laughter again.

"What the *hell* is going on?" I asked Howard.

"Damned if I know. And everybody's laughing at me, too. What a great welcome," he said with a little anger in his voice. "Heck, this is my best shirt."

"I'm wet, too," said Mara, clearly annoyed.

A well-dressed older man who was sitting near us leaned over. "It is the day of San Juan," he said.

We just looked at him. "Saint John. Saint John the Baptist," he explained. "On this day there are many people who will try to baptize you. It is all in fun. The children especially enjoy it. They are the ones who throw the water," he said, pointing to Howard's shirt. He gave us a big smile.

The driver honked his horn loudly. We looked up ahead and saw some half-naked boys with buckets on both sides of the road. Water splashed against the bus as we went by. We joined in the laughter this time. The mood on the bus became festive as people chatted and laughed with one another. It was sweltering hot with the curtains down, but nobody seemed to mind very much. Even Howard was smiling now.

A little farther on we stopped at a crossroads. The bus conductor came back to tell Mara that this was where she would have to catch a jeepney to the barrio where she was going. I felt bad that we were leaving her there by herself at the side of the road. She was pretty self-reliant, but I was glad Howard and I were together.

We got to Casiguran, a pretty good-sized town. Howard and I got down from the bus and got our bags. We were surprised no one was there to meet us. The bus pulled away, and we stood around a few minutes trying to figure out what to do. Some little kids nearby were laughing and pointing at us. I walked toward them and said "Peace Corps? Peace Corps?" They just broke into more laughter and ran away.

"It's no use," I told Howard. "How about if we get a cold drink while we discuss a plan."

"That's what I like," Howard said. "A man who puts first things first."

There was a small restaurant just across the street. We went in, plunked our things down and ordered two Cokes. Cokes, we knew, were safe to drink. Since there was no telling where the guys lived that we had come to visit, I motioned to the waitress and paid the bill.

"Do you know the Peace Corps?" I asked her in careful English.

She shook her head, not understanding me.

"Amerikanos?" Howard asked more astutely.

"Amerikanos," she said. "O, O, Amerikanos." She understood. She led us to the door and motioned to the right, then made a curving motion with her hand to show that we would have to make a left turn farther up the street.

"*Maraming salamat,*"—thank you—we both told her. The language here was Bicolano, but she certainly knew enough Tagalog to understand that. She seemed pleased to be able to help.

We managed to find our way without too much problem. We had to stop a couple of people and say the magic word "Amerikanos," and they simply pointed in the right direction. When we got close enough, we could see one of the guys sitting near the front window on the second floor. We called to him and he waved.

"You guys are early," he said as he came down to greet us. "We thought you'd get here this afternoon."

"Nope. They got us up in the middle of the night to catch the first plane," I said. "I'm Jim Stewart and this is Howard Sansbury."

"Dave Jett," he said, shaking our hands. "Glad you guys managed to find us. We were planning to meet you later."

He took our smaller bags and led us up the stairs. His room-mate came out of a back room looking disheveled from his siesta. He introduced himself as Foster Wiggins.

Their place was kind of a mess. The front room was clut-tered with hundreds of discarded books from the U.S. Navy that they were going to divvy up for their schools. There were triplicate copies of *Time*, *Life*, and a bunch of other magazines. Peace Corps sent a personal copy to each volunteer. There were also open trunks and boxes with more books and some materials I recognized from training.

They also showed us some of the other, less practical, things the Peace Corps had sent them. There was a 96-piece set of expensive glassware and eight place settings of fine Noritake china.

"That stuff was purchased before there was any Peace Corps staff in Manila," Jett explained. "Somebody from the Agency for International Development was sent off to Hong Kong to buy household goods for the volunteers who would be com-ing. Nobody had much of an idea what the Peace Corps was all about. This AID guy figured we'd probably be doing a lot of entertaining, so he set us up in fine style. It's kind of embar-rassing, really, especially out in the rural areas like this. You'll probably get some yourselves. They have a whole warehouse full of it in Manila."

"Come here for a minute if you want to see the real kicker," Wiggins said, motioning us toward the kitchen. "This is our kerosene refrigerator. The same guy bought a bunch of these. It works great. The problem is, it uses so much kerosene that even with our three salaries, it would break us if we tried to keep it running." He opened the door. "When it's turned off like this, it makes a dandy cabinet though. We use it to store our rice and canned goods."

We all had breakfast together the next morning, then went our separate ways. Howard was going to the Casiguran central elementary school with Wiggins. He would be staying in town all week. Jett and I were heading out to his barrio where he stayed with a family during the school week. Howard and I privately wished each other luck, then I joined Jett to go catch a jeepney to his barrio. Along the way I asked Dave how it was that he ended up staying with a local family part of the time.

"We're all pretty free to change our living arrangements once we've settled in," he explained. "With Group I, Peace Corps set up a lot of three and four-person households. They thought we could provide support for each other. Some people liked the arrangement, but a lot of us felt it was too isolating. It was easy to spend so much time together that we never really got out into the community. I wanted to learn more about the local culture and pick up the language. The set-up I have now is ideal for me. I can spend the whole week with my family and then be with the guys on weekends. That way we don't get on each other's nerves so much, either," he said with a laugh.

We bounced along the road through lovely countryside. Riding in a jeepney made everything seem closer than passing by on a bus. You could almost reach out and touch the people walking along the road. I felt like I had really arrived at last.

We got to the school just in time for second period, which was Dave's first class. I met his co-teacher, the male fifth-grade teacher, and watched his classes for the day, which I enjoyed. Dave was an experienced, credentialed teacher. He was comfortable in the classroom, and I worried that I didn't have the training he did.

After classes, Dave suggested that we go for a walk. He said he wanted to meet more of the local people. He had only been living in this barrio for a few weeks since the beginning of the new school year. Before that he rotated between this school and another one up the road while he lived in town. The problem was he hardly got to know anyone then except the teachers and his students.

We first went to a little *sari-sari* store at the crossroads near his house. The stores like this were tiny—sort of like open lunch counters with a small collection of canned goods, assorted snacks, cigarettes, soft drinks and beer. We ordered a couple of beers and sat down on one of the benches in front. Some farmers were just coming in from the surrounding fields, and soon a group of them had gathered near us. Dave began talking to one in the dialect. Another one went over to the counter and bought a large jar of *tuba*, which is fermented coconut juice. The staff had joked about that stuff in training. The man with the *tuba* motioned for us to join the group, and we walked over. He blew the foam off the top of the open jar, poured a full glass, then offered it to Dave.

Dave and I exchanged glances. We both knew it was an invitation that could not be turned down. He drained the glass to the amused satisfaction of everyone around, including the woman storekeeper. The glass was refilled and handed to me. It had a strong smell and a tangy taste, but I finished it off in a couple of big gulps. There were more sounds of approval. The glass went around the circle with each of the farmers quaffing down his share. As it came back toward us, I thought of all the medical warnings we'd had about not drinking *tuba* under any circumstances. I also thought about the chilling statistic that one in ten people in the Philippines had T.B. There were now about a dozen in the group besides us. But to refuse a drink on the second round, when the reason might be painfully obvious to everyone, simply wouldn't do.

This time they handed the glass to me first. I drank about half of it and motioned that it was delicious, but I was full. I gave it to Dave to finish. We stayed for a few more minutes, and then Dave explained that we had to go back to the house. Everyone was feeling pretty good by that time, and they seemed happy that we had accepted their invitation to drink with them. It was as though we had passed some sort of a test.

"I didn't mean to get you into that," Dave apologized on the way back. "Normally, when I'm by myself, I can figure out some way to refuse. But I couldn't come up with a quick excuse for both of us."

"We did the only thing we could," I told him. "Besides, I was curious to see what it tastes like. It's not as bad as it looks."

"Kind of like strong apple cider. And you wouldn't want to know everything that's in the cider back home, either," he laughed.

The whole week was a terrific learning experience. It was a luxury to be able to rely on Dave's contacts and his knowledge of the language. I was only a visitor, and a newcomer at that. If I made any mistakes, they could be excused. This was just a preview to what I would face in my own barrio or town. At least here I wouldn't have to live with the consequences of any missteps I might make. That took some of the pressure off of being in unfamiliar surroundings.

After school each day we had time to walk around the barrio. Everywhere farmers were plowing their fields with their water buffalo in preparation for the first heavy rains of the season. Those were due any day now, Dave said. As soon as they came in full force, the rice could be planted. It was one of the busiest times of the year.

Learning about the culture meant a lot more than walking around, seeing new sights and trying new foods, though. Some cultural lessons were much less tangible and more unexpected.

One like that came from a conversation I had with Dave's principal, Joe. I ended up spending time with him when I wasn't observing classes. He turned out to be a more complicated guy than he seemed at first. Part of it was that he idolized everything American. When he was a teenager, he had a lot of contact with the G.I.s at the end of the war and right afterward. Apparently he picked up a lot of their attitudes along with a colorful vocabulary of English words and slang expressions. One day, out of the blue, he confided in me that Filipinos were basically "a lazy bunch of bastards" who "didn't know their ass from a hole in the ground." That was why the country was so backward, he said. The "goddamned politicians in Manila" were lining their pockets, and the Filipinos were too dumb to do anything about it. The only hope for the Philippines was if it could become a territory of the U.S., like Hawaii had been, and then maybe a state. Otherwise the country "didn't have a snowball's chance in hell."

"Sometimes I think we really *are* too stupid to govern ourselves," he told me.

I was shocked. At first I thought he was just testing me, trying to uncover any prejudices I might have. But he was serious. He really thought of his own people as being inferior. He seemed to have an inferiority complex himself. Maybe that was why he tried so hard to sound like an American. What a terrible legacy that was of the American colonial period and the war. We had convinced the Filipinos, or at least some of them, that they were not our equals and maybe never could be. It was the one sad note of my week with Dave. I don't know why, but I didn't even mention it to him. Maybe I figured he would deal with all that in his own way. It was his barrio, after all.

On Thursday, my last day there, Dave was with me as I said goodbye to Joe. Joe was joking around and trying again to convince me to stay.

"You should find a wife here, and have kids, and improve the race," he said.

"Which race?" I asked him.

That stopped him for a moment. Then he and Dave both laughed. I shook his hand and thanked him for everything.

Back in Casiguran, it was good to see Howard again and swap stories about the past few days. He had enjoyed observing at the central school. He and Wiggins hit it off well, too. But as we traded our stories, I got the feeling that something was wrong. Howard didn't seem to have his usual lighthearted sense of humor. We got off to ourselves just before dinner, and I asked him what was up. He didn't come straight out with it, but finally he said that all the stares, the pointing and the laughing were getting him down. He felt like he was constantly being ridiculed.

"But we all knew there'd be a lot of that," I said. "I've gotten plenty of it myself."

"Not like this," he said. "I could tell the kids on the street were making fun of me. They kept using one word over and over again. I finally found out what it was. It's their word for monkey. That's what they were calling me. You know, it's because of my color, and the way I look to them."

"Son of a bitch," I said lamely. I didn't know how else to respond. We had been told that the cultural adjustment might be especially hard for the Negro volunteers among us, but this had to be really rough. "It's no wonder that got you down."

"Yeah, it hurts. And it's tough to take when you can't say anything back. *We* have to be nice, you know?"

"You gonna be all right?"

"I'll have to be. For two *years* I'll have to be."

James C. Stewart was a Volunteer in the Philippines from 1962-64. "Visits with the Veterans" is an excerpt from the book, Ask What You Can Do, *an account of his own Peace Corps experiences and those of other volunteers he knew. The book was published in March 2011.*

RICHARD G. PETERSON

✦
✳   ✳

Stop, Pig! Drop the Flip-Flop!

Acting on faulty assumptions remains the bane of the Volunteer experience; having two years to make amends is its relief.

IT HAD BEEN VERY MUCH A VACATION UP TO THIS POINT. I HAD left the U.S. for Samoa on October 7, 1975. After we arrived "in country," the Peace Corps put us up in various hotels where we were consumed by dawn-to-midnight classes in language, culture, and the Peace Corps classic training for "How to Teach With One Book and Piece of Chalk." During in-country training, the closest I came to Samoan life was a "White Sunday" holiday visit on the second Sunday in October—a special day that celebrates children—the bar at Aggie Grey's, and the occasional walk on the beach.

My first real village visit hardly qualified as a truly Samoan experience either. It had been to Chanel College, a private Catholic secondary school halfway up Mount Vaea. Robert Louis Stevenson—loved by the Samoans—is buried there. The story goes that his body was carried by forty chiefs to the top of the mountain.

At the college—with its tennis courts, rugby field, and nearby beach—I had not even spoken to a Samoan who was not wearing a tie. Since the college was run by New Zealand priests as a model of New Zealand education, there was very little of a Samoan nature under the green metal roofs. By contrast, my peers had been to real villages, eaten taro, gotten dysentery, and had stories to tell. My tan was coming along nicely, but I was feeling a bit left out.

The training director felt the same way. My time at Chanel had made her question whether I was true Peace Corps stock. "Perhaps you are not clear on why we are here?" The next time we were scheduled to go to a village, she told me, she would make sure I would see the true Samoa.

Departure day for the next village stay and a first teaching assignment was wet. It was raining: not like "lake effect Lake Michigan" rain, but "who pushed me into this damned aquarium?" rain. My leather shoes had been growing mold in my locker since the moment we arrived, so I had changed to a pair of flip flops made from old automobile tires, a product of local industry. We were taken out to our drop points in a canvas-topped two-and-a-half-ton truck that looked like something the Americans might have left there after World War II as not worth saving. When it got to be my turn, the truck stopped, the Samoan driver ran back, threw open the tarp, grabbed my bag and threw it out in the mud. I was "helped" out as well. I was still standing in the puddle in the middle of the road when the truck pulled out and headed off into the monsoon. I had no idea where I was or where I was supposed to go, and the water was running down my glasses and up my khakis. This start in "true Samoa" was not auspicious.

Being volcanic, Samoan dirt makes great mud. It grabs hold and does not let go. Almost immediately, my right flip-flop was sucked off and flowed down the "river," rapidly forming in the center of the "road." Having given up any attempt to stay dry, I tried to follow the shoe while not losing the other one. A large pig, clearly the pride of one of the local families, ran out of the bush, grabbed the floating sandal, and made for the bushes again. At the same time, a small boy ran out from the coconut plantation next to the road, grabbed my bag, jumped over a low stone wall, and started running off through the palm trees.

I had grown up in a poor area of Michigan and knew what to do when someone you don't know takes your stuff. Leaving the one flip flop to the pig, I ran after the boy, all the while stubbing my feet on the volcanic rock under the palm trees, and screaming at my attacker as he disappeared around another wall.

I got there just in time to see the kid run into a nearby concrete house. Raising a hue and cry as I ran (with an epithet or two), I ran up the steps and into the house, prepared to do battle, then more than ready to walk back to town, Aggie's bar, and the airport.

As I tore screaming into the little house, I almost knocked over the nice old man in the spotless *lavalava* standing inside the door looking confused. He introduced himself as the school headmaster. He handed me a towel and a cup of Samoan cocoa. With a bemused—but unimpressed—look, he told me in his dignified way that we would be heading off to school in a moment or two.

To this day I am more than a little embarrassed to tell this story, but after thirty-two years of teaching, every September when school starts, I always remember that first day of school in the Peace Corps. As I survey the new crop of kids, that recollection reminds me not to make assumptions about new people or new situations; each kid deserves the benefit of the doubt, no matter how dodgy he/she may look at first.

Oh, and I found my flip-flop. After teaching in wet clothes for six hours, (with the promised one book and one piece of chalk), I arrived back "home" with my new Samoan family to find my retread flip flop hanging out of their prize pig's mouth.

Richard Peterson taught at St. Peter Chanel College in the community of Moamoa in Samoa from 1975-77.

KAREN BATCHELOR

*

Return to the Land of the Morning Calm

What at one time may have been a cultural handicap may suddenly set a country on a course for spectacular advances.

I HAD ALWAYS WANTED TO GO BACK TO THAT PLACE WHERE MY life was forever altered, so when the job announcement arrived in June of 2006, I did not hesitate to apply.

"Three ESL teacher trainers needed for a training program in Daegu, South Korea." I sent in my application and was delighted to receive a formal invitation from the Ministry of Education.

On the long trip from the San Francisco airport to Incheon/ Seoul International, I spent most of the twelve-hour flight remembering my life in Korea as a Peace Corps Volunteer more than thirty years before. My mind continuously flashed on sights, sounds and tastes. I relived unusual experiences that formed the pieces of the frustrating, fascinating quilt of my life during those two years. Peace Corps was both my first significant time away from home, and a learning experience that I could not have gleaned from classrooms, books or movies.

Like most Volunteers in the early 1970s, I was young, idealistic, adventurous, and recently graduated from college. I could locate Korea on a world map; I knew a little about the Korean War in the 1950s; and I knew that kimchi—spicy, pickled cabbage—was a staple food. Beyond that, I was ignorant about the Land of the Morning Calm.

It was just before Thanksgiving in 1972 when we landed at Kimpo Airport in Seoul. It was dark when we arrived, and there were few people around. The airport consisted of one small building. We walked across the tarmac toward that unassuming building, but snow on the ground made the walkway slippery. Although I was bleary-eyed and exhausted from lack of sleep, the pocket-sized airport made an impression on me. It contained a single check-in counter with three windows and one roped-off area where our luggage was held until claimed. No carousel. Of course, I knew that the Peace Corps sent Volunteers only to developing countries with primitive facilities, but in my young mind, it was hard to imagine that the one major airport for the entire country could be so small and basic.

Our first tasks as Volunteers consisted of learning the language, the culture, and some teaching methodology. After our three months of in-country training, our group—designated K-25—was divided and scattered to middle schools throughout the nation, mostly in villages and small cities in the countryside. I was assigned to Andong Girls' Middle School in Andong, a small city known for its nobility in previous centuries. The only two paved streets intersected in the center of town, and the one paved road in the province ran from Andong to Daegu, the country's third largest city, after Seoul and Pusan.

I lived in a boarding house and had a room of my own, which was highly unusual in this poor country. The Korean language has no direct translation for the word *privacy*, and the word closest in meaning has a negative connotation. Anybody who wants *privacy* is suspect. The widow who ran my boarding house lived with her two teenage children in a room smaller than mine. They ate, slept and watched TV—when the TV worked—in that little room.

This typical boarding house had rice paper doors and an inefficient *yonton* heating system: large cylindrical charcoal chunks were lit and placed under the floor, essentially heating an area of about two square feet only on the floor. This residence was the first place I had ever lived without an indoor toilet; there was no shower or bathtub. We used an outhouse in the backyard, and in two years, I never completely overcame the urge to gag at the stench. When I knew the "honey dippers" would be coming to reap the contents of the outhouse for fertilizer on the rice paddies, I tried to be away. The only Western-style toilets in town were at the Catholic priest's home and in the best upscale restaurant. But those toilets usually didn't work.

Each morning all of the boarders gathered in the courtyard (even in winter), with our individual pans of water—hot in winter, cold in summer—and washed faces, hands and other visible body parts, and brushed our teeth. Once a week, I went to the public bathhouse for a good scrubbing. In winter, I went more often because the hot water and steam made it the one place I could be warm for a little while.

After bathing, we returned to our rooms to eat a breakfast of kimchi, rice and soup our landlady had prepared for us in a cement pit with a charcoal fire attached to the side of the house. This kitchen contained no stove, no refrigerator, and certainly no dishwasher. The young country maid washed dishes in cold water outside in the courtyard during summer, spring, winter and fall. Large brown ceramic pots—filled with garlic, chilies and fermenting cabbage for kimchi—lined the outside walls of the house.

Washed and fed, we dressed for the day. I was expected to be at school until 5:00 P.M., Monday through Friday. Saturday was a regular part of the school week, though we got off at 2:00 P.M. My job was to work with a co-teacher, attempting to teach English to little girls arranged in classes of sixty, in barren rooms with bare-wood floors. The wood-burning stove at the front of each classroom offered scant relief from the cold. In winter we all wore layers of long underwear and heavy socks. In summer, there was no air conditioning, and I could feel the perspiration run down my face and back as I stood in front of the class trying to present an interesting lesson in English.

Because of very complex relationships between South Korea and the U.S., and because of very different cultural systems, Americans were both revered and reviled, depending on the circumstances. As a visiting teacher, I was offered the best at the boarding house, which meant the largest room. As a woman, I had to stand on the train if men were there first. At the restaurant, my food arrived last. I was seldom asked my opinion and not expected to have one. But at school, I was both a woman and an American, making it difficult and confusing for some of the male teachers to know how to relate to me.

I also learned a little bit of what it is like to be a minority. On the streets, I was called "monkey," and "long nose," and "yellow hair" because I did not look like the rest of the population. Children laughed at me until the principal heard them one day and told them that I was a teacher, that they must bow in respect and wish me a good journey. After their brief education, my walks along Andong streets were less emotionally upsetting.

My time in Korea taught me to appreciate what I had always had, both the material wealth of our nation, and the little things—like getting credit for work I had done—that I had taken for granted at home but could not expect in Korea. There were occasions when I could barely contain my anger, as happened the day of a workshop that took place near the end of my service.

One of my jobs was to conduct workshops for the English teachers at my school. One day a graduate student from the university in Daegu came to Andong to give a demonstration lesson at the local boys' high school. He was to demonstrate to all of the English teachers in our little city the "new and right way" to teach English. We were all required to attend, and because I had a workshop scheduled at my school the next day, I thought I would make this demonstration the topic of our workshop. We would analyze this "model lesson" to see if he used techniques I had taught them, or whether he was "breaking the rules" or doing something else entirely. We would make suggestions among ourselves on ways the graduate student could have improved his performance.

So I listened intently and took notes.

During the demo, I noticed many points of sound foreign language methodology that the young man had ignored; he asked a question, but didn't wait for the answer. He used too much Korean and translated everything. When students know there is a translation coming, they stop trying to understand the original. He was too wordy and unclear in his directions. Mrs. Pak, a young teacher sitting next to me, whispered in my ear these same and other observations. Then I felt a tap on my shoulder from behind me. It was a man from the boys' high school, a man we had dubbed "Neanderthal Man" because he could never put two words of English together. He pointed at my notes and, thinking this would be a good learning experience for him, I handed them over.

When the demonstration lesson was finished, we were invited to go outside under the trees with their October leaves in flaming colors. Tables and chairs had been set up so we could have a "discussion" about these "new" techniques of teaching. As I looked around at the teachers I had worked with and those I knew through friends and acquaintances, I felt a wave of satisfaction and fulfillment. I was due to terminate service in two months and return home in December. I felt content that I had been of assistance to this large group of people.

The meeting/discussion was conducted in a very orderly, very Korean manner, and the discussion was entirely in Korean. The first person asked to speak was from my middle school. I was disappointed, but not surprised, that they passed over bright, young Mrs. Pak and instead chose "Fat Pak"—the loud-mouthed town joke—as spokesperson from our school. He was the oldest and spoke fairly understandable English. He carried on and on without saying anything substantial. The next speaker was "Neanderthal Man." I was surprised this time because one of the young men at my boarding house also taught at the boys' high school and spoke terrific English. I thought he should have been chosen to present his views on the demonstration. "Neanderthal Man," however, was older, and the mores of the country are based firmly in Confucianism. Royalty is honored; elders are respected; parents and teachers are held in esteem; and men rule over women.

The next half-hour was the only time in my two years of service that I wished I had been unable to speak or understand Korean. As the man from the high school spoke, I became angrier and more confused. Then Mrs. Pak whispered to me again, "Those are your notes. He translated your notes." There was not one mention of my contribution to his "insights." The man received loud applause as I staunched my tears.

The final insult came when the leader of the discussion, a man whose master's thesis I had corrected, said, "And now we will hear from our Peace Corps Volunteer." For a second, my heart lifted, but fell again when he added, "Mr. Delbert Blume." Del had arrived just two weeks before, had not worked with these people, did not know them, and most hurtful, spoke only about a half dozen words of Korean. I closed my eyes and wished for the ceremony to be over. When I was finally released, I ran all the way back to my boarding house and cried. Delbert came later to explain that he had no idea what was going on there, but I already knew that. "Fat Pak" came by to tell me that I "didn't understand," and laughed his raucous laugh when I got angry. It seemed to me at the time that my two years of dedicated service meant nothing to these people. I wanted to go home. In two months my service was complete, and I did.

In the United States, it was much easier to get credit for what I had done, a fact I had not appreciated until the "model lesson" incident. In Korea, the ignoring of my contributions was never meant to be personal. It was simply the country's over-arching cultural practice, and it was hard to grasp because it was so different from mine. My Peace Corps experience also made me realize that people could live quite differently, could live in poverty, and yet be happy. I appreciated the way nothing in Korea was wasted. Notepads were made from discarded papers and tied together with string. Items were repaired instead of replaced. I began to understand that we Americans were wasteful and could probably be content with a lot fewer things. I started recycling almost immediately upon returning to the United States at the only center in San Francisco. What a difference a few decades have made.

My Peace Corps years set me on a new career path. Instead of becoming an elementary school teacher, I returned to the university for an M.A. and began teaching ESL and training teachers. So when I returned thirty-two years later to the Land of the Morning Calm, I was excited and eager to re-connect with the country. What I found was a completely different world.

My surprise and wonder began when we arrived at the new world-class airport now located between Incheon and Seoul. The complex is huge with elevators, escalators, moving sidewalks, and twelve luggage carousels in each terminal. Ramps connect to arriving and departing planes, meaning no more treks across the tarmac. I saw so many ticket counters that it was difficult to determine where we needed to be.

After catching up on my sleep, I looked forward to seeing the changes I couldn't have predicted. In 1974, telephone service was so unreliable, that when my mother had a heart attack, I received a telegram at my school from the U.S. State Department, signed by Henry Kissinger, advising me of this development and that I would be granted an emergency leave. In 2006, everybody had a cell phone, and in Daegu, PC Bangs (internet cafes) have sprung up all over the city.

The modernization of South Korea has come with wonderful touches that say "Only in Korea." Kitchens regularly contain a dishwasher, stove and two refrigerators, one designated solely for storing kimchi, not only to accommodate the many varieties, but also to contain the pungent odor. The separate refrigerator keeps the smell of fermented cabbage away from the meat, milk, eggs and beer.

At the airport screening station, passengers are offered slippers after removing their shoes. On the toll roads, the women in the tollbooths return your ticket with two hands (Korean custom to show respect) and bow slightly. All along the major freeways, stand shrines to dead ancestors. Paved roads now crisscross this tiny nation set on a peninsula. On my return, I did not see one dirt or gravel road. Those paved roads are necessary because now everybody has an automobile or two. Not just beat up old clunkers, either. These are new, comfortable, state-of-the-art vehicles, made domestically or abroad. Speed traps with cameras are announced with an official sign posted a few hundred feet before the camera appears: Slow down. Police cameras 500 feet ahead.

My job in Daegu that summer of 2006 was to work with Korean educators who were teaching English. The goals were to improve their fluency in the language and to offer some more modern and communicative classroom techniques. Again, I was surprised. The level of English competency had risen dramatically, especially among those people who teach English in middle and high schools. I was also surprised and delighted to discover that one of the attendees in these workshops was a former student at Andong Girls' Middle School, and I was her English teacher in 1974.

Not everything has changed, however. One thing—thankfully—is the respect that Koreans have for teachers. In this Asian country, educators are revered. They must be respected, appreciated, and their needs always considered. The teachers in these workshops, and especially my former student, went out of their way to make us comfortable, take us out to lunch, buy gifts and bow in respect.

Collective thinking patterns still rule. Koreans cannot go swimming before June 15 because you just don't. It's the magic date. Pre-packaged instant coffee is sold at every little shop on the street. The packages contain coffee, sugar, and creamer in tubes because everybody drinks their coffee the same way. I was warned several times that I put too much sea salt into my chicken soup—because, again, everybody seems to share the same tastes.

Yet when I thought about the remarkable economic advances the country has made, I was able to identify collective thinking as a major force behind the advances. I really disliked the group mindset when I lived in Korea, but I realized on this second visit that it is "group think" that has moved the country forward so far in such a short time. And the Peace Corps helped as it sent groups of young people to South Korea between 1966 and 1981 to teach English and to eradicate tuberculosis. The population of the country had to be healthy in order to move forward. And to make such great technological advances, they needed to speak, understand, read and write English.

Peace Corps has sent hundreds of Volunteers to other developing countries that have not made such phenomenal progress as South Korea; the difference here lies in the unity of the people. It's the "group think": the willingness of the vast majority of the population to follow a mandate that, in this case, worked for a very positive communal cause.

The summer Olympics in Seoul in 1988 added more opportunities to advance and for everyone to pull together to achieve a goal. They paved roads. They established modern hotels. They engineered a bullet train from Seoul to Daegu and Pusan—a wonderfully fast and comfortable ride, so different from the trips I used to take. The people banded together to invest in their future and have received positive returns on their investments.

And so it happened that my trip back to the country that taught me so much offered me another awakening. I went back to see the old, but found it mingled with the new.

Karen Batchelor served as a middle school teacher and teacher trainer in South Korea from 1972-74. Since then she has been teaching at City College of San Francisco where she works with ESL students. She also trains teachers at various local universities and through the U.S. State Department as an English Language Specialist. She has published poetry, professional articles, short stories and eight textbooks. In 2006 her novel Murder at Ocean View College, *an adult story at a sixth-grade reading level, was published.*

BRENT R. CROMLEY

✦

A Letter to Sri Padmanabham

Memory gets stored in unlikely places, including the
yellowed pages of a 1964 J.C. Penney catalog.

ALTHOUGH TEACHING MATHEMATICS IN A PUBLIC HIGH SCHOOL IN
India during the early sixties had a profound impact on the
rest of my life, the most moving experience occurred when I
returned to visit more than thirty-five years later.

India IV, the fourth group of Peace Corps Volunteers
sent to India, was a close-knit group. Thirty-three nurses and
science and math teachers, scattered throughout the southern
Indian state of Andhra Pradesh, from its capital Hyderabad in
the center to the Bay of Bengal on the east coast. From June
1963 to June 1965, we endured three months of training in
Milwaukee, travel adventures throughout India, regular Peace
Corps conferences in Bombay, New Delhi and Madras, and a
summer work project that had us clearing fields and planting
fruit trees. We celebrated the birth of a daughter to our
married Volunteers and a marriage between two others. We
mourned the death of one Volunteer who drowned in the Bay
of Bengal and the assassination of President Kennedy.

At the end of those two years, my return to Montana brought me back to a more predictable lifestyle. Three years of law school, a family, and a career practicing law showed little external evidence of my Indian experience. Correspondence with Indian students and friends had eventually tapered off. Other than a few objects, such as a pair of rosewood elephants (purchased after an extended period of intense bargaining in a Calcutta market), my two years in India became less and less a focus of my life.

Despite having been such close friends in India, upon our return in the summer and fall of 1965, there was surprisingly little communication or interaction among the members of India IV. Only a couple of newsletters were circulated. Fortunately, that changed in 1998, when a dedicated few located most of our surviving members and organized our first reunion at the lakeside home of Rick and Georgene Fabian at Holderness, New Hampshire. The excitement, laughter, music, stories and flood of memories that we shared at that first reunion were enough to ensure that the group would continue to hold regular reunions, initially every five years and now every three years.

That first reunion was also enough to awaken a desire to return to India. It was neither a very specific nor a well-formulated desire. I didn't know if I just wanted to again see the Taj Mahal or if I was up to the tasks of trying to find contacts in Tekkali, the town in Andhra Pradesh where I had lived, and enduring the many trains and buses that would be required to reach it. Without a grand plan in mind, I wrote letters addressed to general locations in Tekkali—including the post office and Zilla Parishad Higher Secondary School, the public school where I had taught—inquiring whether anyone recalled the two Americans who had lived there from 1963 to 1965. Finally I received a cryptic email from a man named

Padmanabham who identified himself as a fellow teacher at the school when I had taught there. I was unable to reply, as it had apparently been sent through a public station of some sort. Although Padmanabham had included a telephone number, I was never able to complete a call from Montana. So instead I wrote a letter indicating an approximate time in July 2001 that I would like to visit and saying that I hoped to be accompanied by one of my sons.

Without the encouragement of my son Giano, I doubt that I would have made the trip. He had turned twenty-eight that year, had just received his MFA degree in creative writing, and was up for an adventure, particularly one that he maybe could incorporate into his fiction. And so we firmed up our plans.

Getting there was truly half the fun. The internet assisted us in obtaining maps and a few hotel names, but other than our plane reservation and our first two nights' lodging, we had nothing securely planned until we arrived in New Delhi near midnight early in July 2001. Thankfully, we were greeted by a driver from our hotel, which was located at Connaught Place in the center of the city. The rest of our trip reminded me of my travel in India nearly forty years earlier. On the streets of Delhi we met a driver who could take us to Hyderabad for a modest sum, with stops for wonderful adventures in sightseeing in the city of Jaipur and (of course) at the Taj Mahal.

From Hyderabad, where most of our nurses had been located, it was a surprisingly pleasant train ride to the coast and the city of Vishakhapatnam, where several members of India IV had taught science and math. Then north by bus to Srikakulam, which had many pleasant memories for me. My good friend Tom Bruce had been stationed there and several times hosted some of the Volunteers in our group during holidays or other special events. One was the Srikakulam

District Games at which five of us Volunteers had—when forty years younger—made a fairly decent showing in the championship basketball game. In a barbershop where my son received a shave and a haircut, the barber remembered "Mr. Bruce" and recalled him being a "big man, a very fine athlete." (Despite some gentle prodding, the barber did not recall my own prowess on the basketball court.)

Until we reached Srikakulam, I was unable to establish any contact with Padmanabham or anyone else in Tekkali who may or may not have received my letter. But the evening before we were to catch the morning bus to Tekkali, Padmanabham answered my telephone call and promised that someone would meet us at the station the next morning when we arrived.

A bumpy ride to Tekkali ended with a most spectacular three-day climax. At the bus station were several of my former students, now each eager to introduce my son and me to family and friends. For several days we were feted, fed and entertained. We toured the school where I had haltingly taught math and physics. Although it now had a different name, the school's buildings were astonishingly familiar, as was the respect paid by the students to both their teachers and the American visitors. I think we visited nearly every shop on the main streets. Former students introduced themselves, hosted us with offers of a "cooling drink," and generally made us feel like royalty. We attended banquets, including the annual meeting of the Old Students Association, which had been moved from its normal September schedule to July purely on the basis of the estimated arrival date in my letter to Padmanabham. The Old Students Association, I learned, was a community group that met annually to grant awards and scholarships to teachers and students. At each banquet, both my son and I were called upon to speak. We were presented with flower garlands, shawls and other presents, including the beautiful picture of the goddess Saraswati, goddess of knowledge, hanging in my office.

We accepted as many offers as we could to visit former students and to dine with them, or to just enjoy coffee or a cooling drink. At one point, the son of our former cook introduced himself and explained that his father had told him stories of his two American friends. Many former students recalled how much they had enjoyed visiting with me and the other Volunteer—Fred Schulten, who had taught in the same school—to discuss school work, to play games, or to just talk about our two countries.

On the last day of our visit, a white-haired man came up to me with a plastic bag clutched in front of him. His companion introduced him as "your tailor when you lived in Tekkali." During our Peace Corps tenure, Fred and I would take any opportunity to receive mail, as it was always a welcome diversion and something we could share with our Indian friends to illustrate examples of American tastes and interests. These mailings included J.C. Penney catalogs. Because many clothes are made locally in India, I had brought a catalog to our tailor during my tenure in Tekkali to have him sew two short-sleeved shirts, with button down collars, similar to those pictured. From the plastic bag held tightly in front of him, my old tailor produced the same J.C. Penney catalog, somewhat yellowed with age, but still in fine condition considering that it was now almost forty years old.

Leaving Tekkali was no less difficult in 2001 than it had been in 1965. But I left with a newly discovered feeling of satisfaction and exhilaration. I have always known that my teaching high school math and physics in India, while an extremely valuable and formative experience for me, did nothing to improve or modify India's system of education. And I knew that as a teacher I was probably less proficient in conveying information than my Indian counterparts. But I had now experienced first hand, almost forty years later, the most enduring and valuable accomplishment of Peace Corps.

Brent R. Cromley served in India from 1963-65, where he taught math and physics at Zilla Parishad Higher Secondary School, Tekkali, Andhra Pradesh.Born and raised in Great Falls, Montana, he was educated at Dartmouth College. He is a graduate of the University of Montana School of Law and has practiced in Billings since 1968. He is married to Dorothea Cromley, Professor of Music (piano) at the University of Montana, whom he met during Peace Corps training. His highest award to date is the Distinguished Service Award presented by the Tekkali Old Students Association, July 16, 2001.

KAREN DUNNE

✦

The Fijian Father

What does it mean to live in a land where there is a word
for laughing when in immediate danger of being killed?

HIS BARE CALLOUSED FEET ARE PLATFORM FLAT FROM SIXTY-SIX years of walking sun-baked gravel roads and mangrove swamps. He does not own a shoe, or a pair. He is a fisherman, and one of only two who own a boat in a village that relies on fishing and farming for its survival.

I am nervous. For the first time I am sitting with Esirome, a Fijian elder who will become the most influential person in my life for the next two years. He will be why I complete my Peace Corps service. He will be why I stay when I want to go. I will become his adopted daughter.

Esirome's wiry white beard is his signature. It beams out from coffee-colored skin shining with coconut oil. I can tell who he is from any distance, whether from a passing bus, out in the bush, or in a crowd of others with Melanesian midnight features. His eyes are comforting and kind, above a smile that lights up the world around him, proving that its power has nothing to do with a full set of teeth or just four.

Esirome shares *everything* with me, relentlessly—his language, his culture, his food, his home, his family. He shows me how to live as a Fijian, teaching me the customs, the traditions, the ceremonies, and the intricacies of the land and sea. His life is abundant, with a wife, nine children, seven grandchildren, and a large plentiful farm. His home, his castle, is beside the sea.

Jovial and patient, Esirome speaks slowly, giving me time to translate. I am desperate to speak his language, pleading to my nanosized neurons to make words into meaning. I fidget with my skirt, and my eyes dart from him to my notebook. He giggles at my mistakes, a natural reaction for him. At first it's embarrassing, offensive, especially from my American perspective. But then it's funny. It's Fijian. The tension is gone.

Laughter permeates the culture. It shows in the people and in the Fijian dictionary, with seven variations for the word: 1) to laugh, 2) to laugh at, 3) to cause to laugh, 4) the custom of making merry on the fifth night after a person's death, by way of consoling the relatives of the dead, 5) laughing when one is shamed before others, 6) to call by laughing, and 7) to laugh when in immediate danger of being killed. I usually find it impossible to laugh when I think I'm about to die, even of embarrassment.

Laughter has much to teach me. It's not a topic covered in training, but I rely on it for my survival. It's my ally, my sanity. I chose this kind of life, purposefully, to be surrounded by uncertainty, the unknown, and the discomfort that comes with it. Even if life is nothing more than a chance to champion the choices we make, I still need the salve of laughter.

I am a blockhead at learning a new language. I forget words within seconds of learning them; they don't stick unless I write them down. Not only must I ask how to say a word, but also how to spell it. It's a painfully slow process, and one that mars my self-image. After a page of new words, I start to confuse them. Finally, with my hands up, I ask Esirome, "How do you say, impossible?" He giggles again—a sound I have memorized—replying, "*Drëdrë.*"

I repeat it back, "*Drëdrë.*"

He shakes his head, "*Maka*—no, *drëdrë.*"

I try again. He shakes his head again. There is a speed and inflection to the word that I can't hear, and it's not enough to know the spelling. I master it after countless attempts. Esirome finds this entertaining, not at all bothered by the time it takes me to get it right.

On the northern coast of Vanua Levu, Fiji's second largest island, is Esirome's settlement of Burenitu. It's beside the main village of Korotubu where I live among 155 other Fijians. His farm is dense with coconut trees, cassava, pumpkin, *dalo*, bananas, and vegetables. There are pigs, goats, cows, and chickens. The house is separate from the kitchen, which is separate from the pit toilet, and separate from the water tap.

The kitchen billows with smoke as water simmers in a blackened aluminum pot that sits between two concrete blocks over the fire. The space, only for the women of the family, is sheltered from the wind by three flimsy metal walls that rise about five feet. There is a roof, made from bowed sheets of corrugated iron and weighted down by heavy logs. It's a healthier set-up than most—smoke can escape from the top of the walls, though the roof still traps it. The floor is a fine mixture of dirt and ash residue from generations of cooking boiled fish, boiled cassava, *kuita vakalolo*—boiled octopus in coconut milk—and three-times-a-day boiled black tea.

The water tap, the only tap, is near the kitchen. Everything that needs water occurs at this tap—washing bodies, washing dishes, washing clothes, and cleaning fish. A large *pago*—plastic barrel cut in half—is filled every night when the cows come in to drink. Small chunks of bar soap, remnant fish scales, and empty metal pots are scattered around the cement platform.

The house is made of timber, on wooden posts that rise a few feet above the ground. The doors, opening to a central room, are folded back against the walls, making it appear that there are no doors at all. Its sparse interior creates a welcoming atmosphere with open floor space for plenty of people to sit, or sleep. The food-safe—a wooden cupboard with latching doors to keep the rats out—is next to a plastic basin filled with dishes. A deep freezer, a luxury item used to store fish, is next to the only electrical outlet in the house. There are two pieces of furniture for leaning against—not because the upholstery is missing and all that remains is the wood framing, but because Fijians always sit on the floor.

On each side of the central room are small bedrooms separated by thin colorful cloth hanging from string in the doorways. The unpainted plywood walls are treated no differently than a blackboard, with photographs taped along the top, and scribbles and rhymes written in chalk, in English, by seven-year-old grandson, Bude: *"Father makes a lovo, Mother bakes a cake, Tevita set a table, I sit and wait, It's my birthday."* And, *"Together, This is my family, We do things together, We go to the rugby game, We go to the farm, We go fishing, We go to church, We go together."*

Mesa, the two-year-old grandson, is tenacious in his quest for attention from anyone who enters the house, squealing and running if he must. There is a continuous hum of conversation. Salome and Senraro, the two youngest daughters, twenty-four and sixteen years old, are chatting to each other about where I'm from. Paulini and Sereima, the eldest daughters, can speak some English and help interpret. Esirome's wife, Marica, sits beside him, looking at me with tranquil eyes, as he helps explain some of my mispronounced Fijian words.

Esirome has two sons; they moved to the mainland years ago. Other than Mesa and Bude, he surrounds himself with women. He bellows to Senaca, the third child, to bring tea and biscuits. "S-e-n-a-c-a...S-e-n-a-c-a." When there's no response, he yells again, louder, "S-E-N-A-C-A...S-E-N-A-C-A." Four months passed before I knew that Senaca was his daughter. At first I thought she was a house girl. His demands seemed specific to Senaca; I didn't see him speak that way to his other daughters. I never knew why. Maybe it's just her job in the family. I try to apologize when she arrives with biscuits. It feels uncomfortable to watch her being called to do whatever Esirome asks, especially because my presence, culturally, requires that tea and food be served.

Esirome asks, "How old are you? What is your religion? Are you married? Do you have children? How many brothers and sisters do you have? Where are your parents? Are they healthy? Where do you live in America? What food do you eat in America? Do you know how to fish?"

I answer mechanically—they are typical questions—questions that once struck me as abrasive, too personal. But I've learned that the questions people ask show what they value. Just as an American would ask what you do for work, a Fijian will ask about your family. Americans focus on doing; Fijians focus on relationships. It's personal. It's people. *That* is Fiji.

However, *do I know how to fish?* It isn't a usual question and I sheepishly tell him that I've only been fishing once. His eyes enlarge, he looks to his wife, and with a deep, certain giggle, he turns back to me and says, "*Au na vakavulici O'iko. E dodonu meda kila na qoliva o keda kece nai taukei*—I will teach you, every Fijian must know how to fish."

And I want to spear fish—never mind that Fijian women don't spear fish, that it's men's work. As a Peace Corps Volunteer I have more room to flex the gender roles. In the

U.S. I've had physical and mental freedoms that don't exist in this culture. I was a professional cyclist for almost a decade, traveled to more than a dozen countries, earned a master's degree, owned a business, lived alone, have not married, do not have children. My white skin is as much an oddity as is my past. But Esirome forgives my oddities and shows me how to do things, including things normally reserved for men, like spear fishing.

I want to experience it all, to learn the traditional way of life. Hunting is an everyday occurrence for them; for me it's exotic—raw. It feels primal, in a sexy sort of way. And I want to spear fish; Esirome wants to teach me.

Esirome and Marica ready the boat for the three of us. It's unusual to go out with so few people, but they want the first outing to be closely supervised, ready to turn back if I don't have the tolerance or ability to fish. Their attention is indulgent. I want to help, but they have their routine, working together like a cog and chain. Marica packs the fishing line and some food, and Esirome gathers the spear guns and fuel. I stand ready to carry a load. I am a delighted observer, and a clumsy, want-in participant.

The feeble outboard sounds like a bee buzzing, as we glide on a slick blanket of calm Pacific. The sapphire blue sky feels like a dome over our twenty-three-foot open fiberglass boat, changing to a muted black as it meets the horizon. The sun beams through a colorful reef and the jade green water, and burns the tops of my bare feet. Esirome hands over the throttle, sliding it to the right and left to show me how to steer and warning me not to overheat the engine by going too fast. The sticker says it's a forty-horsepower, but it's barely capable of half that.

We stop frequently to let the engine cool; sometimes it won't start back up. Esirome shows no concern. I follow his lead and the angst is gone. He has a couple of tools in the boat, a rarity among Fijians. While he tinkers, Marica and I paddle using long wooden poles, sometimes pushing along the bottom when it's shallow enough. He's pulling out spark plugs and clearing rubber tubes that are supposed to feed water through the system…he's done this before. We find a place to anchor and get ready to work. The ocean is not a playground; there are no bikinis or water skis. The sea is for life—to eat.

Along with a mask, snorkel, and fins, I wear full-length pants, and a long-sleeve top. Fijian women must have their bodies covered. At first I thought this was odd—to be in the water fully clothed—but I like it, regardless of cultural requirements, the protection from the sun is worth it.

Marica uses a three-prong spear to hunt for *kuita*, or octopus, clam, and sea cucumber; a *pago* is tied to her waist by a thin rope, used to fill with our take. We swim to the edge of the reef to kill our dinner. I am nervous again. *Are there sharks around here?* Fijians believe that sharks will not attack if your soul is pure. I start scanning my past to assess my risk, even searching for things I may have tried to erase from memory. Eventually conclude that I should be safe.

I swim close to him, watching him dive. From a lifetime of hunting in salt water, his actions are habitual and rhythmic. He points out the good areas to find fish and which ones to shoot for. With precision he puts a hole though the belly of a juicy meal—a grouper, large and slow, easier to pierce than lightning fast red-tailed snappers.

The spear gun I use is one of three Esirome owns, simple construction and rusty. The shaft and butt are made from hand-carved pine, light enough to float. The mechanism is similar to a slingshot, but instead of pulling the rubber back by hand, the spear is locked in place inside the trigger. The spear is launched by the rubber tubing, guided through a narrow tunnel made of plastic.

The trigger works well, but I have a hard time pulling the thick rubber into firing position. Red welts form on my stomach from holding the butt of the gun against it, the tension on the tubing is barely within my arm strength. Sometimes Esirome takes it from me to pull it back into position. He rarely fires his gun, but when he does he almost always hits. I'm firing and missing, thinking how difficult it is to kill something that *seemingly* has no intelligence. I feel like I don't belong at the top of the food chain—and I suppose I won't be if a shark finds me unworthy of life on the planet.

Esirome and I continue working the outer reef, and I start to shoot less, but with better accuracy. He continues to guide me, staying next to me, showing me what to do or not to do. After spending most of my time shooting from the surface, I find the courage to dive deep and look under a large coral head. With my feet pointing toward the surface, I peer into the shadows and see two large eyes looking back at me. This is my chance. I shoot at the eyes, without knowing what's attached to them. The water immediately turns cloudy with debris kicked up from the sea floor. I am running out of breath and now I'm scared. I rush up to the surface and call for Esirome, slightly ashamed at having left my spear and the fish under the coral head. A hit and run—*not* very Fijian.

Esirome dives to retrieve my spear and the contents on the end of it. There's a small struggle and more debris churns. I watch weakly from the surface, still scared. He pulls the spear loose and I see for the first time the rest of the big eyes—a porcupine fish, or blowfish, with sharp poisonous spines that radiate outward when inflated. When it's not puffed up, it is actually not a very big fish. My hopes for glory shrivel.

I apologize for not doing the job well, and Esirome giggles, oblivious of any error. He's already on to something new. He calls me by my Fijian name, Kereni, and points to a nearby crevice. I don't notice anything, but Marica comes over and starts poking her spear inside. A trail of murky brown water comes out. She reaches in up to her shoulder, feeling around. Her hand comes back out with nothing. She tries again, this time she's really pulling on something. Octopus tentacles are wrapping all the way up her arm. She shows no concern…she's done this before.

Then Esirome asks me to touch it. *What? Oh, no I can't. Really. I must? Oh, who said I wanted to experience it all?* I hold my breath, close my eyes, and put my hand out. I shriek, pulling back, but the slithering tentacles won't let go. I look to Esirome and Marica in a panic. Then we all start laughing. See, it *is* possible to laugh when you're in immediate danger of being killed. Logically I know this is not *Twenty Thousand Leagues Under the Sea*, but this extraterrestrial-looking creature has my nervous system in flight mode. Marica takes it from my arm and scoops it into the *pago*. I sigh; it seems I can check that off my list. Gratitude overwhelms me, and not because she does the octopus hunting. The richness of my life with them astounds me. There's nothing sterile about it, there are no cubicles, no white walls, no picket fences.

When I miss my friends and family in the U.S., when I want the convenience of a washing machine, when I want to drive a car, when I dream of dressing up for a hot date, or when I dream of having a date, when I want a hot shower and a big cushy bed, when I crave anonymity, or when I want to be free from mosquitoes and heat, I think of the precious relationship that forms between us. There's no way I can go until I have to.

Ask an American for directions and they will explain the way with turns and street names, leaving it for you to figure it out from there. Ask Fijians for directions and they will simply take you there. Esirome didn't tell me how to spear fish and leave me off to venture the reef; he escorted me, willing to slow down in order to share the experience with me. But even thoughts that I've slowed him down are American. The idea wouldn't have entered his mind; it doesn't work that way; speed and production are not his values. Esirome simply wants to be together, there isn't a future to get to, nothing to produce or save. The difference makes me feel as if I've come home. He's taken me under his wing, and it feels like being in a warm bath.

I wonder if I could do the same if I were to introduce him to my culture. I wonder if I would have a wing to take him under, one that wasn't busy flapping like a hummingbird trying to keep up with the American speed of life.

Maroroya me qai kena na baca—to keep it only to feed the worms—is a Fijian expression meaning that it is pointless to keep or accumulate things, not knowing what may happen the next day. One does not live long enough to use all he accumulates, so all must be enjoyed and shared with others while the going is good. There is no pleasure in hoarding possessions. If they are entombed with the dead, the worms will devour them.

Esirome's generosity stuns me. It's not just the sharing of material things; it's his generosity of time. Esirome includes me in everything. That's not easy given that I am a *vulagi*, a guest. Their culture requires that a guest be given the best, whether it's food, or a comfortable place to sit or sleep. Even though I am part of their every day life, my non-nativeness keeps my rank established, no matter how much humility I express. I can only thank them profusely. I am lavished in love and kindness, yet he only wants to know that I am happy in Fiji, that he has treated me well. Most importantly, he wants me to remember him.

When someone is about to leave the village, the family, or the community, a traditional ceremony is required, called a *vakavinavinaka.* There is an exchange of gifts and speeches of thanks. The day before my return to the U.S., the family gathers inside the house and waits for my arrival. We knew this day would come; we've been talking about it constantly for a month, a mixture of excitement and dread. It's a Sunday, the day we usually gather after church to share a big meal, though this Sunday will be unlike any other. No one moves after I sit down. I'm not sure what's supposed to happen next. I'm looking around the room; everyone has their head down. The solemn silence is deafening. Finally, Esirome claps his hands—a *cobo*—to signify the start. He talks to me in English. I've never heard him speak so clearly. I am honored. His voice is breaking, and deep. His words come out, between tears and shallow breaths. He presents me with the family's *tanoa*. Most *tanoas* are simply round, but this one is hand-carved in the shape of a turtle, and it's been in the family for fifty years.

I wrote my speech in Fijian, but I can't sustain it. My throat is tight; I can't form the words. My legs are beading with sweat; my face throbs with heat. I can't look up. I am crying painfully. The room is still; it's O.K. to cry, it's expected. Everyone is crying: Esirome, Marica, Senaca, Senraro. Mesa is not even running around. Bude sits nestled in Paulini's arms. Salome cuddles Kereni. Sereima holds her arm around my shoulders.

For the first time, I tell him that it was because of him, because of his family, that I could bear it when I missed my family and friends in the U.S., when I felt lonely and isolated. I tell him that every time I thought about returning early, I thought of him, I thought of his family, I thought of the sacredness of our relationship. I slide my gifts toward him: my snorkel, mask, fins, a blanket, sheets, a foam mattress, and all my photos. But I have *nothing* that could ever match his generosity.

We are sobbing.

"Don't ever forget us," Esirome says.

Gasping for breath, I reply, "*Drëdrë. Drëdrë.*"

Karen Dunne served in Fiji from 2005-07. She is a retired female professional cyclist best known for winning the gold medal at the women's individual road race at the 1999 Pan American Games in Winnipeg, Canada. She is currently Operations Manager, Test and Development Lab at SRAM Corporation.

JIM RUSSELL

Mending Tarawa

Peace Corps Volunteers and Japanese construction workers
play a friendly game of softball on a bitterly contested
battlefield and do a little to heal an old wound.

ON NOVEMBER 20, 1943, ONE OF THE BLOODIEST WWII battles in the Pacific began on the island of Tarawa, in Kiribati. The mission of that battle was to control the airstrip on Tarawa, and thereby to control the Gilbert Islands. Over one thousand 2nd Division Marines and Sailors were killed in just three days. Only 17 of 4,836 Japanese survived what came to be known as "Bloody Tarawa."

In May of 1999, a battle of a different sort was fought there. Eighteen Volunteers and staff of Peace Corps Kiribati fought eighteen construction workers and management crew of the Japanese firm building a new wharf and warehouse. The battle was a seven-inning softball game, and the battleground was a field constructed by the contractors. The only bloodshed was from a scraped knee suffered by me going for a low line drive in the outfield. I caught it.

This Japanese construction crew had built a softball stadium to rival any field found in the U.S., minus the grass, substituting crushed coral. The field was graded and rolled perfectly flat and level. They built a backstop using scaffolding and chicken wire. Base lines, foul lines and batter boxes were measured and marked with a surveyor's precision. A small scoreboard was erected next to the Japanese third-base "dugout." A three-foot-high fence was constructed in the outfield, a tempting target for their power hitters.

I was included in the line-up because I was visiting Kiribati on temporary duty to facilitate a review of the Education for Development project. This was the second game played by the two squads. The Japanese were missing "*besuboru*" and were excited to have a bunch of Americans on Tarawa who knew the game. The Peace Corps Volunteers there lived on outer islands and came into the Tarawa capital only once every three months. Since it was my first game with them, I arrived not knowing what to expect: a friendly pick-up game? Not quite.

The Japanese team consisted mostly of young strong construction workers, mixed with a few older foremen. The PC team consisted of young PCVs, the Country Director and me (older than the PCVs), and some I-Kiribati staff, who really didn't have much of a clue about the game, but were there for a good time. I was the only one playing in sandals. We had a couple of ringers: recent college athletes, including one woman, a pitcher on her college fast-pitch team who burned my hand when I was warming up with her. However, in the game, we played slow pitch.

The atmosphere was serious in a friendly way. Let me be clear. Both sides wanted to win; and close attention was paid to the scoring, as well as the self-refereeing. Honor and integrity were the cultural values shared by both teams.

We played the seven innings energetically; trading leads every other inning. I'm not 100 percent confident of my memory, but I believe the Japanese team was ahead when the game ended. I'm not sure that anyone really considered it a "W" or an "L."

We then packed up, left the "stadium," and went over to the crew's residential compound of sleeping trailers, as well as a larger temporary "recreation hall." Construction companies take good care of their crews, outfitting them with a variety of diversion and entertainment options, including games, books, large screen television, stereo systems, and, of course, a karaoke machine.

The Japanese hosts went all-out, treating the PC Volunteers to good barbecue and fresh vegetables, accompanied by fresh sashimi and liberal amounts of beer and wine. They gave out prizes for Most Enthusiastic, Most Hits, Most Runs, Most Laughing, Best Play, and I don't recall what else. By the end of the evening everyone had taken a turn singing. Somehow, I was able to remember the Japanese lyrics to "Sukiyaki," thanks to a one-week canoeing trip with a group of high school exchange students I had taken back in my camp counselor days. I sang it as a duet with one of the Japanese, and I must have looked good wearing my Japanese Rising Sun headband, which was awarded to me for my "Warrior Spirit" in the softball game.

These activities probably slowed the construction schedule for the wharf and warehouse. Maybe it was just another softball game. Maybe it was just another potluck dinner. But, maybe, it was a symbol of something a little more meaningful, a little more beneficial, considering that the players came together—on the former battlefield, in plain sight of rusting Japanese big-gun placements—Japanese, American, and I-Kiribati, as friends.

Jim Russell served as a teacher in Thailand from 1985-87 and as a Program and Training Specialist for the Peace Corps in the Pacific from 1996-2002. He is currently a Pacific Sub-Regional Program and Training Officer at Peace Corps. Community youth development, public school education, and adult learning are the themes—he says—that have created a tapestry of experience that can loosely be called a career. He is still adorning that tapestry with guitars, ukulele, bone and stone carving, knot-tying, and continuing life-adventures with his wife Carol.

✶

Second Chances

The perfect project often completes itself in meals and conversation.

IT WAS A WEEK LIKE ANY OTHER. EVERY MORNING I WENT TO THE office, practiced Thai with co-workers, checked my email, had lunch, and then was off to visit my local community store. My friends there told me that they were eager to learn basic accounting skills. When I offered to teach them, they said "Great! Come back tomorrow and we can start." They had been telling me to come back tomorrow for the past three months. I was seven-and-a-half months into site, and I was getting frustrated that the elusive project hadn't materialized. I began to wonder what I was doing in Thailand and what, if any, difference I could make there.

After the community store, I headed off to my weekly music lesson. I had just started learning to play the Thai fiddle, and I enjoyed spending time with my teacher, Ajan Chalaan. He knew some English, and along with my mediocre Thai, we were able to have decent conversations. I asked him where he had learned his English, and he told me that a Peace Corps Volunteer, same as me, had taught him. Surprised, I asked him how long ago that was; it took him a while to calculate the number in his head, but finally he answered forty-four years ago.

"Wow," I said, even more amazed. "Your teacher was probably one of the first Volunteers here in Thailand; probably from Group 1."

"Really," he said. "And what number is your group?" I answered that we were the 118th. My teacher pondered that for a moment and then asked, to no one in particular, "Forty-four years.... Has it really been that long?"

I asked him what he remembered about the Volunteer, and he told me his name (Mr. Tate), how tall he was, and how bad his Thai was. But the one memory that always sticks out in his mind, he told me: How Mr. Tate would play basketball with his students every day after school. As we were saying our goodbyes, I told my teacher that I was amazed he still could remember so many things about Mr. Tate, especially after forty-four years. He seemed surprised himself and, after a moment of silence, thanked me for bringing up some good memories. As I biked away, I wondered if I would ever make any sort of impact the way Mr. Tate had.

Later on in the week I found myself spending the evening, as usual, eating dinner with my Thai family. Over the past seven months, I had come to know and grow close to this family: father, mother, and daughter. They had taken care of me from day one, inviting me for meals, helping me move in, taking me on family trips. One day, I just naturally became a part of their family, their new son and little brother.

This particular evening, my family told me the story of their son. Surprised, I told them that I didn't know they had a son. My Pa told me that their son died while he was very young, but were he alive today, he would be around my age. It was then that my Pa told me that he believed a part of his son was living through me, that some semblance of him was reincarnated in me.

"I am very grateful," my Pa told me. "I am very grateful for this second chance to spend more time with my son."

Listening to their story, on top of the images of Mr. Tate playing basketball with his students, it suddenly became clear to me. All the frustration about not having projects, about not seeing any tangible results, was because I still was not getting what Peace Corps was about. It wasn't about building monuments to yourself, some long-lasting memorial that would remind the host country nationals of your past presence. It was about building relationships with people, connecting with them in a way that transcends the cultural and language barriers. If you are able to do this, then your Peace Corps service will be a success.

It was a week unlike any other week. It was a week of letting go and understanding. As I sat there eating dinner with my family, sharing in their tears as they remembered their son, sharing in their smiles as they believed that a part of him had come back to them, I was filled with a peace that I hadn't felt before. A peace that told me, "Stop worrying, you're doing fine. Enjoy your time here."

Arnold Solamillos (Thailand 2006-08) is an unapologetic idealist whose head is perpetually in the clouds. After graduating from college with a business degree in Finance, he decided to turn his back on corporate America by becoming an AmeriCorps Volunteer, and eventually, a Peace Corps Volunteer. He currently works for the Social Security Administration and was recently accepted into the University of Arizona's Master of Public Administration program as a Peace Corps Fellow. He has been known on occasion to entertain his class by playing the Thai fiddle, where his students' smiles serve as a constant reminder of his time in Thailand and especially of his old teacher, who taught him that music truly is a universal language.

PART TWO

WHY ARE WE HERE?

REILLY RIDGELL

Of Love and Language

*It's a good thing to know exactly what she/
he means when she/he says "I love you."*

The *Truk Islander*, a ninety-five-foot long *copra* and supply ship, pulled slowly away from the Weno dock to begin its journey to a group of atolls 180 miles west of the Chuuk Lagoon. There, at last, I would begin my Peace Corps assignment. I would start teaching school, something I'd never done before. I would live without electricity or plumbing, something I'd never done before. I would go shirtless and wear the brief one-piece loincloth traditional to the Central Carolines, something I'd never done before. And I would, whatever it took, definitely learn to speak the language. Learning to speak a foreign language was something I'd never done before either, despite four years of French classes in high school and college.

As the dock receded, I waved to the three friends who had come to see me off, Volunteers waiting for another ship to take them to their islands. I had been on Weno, at that time called Moen, a vestige of some nineteenth-century explorer's mistake, for about two weeks. Weno had all the charm of a ramshackle, but lively, frontier town. Pick-up taxis with people piled in the back wove their way through pot-holed roads past quaint and musty stores in corrugated tin buildings. These contained some inventory items that probably hadn't been handled, or dusted, since first put on the shelves years ago. It had been an interesting couple of weeks.

Weno at least had power and some plumbing. There were restaurants and stores with cold drinks, a few makeshift movie theaters, and several tacky bars that were best avoided. Most of the Peace Corps and ex-Peace Corps Volunteers who had stayed in country, along with other expat Americans, preferred places like the tin-covered-by-thatch roofed Maramar Hotel. It had a breezy, comfortable, screened-in restaurant where one could have a reasonably decent breakfast or lunch and look past the coconut trees to the broad Chuuk Lagoon.It was easy to pretend that the rusting hulk of a ship in the view was a war relic when it actually was some fishing boat run aground in a storm in the 1950s or 1960s.

Then there was the language. Chuukese was spoken everywhere because, of course, that was their language, and in the 1970s, that's just about all anybody spoke. We had spent ten weeks on the Big Island of Hawaii in training. The language portion of the training had been good: four hours every morning of intense immersion, no English allowed. But in the end, we arrived in Chuuk with only basic language skills. Actually learning to speak and understand would be up to us individually.

It was hard to get used to the sound of Lagoon Chuukese. Choppy and often spoken in a quasi-falsetto, it was hard for us to make sense of it. Then there was that thing with the "N's" and "L's." Speakers of Lagoon Chuukese could not pronounce the "L" sound. It wasn't used in their dialect, and when they spoke English, their "L's" sounded like "N's." Outer islanders who spoke different dialects, however, had no trouble saying "L's."

The *Truk Islander* headed for the Northeast Pass out of the huge Chuuk Lagoon, a forty-mile wide expanse with several mountaintops poking up out of the sea, all surrounded and enclosed by a single barrier reef. Physically, it was beautiful. In the bright tropical sun, the greens of the islands and blues of the water were overpowering. As we slid along the Weno shore with the island of Fefen dropping off to port, the engines thumped reassuringly somewhere in the bowels of the ship. The smell of diesel mixed with the fresh salt air. Yes. I was off to my great adventure.

It took about an hour to reach the pass through the reef. We slipped out between the two flat reef islands and headed into the open ocean. The swells weren't too bad, but it was easy to tell we were no longer in a lagoon. Among the passengers were a Polowat family, returning home to the island where I would be stationed, and a Lagoon Chuukese girl going out to one of the other islands on the ship's itinerary.

By the time we had cleared the pass and hit the open ocean, dusk was approaching. I watched the mountaintops of the lagoon islands turn grey and shrink along the distant horizon. As a Peace Corps Volunteer, I was riding deck passage. I had purchased a pandanus sleeping mat, but there was scant room on the ship's fantail. Besides, the Polowat family was there and had made a tent from a sheet to help keep out the wind. I hadn't thought much about where or how I would sleep. I had been too busy enjoying the experience and watching the scenery.

It was then that I was approached by the Lagoon girl. In her early twenties, she was moderately pretty and had a really nice smile. She tried to converse with me, and we managed a little. But her English was about as good as my Chuukese, so communication was difficult. Finally, she got around to asking me where I was going to sleep. I replied that I didn't know.

She then said something to me in Chuukese that I did, in fact, understand—except that it made no sense. She said "*Ua tonguk.*" Which means, in English, "I love you." I was really caught off guard. I just stared at her with a befuddled expression on my face. So she repeated it, in English this time: "I nove you."

O.K., so I knew the "nove" was actually "love," and I had heard her right the first time in Chuukese. Now I was definitely confused. Here was a girl I'd only known for a couple of hours, and only talked to for about twenty minutes or so, and she was already in love with me. To make matters more puzzling, romance in Chuuk was supposed to be very difficult and always clandestine and discreet. Was I actually going to "get lucky?" Right there on the ship with a girl I'd just met?

Then she told me that she had a cabin bunk, but that I could use it. Now my thoughts were really taking off. I decided not to say anything, or do anything, but just wait to see how things played out. I couldn't believe that anything would happen. But why did she tell me she loved me?

She took me to a small cabin and pointed to the bottom bunk. She insisted that I sleep there and put my pandanus sleeping mat on the floor for herself. There was a Chuukese man using the top bunk. Three in the cabin was not very conducive for amorous activity, but I still made a couple of half-hearted efforts to get her to "share" the bunk with me. She demurred. Then, feeling less than gallant for having the bunk while she had the floor, I tried to get her to switch places with me, but she absolutely refused. Not really understanding much of anything that was going on, I eventually fell asleep. The night passed without incident. Maybe she wanted me there so she wouldn't be alone with the other guy.

We reached Polowat in the morning. It lay flat on the sea like a green pancake, with the spire of the old Japanese lighthouse rising up above the tree line. The *Truk Islander* was small enough to come through the one pass into the tight Polowat lagoon, anchoring just a hundred feet or so off the beach. I said goodbye to the girl and went ashore, eager to meet my new family and settle in to my new home. The ship left the next day, taking the mysterious Lagoon Chuukese girl with it.

For the next few days, I was bombarded with new sights, sounds, and especially people. The women—including my students in school—wore only a wraparound *lavalava* and went topless. The men wore a loincloth and walked with the pride of Polowat, the island of sailing canoes and traditional navigators. The thatched canoe houses were large, cool, and impressive, as were the sea-going twenty-seven-foot sailing canoes they housed.

There was already another Peace Corps Volunteer on Polowat. He had spent a year on Udot in the Chuuk Lagoon and had requested a transfer. We were to become fast friends, but his presence was both helpful and hindering. He already was able to speak the language. I was stumbling along, confusing the hell out of people. So the people would ask him to explain what I was trying to say instead of teaching me how to say it correctly.

One day shortly after I had arrived, he and I were in one of the canoe houses talking with some men. Barefoot, I accidentally stepped on a sharp stem of a coconut leaf from a frond that was on the floor. I let out a slight yelp and pulled my foot back, a drop of blood appearing at the site of the wound. Witnessing my misfortune, one of the men said something in the Polowat dialect that I didn't catch. I looked at him for a moment; then he repeated it in Lagoon Chuukese. "*Ua tonguk.*" There it was again. I just stood there, a puzzled expression on my face, and he said it, haltingly, in English: "I love you." Now I was really confused. I knew there was no homosexual implication at all in the situation; clearly, there was something I just wasn't getting.

By this time, my fellow Volunteer had a big grin on his face. "He just means he feels sorry for you. It's what they say when something bad happens to someone or if someone has an accident or a bad day or doesn't get what they want or misses out on something or whatever. They say 'I love you' to express sympathy, it doesn't mean they're coming on to you."

The light of sudden understanding nearly blinded me. Now everything made sense with the girl on the ship. Indeed, in the weeks and months to come, I'd hear the phrase used over and over again in situations where Americans would never think of saying "I love you." Someone would bump their head, or get really sick, or not catch very many fish, and out would come the "I love you." After a while, I got used to it.

My experience with the love phrase made me even more determined to learn the language. But it wasn't easy. For one thing, we had been taught Lagoon Chuukese; the dialect on Polowat was markedly different. First were the phoneme shifts. An "S" in Lagoon was pronounced as an "H" on Polowat. Likewise a "Ch" in Lagoon became an unrolled "R." And it was very important, when speaking the Polowat dialect, to make sure and use the correct "R," for if you rolled the "R" in a certain word when it was supposed to be unrolled, you could be talking about a rather private part of the female anatomy.

The frustrating thing about learning a language is that it starts so slowly at first. One month on the island, and I still felt lost. Two months on the island, and I realized I knew three times more than I did at one month. By three months I actually began to feel that I could do this. By the end of that school year, with a ship coming to take me back to Weno for the summer, I felt comfortable. I could communicate quite well, could understand easily when questions or comments were addressed to me, and could even pick up the meaning of most overheard conversations.

By the end of my two years, I was fluent in the Polowat dialect. I felt proud of that. I was finally bilingual. My accent, especially, was pretty good, and I was even occasionally able to fool some islanders who heard me talk from behind them. When they turned around to see who it was, they were quite surprised to see me. Of course, I hadn't learned any major language like the French I had studied or the ubiquitous Spanish or even Russian or Chinese. No, I had learned a dialect that, in the early 1970s, was spoken on nine tiny islands by a total of 3,000 people or less. I had also managed a working knowledge of Lagoon Chuukese, a language spoken at that time by about 50,000 people.

To understand how people think, learning the language is a must. But not all PCVs do. A few years ago, I showed slides to a group of Micronesian PCVs who had come to Guam for a mid-term conference. Less than half of them said they were learning the language. Well, O.K. Everybody has different priorities I guess. But to those PCVs who spend at least two years in a place and don't bother to learn the language, I just have this to say: I love you.

Reilly Ridgell earned a master's degree in political science 1970 from UC Santa Barbara. After a year of unsuccessful job hunting, he joined the Peace Corps to teach in the Western Islands (Namonpattiw) of what was then called Truk (now properly called Chuuk) in Micronesia. After two years of Peace Corps (1971-73) and two more years as a teacher, he moved to Guam, where he is currently a dean at Guam Community College. He is the author of Pacific Nations and Territories, Bending to the Trade Winds, *and* Green Pearl Odyssey.

WALTER JAMES MURRAY

*
* *

An Indian Bus Journey

*Behold the Indian bus! A wonder of public
transportation with a corps of drivers to match.*

THE BUS PULLED OUT OF HOSHIAPUR RIGHT ON TIME AT SIX
o'clock in the morning with a full load and all my worldly
belongings piled upon the roof. I had a comfortable window
seat except for lack of legroom, which couldn't come near
accomodating my long legs. I had arrived at Hoshiapur, a
Punjabi town in northwestern India, five months earlier—in
August of 1971—assigned to teach language teaching methods
at a private B.Ed. (Bachelor of Education) college.

In the first days of December, though, a war broke out
between India and Pakistan, forcing me to evacuate. I spent
most of the duration on a beach in the former Portuguese
enclave of Goa on the Indian Ocean. During my absence, the
director of the school had announced that for political reasons
(i.e., the "tilt" toward Pakistan by Nixon), I would no longer
be welcome at his school. As a result I was now en route to
another B.Ed. college: this one at Rewari, in Haryana State,
fourteen hours away from Hoshiapur by bus.

Four hours after departing, the bus pulled into the station at Chandigarh, the state capital of both Punjab and Haryana. There my luggage was shifted to the roof of another bus, its driver impatiently revving the engine. I hopped aboard to find the last (and worst) seat on the bus: the one right behind the driver where, if I didn't get them out of the way in time, my knees were rapped by the floor shift every time he changed gears.

Just south of Chandigarh and across the border from Punjab, we were stopped at the *octroi* (a customs post) where the Haryana State government collected duty. At least a dozen agents inspected passenger luggage inside the bus and atop as well. Soon a controversy ensued outside the bus, with agents confronting the passengers and the passengers angrily shouting what sounded like denials. Both sides were waving their arms and glaring at one another. Not knowing what the problem was, I could only observe the scene from my seat inside the bus with bemused detachment.

The argument finally petered out, and the passengers got back on, including a man who had been sitting in a seat behind me. The bus started up and we sped off. As soon as I could, I turned around and asked the man, who spoke English, what had gone on back there. He said the customs men wanted somebody to pay duty on a table fan they had found on the roof and nobody on the bus had claimed it as theirs. Realization that I was the culprit hit me at once: It was my fan. When I was able to speak again, I told him offhandedly that it belonged to me. He laughed and turned to the others and repeated what I had said. There was more laughter. Who would have thought the sahib would be having a fan atop a bus in India? I had inadvertently put one over on the customs agents and delighted in the momentary fame bestowed on me by my fellow passengers.

At Ambala, a fair-sized town in Haryana, I was able to change seats, taking the one on the left next to the driver where I had a good view of the road. The bus motored on to Rohtak, where we would arrive early in the afternoon. The road was a narrow, two-lane blacktop going through a populous area accommodating vehicles from large, overladen trucks to wooden-wheeled carts pulled by various combinations of muscle power, including cow, buffalo, horse, oxen and man. Our driver skillfully wound his way through and around the continually evolving challenges, his left hand deftly and repeatedly moving the gearshift through its range of options. From my seat I could share with the driver his every crisis and solution.

By the time we pulled into Rohtak, I was famished. There had been opportunities to buy food along the way, but they were usually offered through the bus windows by raggedy vendors. Because I had already found that bus station food was quite good and no problem for me, I managed to be the first off the bus and hurried through the crowd looking for a restaurant. There were a number of them , and I chose one that had the popular samosas, a meat-filled pastry that was filling and appetizing. I sat down at a table already claimed by mynah birds pecking crumbs at my feet and ate my fill, along with a bottle of soda. Satisfied, I went back to the bus.

But it wasn't there! The dock where the bus had parked was empty and there was not a bus anywhere to be seen. Had I missed the bus? Had it gone without me? A feeling of having been abandoned, of losing my belongings and of being stranded miles from my destination swept over me.

My plight attracted the attention of a policeman who came out of nowhere and in skimpy, but adequate, English asked me what the trouble was. I said my bus had gone without me and I didn't know what to do. He asked me a few questions and then took me to the station office to make inquiries. There I listened apprehensively to the talk going back and forth without catching a word. I was relieved when he smiled broadly, took my hand in his, and, as with a child in tow, escorted me back to the platform. It seemed the bus was in need of servicing, he said, all the while holding my hand, and had been driven away from the station to be cleaned and refueled. The relief I felt was enormous.

Holding hands with another man was something I was not accustomed to even after seven months in India, where the practice was commonplace. I had experienced it briefly in my short stay, but always reluctantly. I knew that in South Asia and in the Arab lands to the west, hand-holding between men didn't raise an eyebrow, but where I came from, it was decidedly out of place. Now I was holding hands with a man and feeling entirely at ease, like I'd been holding hands all my life. I inwardly hoped he wouldn't take his hand away because the warmth and touch and intimacy gave me the sense of security I needed. Looking at one another amiably, we exchanged small talk and basked in our new-found friendship. Why, I could hold hands forever. Then the sound of an approaching bus got our attention, and he let go of my hand to point it out. "That you bus," he announced triumphantly. As the bus came nearer, my eyes focused on the roof: I could see my belongings were still there, the fan the most prominent of all.

It was now about twelve hours since I'd boarded the bus in Hoshiapur, and there were still two to three hours to go. It was becoming a long day. The steady droning of the bus over the endless road was trying. It was time for something to shake us, the driver and me, out of a growing lethargy.

At the instant I saw that "something," I felt the driver ease up on the accelerator. He had seen it, too. There was a large object in the middle of the road blocking our way. There was no telling yet what it was, but I knew we would have to go around it on the shoulder. The distance narrowed. At about two hundred feet I could see what it was: a four-wheeled oxcart with rubber tires covered with a tarpaulin. Two animals, one a buffalo and the other a cow, were tethered to a tree by the side of the road, but there was no sign of the owner. As we rolled to about thirty feet from the cart, the tarpaulin lifted and a head poked out with a look of bewilderment and amazement written all over it. The bus driver set the right wheels on the shoulder, and we passed by, mere inches from the cart, as the man lying in it simply stared at us, evidently without a clue as to where he was.

I was taken aback, finding it hard to believe that, even in India, anyone would park a vehicle in the middle of a main road, such as it was, and retire for the night. The bus driver showed no reaction whatsoever; he put his foot to the pedal and drove on without the slightest indication anything unusual had happened. Bus drivers in India have to be inured to everything.

We now had the road entirely to ourselves. As we drove in the moonlight, I started to think of what was in store for me. I had been assigned to a teacher training college called the Satish Public College of Education, a private college with no more than two hundred students, most of whom were ostensibly preparing to become high school teachers. The college was owned by a group of local businessmen and supervised by a principal hired by them. There would be a room in the dormitory for me, and I would have a co-lecturer, an Indian national, to work with in the English department.

My reverie ended when the bus pulled up at Rewari. It was 8:30, and the town had already gone to bed when the bus pulled up to a stop. From the bus window I could see no sign of a welcome committee. But because all the other passengers were getting off, I thought it prudent to get off as well. I was the last to climb up to the roof of the bus to retrieve my belongings, making five trips. I piled them on the bare, dusty ground. I stood for a time watching for anyone who was looking for me, but there was nobody. The bus drove off, and one by one the passengers disappeared. I was alone. Picking the sturdiest piece of luggage, an aluminum suitcase, I upended it, sat, and started to sort out my unexpected, unpromising situation.

It is disconcerting to be alone in a strange city on the other side of the world late at night burdened with five pieces of luggage. I couldn't leave the luggage alone on the street and go looking for help. I would just have to sit in isolation and wait for events to unfold. Looking left and right, I could see only vacant streets and closed-up shops. Even the ubiquitous Indian street dogs were absent, and the birds had long since found a roost. I shook off a growing feeling of estrangement. But what to do?

A hotel might be the answer, if I could find such a place, one that wasn't a flophouse with, in my imagination, seedy rooms crawling with vermin and peopled with villains intent on taking advantage of me. I would be an easy mark. Railroad stations were good places to go; they were cheap, clean and safe. If I had known one existed only a short walk away, I'd have felt better.

The stillness deepened. Then far off down a street I saw the approaching lights of a vehicle. It was a jeep, the color of the jeeps the Peace Corps used in India. It pulled up next to me, and Les and Clyde, two fellow Volunteers from my group, India 122, got out and greeted me. Along with them was my new co-lecturer, Ashok Kumar Nagar.

I had not gotten off at the last stop after all. That was where the bus went after leaving me on the road and where my friends were waiting. When to their dismay I didn't get off, they immediately asked the driver if he knew where I was. They came at once, making a happy ending to my first very long Indian bus journey.

Walter James Murray served in India from 1971-73, teaching language teaching methods on the college level. He had previously volunteered in Brazil from 1962-64 (his story "The Dinner Pet" appears in The Americas volume). Before joining the Peace Corps, Murray served in the Air Force during the military occupation of Japan after World War II. In addition to India and Brazil, his teaching career has taken him to Laos, Saudi Arabia, Colombia, Japan, China, South Korea, and Turkey.

KRISTINE ALANIZ

✦

Sloslo Nomo

*It's the small things that sometimes matter the most,
and sometimes those small things are words.*

VANUATU, A TINY ISLAND NATION IN THE SOUTH PACIFIC, IS SAID to have the most indigenous languages per capita in the world: 113 to be exact, not counting dialects. While serving as a Peace Corps Volunteer there from 2007 to 2009, I took on the daunting task of attempting to learn Namakura, an entirely oral language that maybe only a couple of thousand people speak.

One of my best friends in the small seaside village where I lived was an elder named Bubu Bong. He was an 80-year-old gardener, chief, father to eight or nine (he couldn't remember), and total Casanova. Most days of the week, he—along with his dogs, named Trouble and Manioc—would saunter down the forest path, walking stick in hand, blue cataracted eyes sparking over a mostly toothless grin. He was the self-appointed Namakura teacher for my husband Javier and me, but there is reason to suspect he was motivated by my papaya tree, cups of Nescafé, and a captive audience to share his thoughts on current events and to relive World War II.

Our language lessons were confusing and hilarious. Bubu Bong would spout off syllables and syllables of gibberish and demand that I repeat. "That means, 'I need someone to help me collect firewood before it rains.' An important one," he'd say, eyeing my coconut leaf kitchen, totally devoid of firewood.

I'd try to break it down. "Let's start with one word," I'd plead. "How to do you say, *I, someone, collect, rain.*" But that's not how Namakura works.

Once, early on, Javier and I—diligent language students that we were—spent an entire afternoon making up a skit for our language lesson. It had an elaborate plot, set in the garden, with three acts. We performed it the next day with what we thought was flawless and flowing Namakura. We finished, huge smiles, arms open, as if to say, "ta–da!" We waited for the praise to begin, but instead Bubu stared at us, one scraggly eyebrow raised, with a look of complete and utter confusion. He finally stamped his walking stick in the dirt, in a very final sort of way. "So," he cleared his throat, "did I ever tell you about the time I went to a nightclub in New Caledonia?" Our skit was never mentioned again.

In the end, my Namakura language skills never passed the preschool level, but I am actually quite proud of that. This meant, though, that most of the time I depended on my trusty Bislama, the national language of Vanuatu. Bislama was developed during Blackbirding, a dark time in Vanuatu's history when islanders were forced to work on plantations in Australia and Fiji. A mixture of English, French, and local languages, it has evolved over the last 200 years from a simple pidgin into a genuine language with its own dictionary. Though the majority of Ni-Vanuatu rely on local languages, most also speak Bislama to communicate with people from other villages and islands.

Bislama was easy to learn and fun to speak, especially after I was able to master the sing-song style and nonsensical slang words. But it was also painfully simplified. In Namakura, for example, each finger has a different name. In Bislama, everything from your shoulder down to the tips of your fingers is called "hand." As a community health Volunteer, not being able to describe body parts was tough, but it was the deeper things that could be downright frustrating. Saying you are *kros* (cross), for example, covers up everything from mildly annoyed to red-faced, steam-coming-out-your-ears pissed off.

Bislama also has little catch phrases that can be used in a variety of situations. Everyone from two-year-olds to teenagers to elders uses them, making them unavoidable. One of my favorites was, *"Bae yumi luk"* (pronounced *bye you-mi look*). Literally, "In the future, we will see!" However, this bit of wisdom is not offered as sage advice in a serious tone. You have to sing it, cheerfully. Try it. Say it out loud right now in your most cheerful voice, and you will see how it might be annoying to people, especially if you were hoping for a more definitive answer. This phrase can be offered as a vague answer to any question or dilemma.

The phrase I heard the most was *"Sloslo nomo."* Literally, "Just take it slow." I heard this on a daily basis, but with increased frequency while in, or around, a boat. The cheapest way to travel between the 82 islands in Vanuatu is via cargo ship. One particular time, another Volunteer and I opted to take the $10 cargo ship instead of the $75 flight to a nearby island. The speedboat picked us up on the shore and brought us to where the ship was docked. To transfer to the cargo ship, I was expected to wait for the waves to shift the speed boat, then I was to climb on a tire swing and sort of fling myself through a rusty hole in the side of the ship, while wearing the required ankle-length skirt.

On my first attempt, I softly crashed into the side of the ship and tried to kick a leg up into the rusty hole. "*Sloslo nomo!*" The ship captain called out, frantically. "Please don't die!" was what I heard. *Sloslo nomo* was muttered and screamed at me at least ten more times over our eighteen-and-a-half-hour ride to the next island: while walking on deck and nearly plummeting overboard, or attempting to go into the bathroom without falling in a pile of crap.

Another common setting for *sloslo nomo* was during trips to "the bush." Javier and I spent our entire first year of service working with a village committee to plan, build, and maintain a direct gravity-fed water system. The source was a spring located straight up a mountain; from it, pipes were laid down to the village. Walking the four kilometers was slippery, there were biting black ants and ridges where you could easily plummet to your death. One particularly hot day, the committee organized a "community work day" where everyone had to carry materials up to the source. Mamas loaded bags of cement and sand on their heads, and men carried tools and timber. As an honorary mama, I hefted a rice-bag-backpack full of sand and started hiking. It had rained the night before, and by the time we were halfway there, I had fallen on my butt at least five times. After the sixth time, I laid in the mud for a while, sweat stinging my eyes, leaking a trail of sand behind me. A grandma, who must have been eighty years old sauntered by and paused briefly to check me out. She was barefoot, wearing an island dress (a muumuu with lots of ruffles) with a huge bag of cement balanced on her head. She could not have weighed over eighty pounds. She looked at me and smiled. I slowly got up as she sang, "*Sloslo nomo!*" Translation: get off your ass and start walking, girl.

We had many committee meetings for this water project. Sometimes they were urgent: we had to make a decision about something for our grant, or we needed the secretary to withdraw some money. Invariably, no one besides the chief would show up. We'd wait, eat a few bananas, and wait some more. Finally he'd sigh and say, "*Lego.*" Just let it go. I'd protest, but my reasoning would trail off. *Lego.* We'll put it off for another week. Or month. It will get done. And it did...mostly. "*Lego*" turned out to be another one of those phrases people integrated into everyday occurrences.

On New Year's Day 2008, our Country Director called the village to let me know my grandfather had passed away. When I left the U.S., all four of my grandparents were alive and well. Even though I knew it was a possibility that one could pass away, I wasn't prepared for the sadness, helplessness, and isolation I felt. When my counterpart and local village health worker, Annie, heard the news, she and her three sisters came to pay a visit. Following their custom, when they neared my tin shack, they began wailing loudly. They entered my veranda and draped bright pieces of fabric around my shoulders. They held me tight, still wailing, for a few minutes, then sat down on the mats and stared at me.

"We are so sorry. We are sorry for your mom, for your dad, for your grandma."

Tears were streaming down my face. I told them stories about my grandpa, a dairy farmer. He didn't go to school for very long, just like a lot of people here. He had six kids and many, many grandkids. He was married to my grandma for sixty years. I started crying again, thinking about my grandma. Sixty years is a really, really long time.

"Krissy," they said with finality. "You must *lego*. Your grandpa had a good, long life. Many kids. He worked hard and loved his family. Death is part of living. Its time to *lego*."

I was amazed by how soothing those words were, despite the fact that I didn't want to *lego*. I wanted to hold on. But they were right. When my other grandfather died, six months later, their words came back to me. He too, had a long, wonderful life. It was his time to *lego* and ours to *lego* him.

It was soon after that I began to realize the complexity of these expressions, *lego, sloslo nomo, bae yumi luk.* They went beyond just words used to command you to do something, or not do something. They even went beyond a state of mind, or an attitude you could adopt to deal with the situation. These phrases embodied the culture of Vanuatu. They summed it up in a few words and provided important mantras to get you through tough or stressful times. People in Vanuatu live "in the moment" as we in the West might say. Not because they are looking for nirvana, but because there is no other way to live.

Much of this view of life is linked to the natural world. Vanuatu gardens and the bush provide everything: food, shelter, warmth, ceremonial objects. There is a sense of security, but people are also completely accepting of life's hiccups and possess deep knowledge that at any point life could completely change. Vanuatu is one of the most disaster-prone countries in the world. Volcanoes, earthquakes, land slides, tsunamis are a huge part of life here. So there is no sense in planning beyond the next crop; you have no control over the weather.

My last year of service, I tried to embrace these catch-phrases. The truck is thirty minutes late, meaning I am going to be late for my workshop. *Lego!* No one was going to show up on time anyway. Should I extend my service? I see so many benefits, but drawbacks, too! *Bae yumi luk.* No sense in worrying about it twice. Just make a decision and then deal with the consequences as they come.

My husband made fun of my list of intangible things I planned to "bring back to America." This list included harvesting rainwater, eating grapefruit daily, gardening, spending more time with old people, and the Vanuatu stroll (walking excruciatingly slow and smiling at everyone). I hoped that these mantras would make it back into life in the U.S., amidst stressed-out people and a fast-paced environment. Before a job interview: *"Sloslo nomo."* Stock market crashing: *"Bae yumi luk."* Dealing with loss and death: *"Lego."*

Before I left for the Peace Corps, I had heard many returned Volunteers say: "I gained so much more than I gave. I learned so much more than I taught." So I moved to Vanuatu with the mindset that I would grow and learn and gain. But I never could have imagined how uttering one, two, or three tiny words could bring me so much peace and tranquility. How these expressions could influence my life and, hopefully, will continue to do so. *Bae yumi luk.*

Kristine Alaniz served in Vanuatu from 2007-09 with her husband Javier as a health Volunteer. She now works to improve the health of women and children in inner city Milwaukee. She and Javier find the lessons they learned in Vanuatu helpful in raising their spunky toddler Aya and preparing for the arrival of Baby #2 in September 2011.

Families

Being close to the families we were born into is no bar to
becoming a part of a larger family half a world away.

I AM HERE IN THE PHILIPPINES AGAIN IN 2006 AT CHRISTMAS, with the Escaler family, sitting in the bamboo *kubo* with the thatched roof out front of the house that was my home for three Peace Corps years, 1968-71. Raul, the youngest, and his family live here now with Nanay. Raul turned fifty last month, and I joined all the family for a party with lots of food, song, and stories. Nowadays there is the addition of a video with music and pictures of Raul's life. How times have changed.

This year I brought a copy of Nanay's letters that she sent to me back in October of 1991 after Tatay died. I had told Raul about the letters that reminisced about her life with Tatay in the early years, but only now did I bring a copy. Although I had been exchanging letters and Christmas cards with Nanay since I was a Volunteer and had even managed a brief visit back the Christmas of 1976, the obligations of husband, house payments and work with only two weeks of vacation had kept me from visiting again. Then in 1991, I knew it was time to return because all their five kids would be there for the wedding anniversary, coming from overseas jobs in Saudi Arabia and Dubai.

So I arrived back in Limay, Bataan, to stay in my old room at the back corner upstairs in the hollow-block house that Tatay built on Villafranca Street. There in the corner was my old flower-decorated dresser and the Peace Corps issued fan that still worked. They don't build solid metal fans like that any more, and Kuya Eddie had kept it alive for twenty years with his repair magic.

A fiftieth wedding anniversary celebration calls for a repeat of wedding vows in the Catholic church located just down the street over the bridge. Nanay, Tatay, five children and their spouses, fourteen grandchildren and the great grandchildren were all dressed up in traditional dresses and *barong* shirts. I wasn't told to bring a special dress and felt that I stood out more than usual with my turquoise sundress. But I was included in all the preparation, festivities and pictures anyway—even getting all done up with makeup that I never wore at home. The photographer carefully got pictures of Nanay's gown as well as the church ceremony and all the family standing for photos after the ceremony. All this was carefully preserved in a golden wedding photo album. There I am standing in the back row in bright turquoise with a big grin on my face.

I was back home only two months when disaster struck, and Raul called me with the news that Tatay was dead. He had been inspecting the possible storm damage to his son Efren's house that was being built under Tatay's supervision when he slipped, fell, hit his head, and died. It was a freak accident. A sad end to a wonderful life just celebrated together with Nanay.

I was surprised when Nanay's letter arrived in October just after the town fiesta. "Do you like to hear about Tatay and me?" she wrote, continuing in both English and Tagalog to tell me of their growing up together and the courtship starting December 16, 1940. Her guardians did not approve because Tatay had no work. So they eloped on May 2, 1941. "*Mabait si Tatay.* (Tatay was kind) He loved me very much. Remembering those days. It's hard to forget."

Soon after they married, war came to the Philippines, and Bataan was in the center of the resistance to the Japanese invasion. Their eldest, Eddie, was born on April 9, 1942, in hiding. It was the day the Japanese took over Bataan as the American soldiers retreated to the island of Corregedor. The next morning Nanay, Tatay and infant Eddie walked to the town of Balanga. Nanay told of encounters with Japanese soldiers and relief at being let to continue on their way. "We were one of those joining the Death March."

Tatay found work where he could, and soon the new family was able to take a boat with Tatay's brother to the other side of Manila Bay, then to Manila, and eventually to the Bicol region for the rest of the war. There they lived between the mountains and the sea with fishing and "rice, fruits, sugar cane, coconuts to eat." In 1945 Nanay saw U.S. airplanes "dropping some apples and cigarettes on which was written a message by General MacArthur: *na may sulat na* (I shall return) *ni Mac Arthur.*" When the Japanese left, Nanay and Tatay returned to Bataan. Tatay built the house where they raised their family.

My own family ties almost kept me from being a Peace Corps Volunteer. When I joined the Peace Corps in 1968 after college, I was offered the Philippines for a secondary science teaching assignment. We trained for two months in San Jose, California, studying Tagalog, Filipino culture and teaching techniques. Toward the end of the two months, I was called in for a special interview and was told they were unsure whether

I would stay long as a Volunteer. My responses showed that I was very close to my family and spent much of my time, including vacations, with them. The Peace Corps worried that I would get too homesick or something and not stay. I asked the interviewer if he had ever lived in another country, and the answer was "no." I told him that living and teaching in another country was a life-long dream of mine and that my family supported me. I guess they figured to give me a chance, and I was much relieved to be able to join the group heading for the Philippines in September 1968.

Arriving to teach biology and general science in Limay Municipal High School, I met my host parents Mr. and Mrs. Silvestre Escaler, whom I was invited to call Tatay and Nanay (father and mother). There had been another Peace Corps Volunteer boarding with them, but she had left after only one month in the country. The three upstairs rooms in the house were occupied by Carmen, the middle daughter; Miss Auring Pasqual, the Filipino teacher at the high school; and me. The two youngest boys slept on mats in the living room under their mosquito nets. Nanay and Tatay had their own room downstairs.

I loved teaching. My colleagues, principal and I put together a school library, held science fairs and went on field trips in science class. I made friends. In the traditional Filipino way, Nanay always asked where I was going and who my companions were. If I wanted to go someplace and had no companion, twelve-year-old Raul was offered as my companion, and off we would go. He remembers so much better than I the little adventures we had when he trailed along as I explored the mountains, rice fields, the shore of Manila Bay or went to other towns visiting Peace Corps friends.

There were, of course, rough spots in my life in the Philippines that have become part of the Escaler family memory. The first birthday that I celebrated in the Philippines was especially hard. On the morning of my birthday, Tatay heard me crying in my room and asked what the matter was. I explained that my family at home always treated me special on my birthday. I got to choose the day's activities, and my mother made my favorite foods and arranged for friends to come over if we had a party. I said that I was uncomfortable with the Filipino tradition of being responsible for asking my friends over for food and celebration. He said he understood and to come on down to breakfast with the family. Later that day, I was surprised when brothers Eddie and Vic and their families and my friends arrived to eat the ice cream Tatay had bought for us to share. It wasn't the same as being back home, but how special I felt. Ice cream came only once a week to the only store in town with a freezer.

Over the years my family bonds with the Escaler family have grown. So many more events—it's called life—have continued to bind us since 1991 when I returned to the Philippines for Nanay's fiftieth wedding anniversary. Since I have been a diabetes nurse educator for the last thirty years, my family visits have expanded to include yearly volunteer activities at medical missions, diabetes camps and lecturing. I continue to expand my friends and contacts in the Philippines. I have brought my husband, friends, sister and niece with me to meet my Filipino family. The Escaler family was expanding when I returned for the wedding of Ivy, Raul's eldest daughter. On May 17, 2008, she married Alfred Baldwin, a current Peace Corps Volunteer in the Philippines. Alfred and I compared notes from my Volunteer days and his time there now. We rejoiced that we have been fortunate enough to become the American members of the Escaler family.

Dory Mehdenhall Blobner taught in the Philippines from 1968-71. After earning a masters degree in health education, she switched her field to health education, got a nursing degree and started a 28-year career as a diabetes nurse educator. Officially retired, she still enjoys the diabetes volunteer work she has done in the Philippines since 1991 and Vietnam since 2002. She went back to the University of Wisconsin for Tagalog classes in 1991 and continued taking courses, one class each semester, until she received a masters degree in Southeast Asian Studies in 1998.

✳
* *

Taking Out Smallpox

*The young women of Afghanistan Group 15 worked as
a group and share an ongoing conversation here.*

OUR SMALL GROUP OF ALL-FEMALE VOLUNTEERS TRAVELED
around Afghanistan with male Afghan health workers, relying
on villagers hospitality for food and shelter and under orders
to vaccinate every man, woman, and child as part of the
World Health Organization (WHO) effort to eradicate smallpox. "Who are we supposed to vaccinate?" we wondered,
flying into Afghanistan on New Year's Day 1969, gazing at
the endless miles of undulating bare mountains and empty
desert to the south and snow-covered peaks around Kabul
further north.

The answer unfolded over two years, over endless cups
of tea and days of walking, riding, extreme heat, and biting
cold—both easy times and hard—until the Afghan people and
landscape permeated our hearts and thoughts. Now, so many
years later, it is hard to bear the presence of Afghanistan on the
nightly news and the sorrow we feel at the continuing scenes
of violence and confusion.

These memories are offered in honor of the country and people we knew so long ago, and in hopes that peace will return some day to this rugged, beautiful land.

> *"Vaccinating is just what it sounds like; you go out and you vaccinate people. That was the easy part."*
>
> —Linda Berryhill

To The North: Kunduz, Baghlan, Pul-i-Khumri

Jill Vickers: Kunduz, base for about half of our group of twenty-one female vaccinators, was close to Afghanistan's northern border with the Soviet Union and over the Salang Pass of the Hindu Kush, a harrowing road trip from Kabul. We arrived in January and stayed for months in the Hotel Spinzar, whose name and whose friendly proprietor were its only good features. Our counterparts, the Afghan males, away from home as well, unpaid and cold, were waiting to work, if and when their money arrived. Consequently, I did little vaccinating those first weeks. Farsi lessons, whist games, and forays to the bazaar were the high points.

I bought long woolen *buzkashi* socks of many colors, a man's corduroy tunic, and imported cookies and chocolate—all useful in acclimating. We frequented a favorite teahouse and could hail a horse-drawn cart on the side street where we lived and be driven over the snow-covered streets for a few pennies. The lights, the aroma of kabobs on the grill in front, and the wailing of Indian torch songs beckoned to us.

Katherine White Dawa: The one thing really embedded in my cranium was how popular I was with the Afghans. Before arriving in Afghanistan, I wasn't shy about getting attention. I truly got my share. But this was different.

While vaccinating on one typical occasion, even before I had time to enter the house, I was surrounded by eight or ten animated, giggling women. Because of the language limitation on my part, they began to make gestures toward my anatomy. Several women were bold enough to feel my breast and—yes—go further. I guess they were satisfied that I lacked the male anatomy. Once satisfied of my gender, they allowed me to vaccinate them.

Another memory I have was about my hair: I had short hair and many times it was referred to as wool. Somehow I didn't get offended. I was the very popular *siya poste*—black skin.

Jacki Davidson: The Afghani people we met took much pleasure in trying to please. I remember how honored and special I felt to be invited to the home of a woman who had befriended me in Kunduz. After a wonderful dinner, including fried sparrows, with great pride she played the drum while her daughter danced for us. Only later did I learn from Doris Lessing's book *The Wind Blows Away Our Words* that she had been imprisoned and tortured by the KHAD (secret police) for her resistance activities during the Soviet invasion.

Then there were the faces of laughing children who would gather around us, sometimes taking us down a muddy path between compound walls to vaccinate. They were so curious and light-hearted. On too many occasions, however, I saw the pain and despair in the eyes of mothers and fathers who told of their child dying of smallpox or felt the desperation of a parent who took us to a sick or dying baby, asking for medical help. These were the faces of a people trying to survive and doing the best they could to peacefully feed and care for their families without the amenities of the Western world. It was a country of fruit and almond trees, gardens, flowers, and clear night skies with stars so bright they seemed unreal.

Charlene McGrath: The airport in Kabul wasn't a hive of activity in 1969. The ride into the city center previewed the contrasts that were typical of Afghanistan. On one side of the road the American Embassy, white and clean and modern, sat behind iron gates barricading this American soil from the motley camel trains and nomads that passed by and the braying, overloaded donkeys that grazed on the grass and waste.

Dinner the first night in Baghlan, where we were posted, was at a teahouse in the bazaar. It was dark when we set out, and the lights from the teahouse were reflected on the snow.

When we walked through the door, everything stopped; the men became silent, hands raised with fistfuls of rice in mid-air. We entered, took off our shoes, and sat on a raised platform with the rest of the diners. Food was ordered. All eyes were on us. Indian music blared from the radio. After several minutes, the murmured conversations resumed. We could make out Dari words like "women," "black" (in honor of our African-American Volunteer), "Kabul," "America." Halfway through the meal of kabob, rice, bread, and tea, "Strangers in the Night" by Frank Sinatra came on the radio. It seems that every night at 10:00 P.M., Radio Kabul played an English-language song. Everyone in the tea house looked at us and the waiter gestured with his hand as if to say, "This is your music." We laughed and the men in the teahouse nodded their heads, knowing who the strangers in the night were.

Carol Crawford Omar: After walking up and down parched hillsides through dry, hot valleys, along dried-up creek beds and over countless empty irrigation ditches, we'd arrive at a village. Ushered by our counterparts and the village elders to cushions, soft mats and carpets on a raised platform, often in the shade of a few wonderful trees, we'd always be served the ubiquitous tea and condiments. But also, to my utter astonishment, would occasionally appear out of nowhere platters of glorious fresh fruit: juicy, sweet watermelons and white-fleshed honeydew-like cantaloupes; grapes more delicious than any I'd ever eaten: sweet, crisp, and served on a bed of grape leaves; and to drink, *mast*, a yogurt, dill, cucumber, and salt drink sure to quench one's thirst like nothing else, served from cool pottery jugs. Out of their stark and austere environment, through creative and judicious use of resources, the Afghans had created gardens of Eden. I honor their ability to create such abundance from a difficult environment. I've never been the same since.

To this day, I never use more water than necessary, never waste water left over in a teapot, never use drinking water if some other cleaning method is available, never stay in the shower longer than necessary, and am continually conscious of my good fortune to be blessed with an abundance of potable water. To me, every drop is precious.

Patricia G. Mittendorff: My grasp of the Farsi language was shaky in our first days in–country, but there was no mistaking the meaning of the women of a small Turkomen village in northern Afghanistan as they pointed to empty cradles and cried. The translator confirmed that the babies who had slept in those cradles had died within the past two weeks of smallpox. Their question for us: Why didn't you come sooner? I could feel a crack in my heart.

After that first meeting with the grieving mothers and the scene of devastation that smallpox had left behind, we caught up with the disease. This time, we got to a village when there was active pox, but we were no more help in this village than in the last. I remember the terrible moment of coming face to face with this scourge. I entered a tiny mud hut to find a young mother and her two children covered with pox. There was nothing I could offer, and I suspect that realization could easily be read on my face.

We were too late. But a terrified young woman, herself appearing to be developing a rash, brought a baby to us and begged us to vaccinate her. The baby seemed quite young, and we had been cautioned not to vaccinate children under six months. We couldn't quite determine from the woman just how old the baby was or if the baby was even hers. But she was begging for the baby's life. We stood in the cold and mud debating. For better or worse, we vaccinated the little girl. I have often wondered her fate.

If there was any lesson, it was to get ahead of the disease! Our little troupe of odd-appearing young American women combed the area for villages that had not yet been affected. By then, we were crazed with the need to vaccinate anyone who moved.

Lizette Echols: I always liked desert villages because they were very discrete and you could organize the people, get through it, and then you would have a whole stretch of not doing anything but getting to the next village. But in Afghanistan's northern rice valleys, it was like one endless village. We'd start when we could not see daylight. The work was constant.

There were four of us, two Peace Corps vaccinators and two Afghan counterparts, so one day we split up. Martie went with her guy and I went with mine. It was hot, and I had menstrual cramps. It was the sixth month, and I guess it's between the fourth and sixth months when Volunteers get really homesick. My guy was very shy and would never ask for tea, so I was dehydrated, too. He would swing a stick at the dogs that were coming after us and hit me instead. He didn't understand how to deal with those dogs, and he couldn't organize the people. He wasn't very well equipped for the job, and I wasn't either; but we were out there. I was feeling put upon by the world and wanted a helicopter to come down and take me away.

Toward the end of the day, I came to this broken-down compound wall and there was a lady—probably about thirty-five, but she looked twenty years older—sitting there. She was blind, but I knew she also had bone TB because her neck had an open sore. She knew she was dying. I explained to her why we were there, and she immediately called her children over, unlike my experience the whole day of fighting to get the children.

She said, "I want them to have everything to protect them." Just a lovely woman.

I walked out of that compound saying to myself the world doesn't owe me a damn thing, and that's the lesson of life.

"At the Ministry of Health, they laughed at my Farsi because it was village Farsi. That's where we fit in, in the villages."

—Jane (Deezie) Flower

To The South: Kandahar, Jalalabad

Carolyn Moll: Peace Corps experiences in Afghanistan are so woven into the fabric of my life that it is difficult to isolate the individual threads that form the whole. As a smallpox vaccinator working under WHO, I recall vividly seeing an unforgettable case: a young boy dying in an empty room, with only a blanket and a jug of water as companions. A very lonely end to a very young life. Now, forty years later, smallpox is considered to be eradicated worldwide. I'm glad to think we may have helped!

Maggie Eccles: Flies crawled over the baby's face; the mother, seemingly unconcerned, continued serving us tea and bread as we sat in the village's guesthouse, then quickly left, the baby slung at her side. It was 5 A.M. and time for us to start walking with our male Afghan counterparts to ensure we could reach and vaccinate several villages before the desert summer sun got completely unbearable. In this weather we had early, short days, napping through the hot mid-day and sometimes continuing our work until dusk. We were like apparitions appearing out of the dusty brown desert, claiming to be women, but acting like men; traveling with men not our husbands; trying to communicate in fractured Farsi in a land of Pashto speakers.

"Why does your father let you go so far?" the women asked us. "How many sheep will he give for your dowry?"

That next winter, a group of us piled into a Land Rover to drive south through Jalalabad, home to abundant fruit trees and the occasional palm tree. At dark we stopped to pick up a couple of Afghan soldiers who clung to the outside of the vehicle: "to protect us against bandits," our counterparts explained, though the skinny frames of the soldiers in over-large uniforms didn't inspire confidence. Miles later, after bumping over stony fields on no discernible road, we arrived at a small mud house in what seemed the middle of nowhere.

"The local health clinic," our companions told us. Propane lanterns cast yellow light on the walls of the clinic as, without any further discussion, we lay down on the mud floor on thin *tushaks*, mattresses, and pulled quilts over us against the biting cold.

I lay awake for some time, watching the light shadows dance on the mud walls and contemplating the mounds that were my fellow vaccinators. Most of them seemed instantly asleep. For a few moments before sleep overtook me, I thought how strange this scene was and marveled at how calmly our group of mostly twenty-something young women from America adjusted to whatever came along. As the years have gone by, I've come to realize how key this quality was to our ability to participate successfully in the vaccinating program and how useful this same quality has proven to me over and over again, in situations far removed from—yet oddly similar to—this dark night in an isolated mud hut in Afghanistan.

"My mother was absolutely convinced I was going off to die."
—Martie Haynes

Rita Hackett: Sometime in school I learned that the most beautiful sounds in the English language were found in the words "cellar door." Shortly after John Kennedy's inauguration, I replaced them with what became for me the most beautiful, powerful, and evocative sounding words: Peace Corps. I was merely a freshman in high school, but the notion of volunteering overseas kindled a spark in me that did not die.

Our work was challenging for us and intrusive for the Afghans. We would arrive unannounced, sometimes breaking up funerals and weddings to vaccinate, sometimes becoming the guests of honor at the wedding. The job provided us with the opportunity to travel widely within the country, to places where foreigners had never been. In keeping with the Afghan code of hospitality, we were treated with great respect and curiosity and given the best of what they had. Even up to my final days when I admittedly grew weary of certain aspects of life in a conservative culture, I never ceased to be deeply touched by the kind hearts of the Afghan people.

These many years later, those two invaluable years are still with me like nothing else from my youth. I like to think that they've enabled me to reserve judgment, knowing that things are seldom as they appear to be, making me more open and tolerant of different people and ways of thinking. I like to think that all of us who served have had a positive impact on our families and communities. Peace Corps...how sweet the sound.

Jan Reimer: As we hear of the ongoing violence and the influence of the Taliban on the villagers, I often think of our Afghan counterparts. I remember that there were some who were particularly "good guys." They were the ones who were able to win the cooperation of the village leaders/mullahs when convincing them to let their people be vaccinated. They won their confidence by being respectful, honest, and patient.

The "good guys" were the ones who were able to vaccinate children and women alongside us because they assured the leaders that they would not attempt to look at the women as we vaccinated. Near the end of the first year, we pushed for being allowed to go out in the field with just one female Volunteer per team of male vaccinators. What we had found was that the two women Volunteers on each team ended up vaccinating three-fourths or more of most villages, while our counterparts remained idle, waiting for us to finish. With only one woman per team, the male health workers were more likely to be allowed to vaccinate women and children alongside us—but only if they abided by strict rules governing the looking at or touching of village women (a husband might tear a hole in his wife's dress sleeve rather than let her expose a bare arm to a strange male). It was imperative that all the males on the team be "good guys," and most were.

Barbara Runyan: I remember the trip—maybe it was to Uruzgan in central Afghanistan—where we traveled in an International Harvester truck, along a single-lane dirt path. You could see for miles, and there was no curb or edge to the road. Everything was flat. In the horizon, a bus appeared. Both vehicles kept approaching each other. We did not slow down as we came nearer. Finally, when we were about twenty feet apart, our driver slammed on the brakes, as did the bus driver. Everyone got out of our vehicle and everyone got out of the bus. Everyone on both sides yelled as to who had more right of way. After about ten minutes, one person said *Birum bakhi!*—Let's go! Everyone climbed back in their vehicles, both vehicles backed up, one going off the road to the left, the other to the right, and continued on their way.

The stories here are told by women of Afghan 15 who in 1969-71 were part of the World Health Organization's initiative to eradicate smallpox. They were responsible primarily for reaching the women and girls in Afghanistan's traditional Muslim culture by traveling to remote areas and working house by house. Their story is documented in the film Once in Afghanistan, *by Jill Vickers, Jody Bergedick, and Katherine Wheatley.*

HOWARD E. DANIEL

✦

Earstaches and a Message from Chiang Kai-Shek

*Being a Hindi-speaking foreigner gets you all
the plum jobs in police investigations.*

A FUNNY ARTICLE ABOUT EAR HAIR IN THE NEWSPAPER TRANS-
ported me back to my Peace Corps days in village India, half
a lifetime ago. Local columnist David Shapiro, who must be
about my age wrote, quite entertainingly, about a battery-
powered ear- and nose-hair trimmer, a gift idea for males who,
like me, have started on their second half-century.

"Can you imagine if teenagers had nose and ear hair?" he
wrote. "They'd incorporate it into their fashion statements,
and we'd see kids walking around with nose-hair dreadlocks
and ear-hair pigtails."

That article sent me back to Rajnagar (informal translation
from the Hindi: Kingston), the north-central village in which
I learned a few of life's lessons while working as a Peace Corps
volunteer from 1968 to 1970.

It was in Rajnagar that I met a guy with the most astonishing ear hair I've ever seen. He was the local police chief. Like
a great many of those in law enforcement and the military in
India, Singh—which means Lion—belonged to one of the

warrior castes, many of whom have adopted this family name. (Singh is also the most common surname among India's Sikhs, a people with a proud martial heritage.) Men of such castes often take pride in outward manifestations of virility, usually involving hair. Outrageously long moustaches are most common. I remember one handlebar job whose owner doubled it back on itself, creating a horizontal figure eight, the mathematical symbol for infinity.

But Rajnagar's police chief was a man who wished to display not merely virility, but individuality. He did not wear a moustache. Perhaps he preferred to save his moustache wax for his luxuriant ear hair. No, he did not wear it in pigtails. His fashion statement was two stiff, brush-like appendages, which protruded the better part of an inch on either side of his face. They jutted out horizontally, carefully waxed, groomed and trimmed, each the diameter of a small, jet-black dowel. They looked like perches for a pet finch.

Singh and his "earstaches" would doubtless have occupied a modest niche in my memory in any case, but an incident that took place midway through my service in Rajnagar absolutely assured his immortality in my mind.

It began one evening as I was returning to Rajnagar by bus from a day-trip to Chhatarpur, the district town (equivalent to a county seat in the United States), about thirty miles away. When my bus pulled into the village just before Rajnagar, a young man at the bus stop spotted me in the window and said, "Your friend has come to see you. He came by parachute, or maybe balloon. I'm not sure which. He landed in a wheat field a mile or so past Rajnagar."

I've got to explain a couple of things. Unlike most Indian villages, Rajnagar was not completely off the beaten track. It was just three miles up the road from Khajuraho, famed for a fine complex of ancient temples. As an architectural monument alone, even in a country like India that is awash in such riches, it would still be a notable draw. But the temples at Khajuraho share a distinction with only one other site in India and few others in the world: its series of thousand-year-old stone reliefs as explicitly erotic as anything you'll ever see on the internet.

A place like this draws its share of foreign tourists. During my time in India, most of them flew in and out and never made it up the road to Rajnagar. But every few months, some intrepid explorers would show up in a car, having driven all the way from Europe, and a few of these occasionally ventured past Khajuraho, to Rajnagar. Invariably, someone would tell me my "friends" had arrived.

Of course, none of them were actually friends of mine. And certainly none had ever arrived by balloon or parachute. This was a distinctly new twist with a hint of espionage to it. For the espionage part, I did have a tiny bit of context with which to try to assimilate this peculiar bit of news. In the 1960s, the Soviet Union, which enjoyed warm relations with the Indian government, was trying to discredit the Peace Corps, accusing us in pamphlets available in a wide selection of Indian languages, as well as in English, of being spies. With that in mind, I felt that the best course would be to stifle my curiosity, and just go straight home and mind my own business. As expected, no foreign visitor came to see me that evening.

The next morning, as usual, I got on my bicycle and headed over to the bus stop, the social center of the village, where I generally had breakfast at a tea stall. Just as I coasted to a stop, a bus pulled in. It was way too early for a regularly scheduled bus, and this one was coming from the wrong direction, too.

When the door opened, out came Singh, followed by several policemen. He marched up the street toward police headquarters, subordinates close behind. They were bearing booty. One of them carried what looked like a modest-sized Styrofoam cooler. It trailed a spaghetti-like tangle of cords that were still connected to a hastily folded heap of plastic sheeting: a large, deflated balloon. The rest of the khaki-clad policemen carried the pile of cords and sheeting and marched up the hill behind Singh and the cooler carrier. Following them, was virtually every small boy in the village, and quite a few of the men, a procession that would have done the Pied Piper proud. I joined in, of course, and quickly worked my way toward the front.

Arriving at the police station, I took advantage of my status—as a Hindi-speaking foreigner, I was basically everybody's friend—and stepped inside. Singh sat at his desk, ear hair at rigid attention, as a subordinate began opening the "cooler," whose "lid" was fastened by wing nuts, not at the top, but the side.

Once the side panel was removed, we could see that the "cooler" was divided into compartments. In one was a timing device with a dial, marked from 0 to 72. From behind the dial, wires snaked out, leading to a good-sized Eveready battery. This told me instantly that the device, whatever it was, was not of Indian origin, since Eveready batteries were not then sold in India. Another compartment was filled with granules that looked like fertilizer, but which I guessed were a type of explosive.

The largest compartment held the solution to the puzzle. It was packed with water-stained leaflets. Printed in color, on high-gloss paper, the front was emblazoned with the flag of Nationalist China (Taiwan) and a portrait of its then-president, Chiang Kai-shek. It was not a contemporary photo of the aging leader, but one from a distinctly more youthful period. The message, scrolling vertically down the pages, was entirely in Chinese.

From my interest in world affairs, I put it together in an instant. The device had been launched from Taiwan—some

2,500 miles away—with the intention of having it drift over the Chinese mainland, where the timer would trigger an explosion and scatter Chinese Nationalist propaganda to those living under communist rule. This, after all, was at the height of the Cold War. But water had infiltrated the "cooler," and the device had failed to explode, drifting instead over practically the entire breadth of China, finally coming to rest in an Indian wheat field.

The picture was not quite so clear to Singh. As soon as he laid eyes on the pamphlets, he stared at the strange-looking script. This was not the sort of man who might let unfamiliarity with something stand in the way of an authoritative pronouncement.

"Aha!" he said in the tone of one who has made a momentous discovery—and in English, no doubt to impress his subordinates. "It's in *French*."

French, as in "French leave" and "French kissing," was a concept I'd heard applied in India to anything improper or suspicious. A little-known legacy of the British Raj, it would often elicit snickers even in the lower, non-English-speaking echelons of India's rural civil service. So Singh's conclusion, while comical to me, was quite understandable. I gave him a sketch of the relevant history. He'd never heard of Chiang or the Nationalists. The English teacher at the village school vouched for my information. Judging by the way Singh's eyes lit up, this made his prize even more valuable. India had fought a fierce border war with China only a few years earlier, in 1962.

Singh's "French" remark would probably have immortalized him for me even if he had not worn his ear hair in faux finch perches. But the twin images are ineradicable, creating a mental picture far more vivid than any columnist's imagined "ear-hair pigtails."

And I've always wondered how he wrote the balloon incident up.

Howard E. Daniel served in India (India 55) from 1968-70. He is a writer and editor, living on the island of Oahu, Hawaii.

The Great Upolu Rental Car Adventure

Sometimes, the little regrets contribute to big understandings.

OTHER THAN MY VISIT TO THE SAMOAN LUNCHEON CLUB ON Monday, that week in July 2002 was pleasant and uneventful up until Thursday, the day that would begin the great rental car adventure. The Luncheon Club is a group of mostly *palagi* (Caucasian) ladies who eat lunch together once a month, listen to a guest speaker, and organize various charitable endeavors. My impression is that it's mostly to give people something to do when they're in Samoa only because of their husbands' jobs. It was nice to meet new people, and fascinating to hear how utterly different their experiences of Samoa were from mine. One of them commented how she'd never gotten around to taking a bus yet. It's amazing how much difference a car can make.

At 8:00 Thursday morning, I reported to the Blue Pacific Car Hire office to pick up my reserved rental car. We Peace Corps Volunteers were not allowed to drive, unless we took official vacation and filled out forms saying that it's not Peace Corps' fault if we get ourselves killed. Which isn't really funny.

The car was in good condition, the one complication being that I'd forgotten to ask for an automatic: turns out they didn't have any! I know HOW to drive a stick, but I'm just not very good at it. I wasn't worried: my friend Claire could drive a manual very well, and so I proceeded (a little jerkily) into town to pick her up, and off we went.

Samoa's main island of Upolu is oblong, with Apia, the capital, on the north side a little east of center. Until a few months before, the road heading west from Apia had dead-ended at the southwest corner of the island because of mountains. New construction had just recently connected that up with the road on the other side of the mountain, and so I thought it'd be cool to drive on the new road up over the mountain. It *was* cool: great views of both the west—including the other three islands of Samoa—and the south coasts.

On Friday, I picked up our friend Shawn when he arrived on the ferry from the island of Savaii. Then Shawn, Claire, and I set off across the Cross-Island Road, which is the one straight down the middle of the island. After we crossed the mountain, we turned east on the south road and stopped for a hike along the sea cliffs in the National Forest. This is one of the few places on Upolu where you can see nice lava rocks—most of the rest of it is covered by topsoil and vegetation. We decided to go for lunch at the only restaurant on the south road, close to the southeast corner of the island. There the road makes a loop, so we figured we'd just swing around and go back to Apia from the east. Imagine our surprise, then, when just after we passed the T-intersection heading west, we found the road completely blocked by a landslide! This would've been only a minor frustration, except we'd said we would pick up a friend in town at 4:00 P.M. and it was 3:30. There was nothing we could do, so we headed back to that T-junction and went south, to get back on the south coast road going west.

It was on the road to Apia that I was reminded, to my embarrassment, that when I don't concentrate I still automatically act like an American. See, there were these two old women walking along the road as we came away from the landslide; they'd obviously gotten off one of the buses beyond it, clambered over all the mud, rocks, and fallen trees, and set off on foot for home. We pulled over and offered them a ride. That's all fine, but when we discovered that they were headed for a village back near where we'd had lunch, we thought we could just drop them off at the intersection where we were turning west and they east, and they'd get another ride shortly. So that's what we did.

About thirty seconds after they got out of the car, it hit us how incredibly rude we'd been. Any Samoan, once they'd offered those old ladies a ride, would've driven them ANYWHERE, unconditionally, even if it made them five hours late for something. We sat there for a minute, trying to decide if we should go back and pick them up again, but then we saw a car turn down their road with Samoans driving, so we felt relieved of responsibility. I always felt guilty when Samoans went out of their way to drive me somewhere or do me a favor, and it turned out that's because I don't generally expect to go out of my way that much for other people. A nice illustration of the principle we discussed in training: cultural misunderstandings arise from differing expectations.

I have no idea what those two old ladies thought of us after we so rudely dropped them off. I like to think that they were more amused than offended, a hope that recurred throughout my service, in a variety of situations. That's the foundation of why Peace Corps works: while we Volunteers provide some useful skills, we must always depend on the generous spirits of the people we meet in our host countries, and both we and they know it.

Miriam Krause taught high school science as a Peace Corps Volunteer in Samoa from 2000-02. As of fall 2011, she has just finished her Ph.D. in Speech-Language Pathology and is joining the faculty at Bowling Green State University in Ohio, researching how traumatic brain injury affects cognition and communication. She is already thinking ahead (30 years or so) to her next stint in the Peace Corps.

✦

Digging for Fish

In Isaan it is possible to be "bitten" by a catfish and to be cured from the swelling by a little smoke, smashed herbs, and a banana leaf.

"And I will roast some of the whitefish and make jaew *for everybody,"
Uncle Gah offered. Then he returned to Tid-joon, and sat beside him
and said, "It won't hurt for long." He took Tid-joon's hand in his,
and mumbled his chanting prayers, and blew on the sore place a few
times. When he had finished the treatment, he said, "Kamgong, you
roast one of these* ee-ooy *on the fire until it is well done, then take
the brain and smear it on the hurt place."*

—Kampoon Boontawee, from the novel *Luk Isaan*

GETTING LOST ON THE WAY TO BEN'S WAS JUST THE BEGINNING.
It was the early part of 1997, sometime in February or
March—I cannot remember exactly. My group of Peace
Corps Volunteers, the 108th to come to Thailand, had been
in-country for only three or four weeks, living with rural rice-
farming families in a homestay arrangement in the province
of Korat. Korat, or Nakorn Ratchasima as it is labeled on the
map and officially known, is located in a northeastern region
of the country called Isaan by the Thais. More or less settled

141

into homestay conditions by now, the members of Group 108 were brought together for a group meeting in Korat and given the names and locations of currently serving Volunteers we would be sent out alone to visit the following week. The purpose of this three-day visit, our Thai and American trainers told us, was to spend some time with a Volunteer who was currently working in the field and nearing the completion of his or her tour of service. At this point, technically, we were still "trainees" and would remain so until the twelve-week period of training came to an end, officially punctuated by the starched-cuff brouhaha known as the "swearing in" ceremony. Our objectives were to observe our assigned Volunteer's inter- action with the community, see how he or she functioned and dealt with problems on a day-to-day basis, ask questions, learn from them. Not incidentally, this would be the first time, after a month or more in Thailand, that we would spend more than twenty-four hours outside the immediate custodial and admin- istrative clutches of Peace Corps. This fact in itself was reason enough to look forward to the trip.

There were other reasons as well. I was looking forward to getting away from my homestay family for a time. A rice- farming unit of five, they lived in a small, cheaply constructed concrete house across from the village *wat*. The village was very traditional in this regard, with houses distributed around the *wat*, like spokes radiating from a wheel. The position of my "father" in the community—headman of the village— belied the poverty of his circumstances. Income was sporadic and earned primarily via the sweat of his brow. Financial security? Unknown. Like most Isaan residents, my family eked a hardscrabble, precarious existence out of an uncompromising environment. My family and I were still new to each other. I spoke very poor Thai at this point. I also knew that my presence in their household required continuous accommodation on their part, not to mention an outlay of patience, space and resources they could ill afford. Our dealings with each other were cordial, yet strained. Thus they were probably looking forward to my trip as much as I was.

But most importantly, I was excited at the prospect of receiving straight answers to my questions. After a month in Thailand, we still knew very little about what we would be doing once training was over and we were promoted to full-fledged Volunteers. Reliable information was hard to come by. To put it bluntly, our Thai and American handlers had been coached well in the subtle art of equivocation. Their artistry was brilliant, albeit frustrating. With the impending Volunteer Visit, however, perhaps finally we would have an opportunity to have our questions answered without any of the mincing jargon with which our trainers were so fond of confusing us. The volunteer I was assigned to visit I will call Ben. According to the fact-sheet given me, Ben worked in the Isaan province of Chaiyaphum. *Ben will give me the straight skinny*, I thought, although I had never met him. I began a list of questions to ask him several days before I left Korat.

The name of Ben's village now escapes me, although I remember clearly that it was perfectly unpronounceable. Ben had sent the directions himself, care of Peace Corps. I felt cocky. While everyone else left early, on the morning of departure, I succeeded in doing what was impossible in our homestay villages. I slept in late. The province of Chaiyaphum is directly north and west of Korat; I was promised it would be a short trip. With Ben's directions folded in my front pocket, I left our hotel in Korat and headed out to the bus station in the early afternoon. I had every confidence I would be swigging back some beers with Ben in less than three hours.

Instead I got horribly lost.

Eight hours later—tired, covered in dust and dragging my pack—I found myself standing under the stars staring at an old cement-and-wood two-story house. Behind me was the Thai man whose vehicle I had just exited. I turned back to look at him. He was standing outside the driver-side door, clutching my money in his fist and waving me on to approach the house whose driveway I now faced.

"*Farang*? Ben?" I asked him in baby-Thai, seeking some assurance that he had indeed brought me to the right place.

"*Farang!*" exclaimed the man excitedly. "*Doo muan you!*" ["He looks like you!"] he added, using, for my convenience, the English word for *you,* which every Thai knows. Again he began waving me on towards the house with both hands.

His comment was a good sign, at least. A few Thai trainers back in Korat had impressed upon me how much Ben and I resembled each other. Perhaps this was the right place after all. My trepidation slightly alleviated, I approached what looked like the front door. A light left the second floor and allowed a splinter of luminosity to quiver weakly over the driveway before me. Except for this, it was completely dark. The man behind me drove off.

Quietly approaching the front, I saw through the screen door a large Western man with features arguably resembling mine asleep in a hammock in the front room. Behind him a row of Elephant Beer bottles lined the wall. The figure was snoring tranquilly, gently. A huge electric floor fan was pointed directly at his face. *This must be Ben*, I thought. I liked him already. I knocked hard.

"Whoa," said Ben, nearly falling out of his hammock to answer the door. It was about nine at night. Not late, but late enough. "You the guy come to visit?" he snarled from some scorched corner in the back of his throat.

"Yeah, that's me," I answered through the screen door.

"You're late. I didn't think you'd make it." He opened the door. He was a tall, dirty-blond-haired man in his mid-twenties. My Thai trainers were right. We *did* look a little alike. I could understand how the trainers—so unused to Western physiognomies—could find a certain resemblance.

"Sorry. My Thai still sucks," I said. "I got lost. Besides, no one understood me. I had to pay a ton of money to have some guy drive me here in his pickup. My name's Blaine."

"I know. Peace Corps sent me a letter. Nice to meet you." We shook hands. Rubbing his eyes and closing the screen behind me Ben said: "I bet you said ★&%$#' instead of @+-$#%,"—implying I had probably pronounced the name of his village incorrectly.

"How long you supposed to stay?"

"Three days I think."

We chatted for a while. After asking me about some of the current Thai trainers training our group—for Ben was curious to hear the latest gossip on all of them—he turned to me abruptly and said:

"So, you ready to go?"

"Go where?" I asked, swallowing another mouthful of beer. I was still trying to dislodge the thick layer of dust that had congealed in my throat.

"Bangkok. Have some fun! I'm bored. Let's get the hell out of this province. Let's go to Bangkok and get drunk and have sex! What d'ya say?" Ben was fairly beaming.

"Uh, well…sex…"

"Not with me, stupid! I mean with women! Peace Corps gave you money to come here, right?"

"Well, yeah," I said, shrugging to communicate that, after all, it really wasn't much.

"So you're all set!"

"Bangkok? Now?"

"Yeah, they got air-con buses all night. I can have my neighbor take us to the bus station down the road. What d'ya say?"

"Uh, well," I mumbled searchingly, "I mean, I just got here. I'm supposed to be here to observe you or something. Ask questions and stuff." I was speechless, taken aback. Was he serious? I had yet to see Ben's village in the daytime and now he was suggesting we leave for Bangkok? Just the same, I was getting accustomed to this kind of thing. We were trainees still wet behind the ears. Still idealistic. The relaxed attitudes and cool indifference to PC regulations that many Volunteers of long duration evinced in our presence was a recurrent eye-opener to us. The unavoidable question was: Would we become this way one day? This disillusioned and bored? This blasé? (We would. Everyone does. But that's another story).

"But Ben," I pleaded, "I still don't know what I'm gonna be doing when *I* get to *my* village. I'm supposed to…you know…observe you…" In retrospect I must have come across as an absolute prig.

Ben opened another bottle of beer and burst out laughing. "I was just kidding!"

I wasn't entirely convinced of it.

At cockcrow the next morning I awoke bright and early to the sounds of rooting pigs and pounding hammers next door. A neighbor was doing work on his house just a few feet away. What's more, habituated to waking early with my homestay family, I couldn't have slept longer had I even wished to. Six A.M. is mid-day in the village. Determined to get a closer look at Ben's worksite, I bathed, dressed and headed out for a walk.

The scene was typical, one replayed to the point of redundancy every day in thousands of villages across Isaan. There were makeshift mom-and-pop noodle stands here and there; dirt roads crosshatched by the tracks of numberless motorbikes; uniformed schoolchildren shuffling fussily off to school; the flushed, mindful faces of monks on their morning alms round; clouds of dust so bulldogged and invasive they are reckoned independent forces of nature; stands of bamboo trees and piles of wind-blown refuse lining the roadside; wooden houses on wobbly stilts; the tip of the local *wat*'s crematorium jutting out over a clump of trees, a man selling homemade brooms door-to-door, bent over from their weight. And, of course, off in the distance everywhere a brown rippled sea of dry rice fields. After circling the *wat* two more times I headed back to Ben's.

There was a pot of boiling water on the gas burner. Ben, just out of the bathroom, told me he had something special arranged for our first day together as mentor/protégé. He explained his plan as he poured coffee. After his morning lessons were finished at the local high school—which I would attend and help him with—a local friend of his would pick us up and take us to a spot in the paddy where some villagers were draining a small pond of its water.

"Why?" I interrupted.

"To get the fish out!" Ben's delivery told me I probably should have figured this one out for myself.

"And what are *we* going to do?" It sounded interesting. *But what does this have to do with us?*

"To watch of course," said Ben. "And maybe give them a hand."

"But why?" It seemed to me a legitimate question at the time.

"Have you ever seen how they get the fish out?" Ben probed.

"No," I said.

"O.K. then. It'll be something new for you. Something fun."

"But…"

"You see!" he shot back. "We could be sleeping in an air-con hotel in Bangkok right now!"

I decided to keep my mouth closed. And as these things go, it turned out to be one of the most interesting days I ever spent in a village. More, one of my most memorable days of my life, in Thailand or otherwise.

Before going on, it's worth describing these ponds. Take a walk into an Isaan rice field. Out in the paddies one finds—spaced every half-mile or so—large rectangular, bulldozer-dug ponds. They're right in the middle of the paddies and full of fish. The rains fill them up between drainings, although how they initially get filled with fish I do not know. Theories abound. Perhaps—like herpes or communists—the fish just kind of flare up and come to life at odd moments when the time and conditions are right.

Following classes with Ben that afternoon, we were picked up by Ben's friend in front of the school's canteen. Two or three quick turns not far from the school, and we were suddenly in the midst of one rolling, seemingly horizonless rice field. The fields were dotted here and there by large out-of-place trees or rickety bamboo huts. Small berms, built to keep water in and used as footpaths in the wet season, divided the landscape into squares as far as the eye could see, protruding from the earth like bony exoskeletons. Though ivy-green at other times of the year, today the land appeared sun-baked, dormant.

About one hundred yards to our left was a crowd, and the growling sounds of an engine. We walked across three fields. At the far end of the third, a copse of trees and slight rise in elevation hid the pond from sight. We joined the villagers and stood looking down at a fast-emptying hole in the ground. It must have been fifteen feet deep, by twenty yards wide. Up top, one of those ubiquitous Kubota engines was hooked up and siphoning out water at an enormous rate. Below us a man was packing mud around the exposed part of the tubing, so that it would draw water and not air. It was hot. My undershorts were already sticky-taped to my bottom. I squinted against the glare.

The villagers around the pond seemed to know Ben. They reacted to his arrival either with indifference—the rarest honorarium for the *farang* in Isaan—or with a modest greeting suggestive of close familiarity. It was me they were interested in. I did my best to explain myself. Yet after entertaining the crowd for a minute or two by saying, again and again in Thai, "My name is Blaine," more questions were asked. These were wide of my abilities. Alas, at this point of my stay in Thailand I understood spoken Thai like a camel understands a clarinet. In no time the novelty of having a new *farang* around wore off, and everyone went back to work.

And how they worked! Down in the mud in the bottom of the pond were about ten people. Men, women and children. Some had thatched, wide-brimmed volcano hats on, or a sarong wrapped around their head for protection from the sun. Long-sleeved shirts were also common. Each person seemed to have different duties. Some of the smaller children, without baskets of their own, sloshed around in the foot-deep mud, slapping the water with their fists to scare the fish over to others nearby, who grabbed them by the heads and shoved them into baskets. Others worked independently. With bent backs they moved about slowly, plunging their hands into the mud and feeling around for anything alive.

I squatted by the edge and watched. The villagers were methodical. If someone's basket was full, or they couldn't open the top for some reason, they would simply fling the fish to those on top. Whereupon the children would let out a shout of laughter and sprint after them, flailing almost as much as the fish themselves. Once, a flying fish hit a little girl in the back. She immediately turned around and stomped on it, muttering something nasty under her breath.

The fish were sorted by women and put into different barrels after being gathered up and rinsed. They were sorted according to size and type. From time to time the people up top would send down a boy or girl with a near-full glass of whiskey to be shared by the men (and some women) at work down below. Sometimes it was just a tall decanter of water. A few yards from us someone had started a small fire in a makeshift fire pit. A dozen or so fish were being cooked up on the spot, for a snack. I took a shot from the communal whiskey glass when it came around. After socializing for a time, Ben came over and sat down next to me. More squatting and watching, as Ben helped me understand what I was seeing. He answered my questions and pointed out fish species—and their Thai names—as they rained down around our feet.

Then someone abruptly turned off the Kubota engine. What was going on? Ben said they had drained as much water out of the pond as possible.

"So now what?" I asked. Ben turned and squawked something to a chain-smoking, elderly man dressed in a sarong to his right. They talked for a few minutes.

"Well," said Ben, turning to me and grinning, "I guess you and I should get down there and help them. I think they want us to help."

"What! They want me to get down there!" This changed everything. What had looked so quaintly rustic a minute ago now appeared like a pool of soupy shit.

"Yeah," reiterated my interpreter and friend. "You're not worried, are ya?"

"Well, no," I balked. "I'm not *scared* or anything. It's just.... I mean...."

"Look, we should help. We're two big healthy men, and we're just sittin' here like idiots, drinking their whiskey. Why shouldn't they expect us to help? What d'ya say? You don't want to *offend them*, do you?" This last question was pure brilliance on Ben's part. He had been a trainee at one time, too. He knew how excitable we trainees were to notions of *fitting in, not offending, doing it the Thai way*, etc. Fresh off the boat, I for one was still terrified of appearing even obliquely discourteous.

"Well, what d'ya say?" he repeated.

I looked again at the people in the mud, and at the fish thrashing about. The more I thought about the idea, the less disagreeable it seemed. Why not?

"O.K.," I answered. "Let's go!"

When the villagers saw us take off our sandals, roll up our pants and make our way down one side of the pond, they sent up a whoop of encouragement. Some people even started clapping. *What a strange reaction*, I noted, *especially for people who expect us to help!* One old woman near us stopped plucking at fish long enough to squat in the mud and watch. Her mouth was a bright carroty color from betel-nut.

For the next hour or so Ben and I went digging for fish. We worked hard. Between the two of us, we pulled up twenty or thirty fish in just the first few minutes. At times, weary of being bent over, we helped the children scare the fish over to the people with nets. This was easy, since it only required you to stumble and cause a lot of splashing. I was perfect for it.

The poor fish. They were frantic, doing their best to keep moving and not get caught. From their point of view the situation must have appeared nothing short of eschatological. Some sort of scaleless, non-gilled devil was now wreaking murderous upheaval upon their world, sucking the universe of water. A piscine holocaust!

Because I did not have a net of my own, I found myself staying close to the old woman who had squatted and smiled at us when we first got in the pond. She had a big net, which she dragged around behind her. I tossed my fish in her net. In no time she got used to me following her around. We built up a kind of rapport—based chiefly on fish, grunts, mud and carroty smiles.

Then she looked like she wanted to tell me something. I was putting a particularly large fish in her basket when she finally got around to it. While both of us were bent over, she slapped me on the shoulder and said something in the Isaan dialect. Her voice was harsh, like a cracked drum.

"*Alai*?" [what?] I asked, standing up straight.

This time she shouted at me. It went on for several seconds. At the conclusion, we stood looking at each other. The basket of squirming fish lay in the mud between us. What should I do? On the odd chance that she might have been asking my name, I said: "My name is Blaine," in slow central Thai. But she didn't seem satisfied. Again she yelled at me. She began waving her hands, too.

"Ben!" I screamed. He was across the pond, helping some friends scoop minnows out of a depression. Ben stood upright, a fishy specimen in one hand.

"What is it?" he yelled back.

"What is this woman saying?"

All talking in the pond ground to a halt. Everyone wanted to know what was happening. Ben carried on a conversation with the matriarch from across the pond. After yelling back and forth, Ben said:

"She says you should probably stop now."

"Really? Why?"

"She doesn't want you to get hurt."

"Get hurt!"

"That's what she's saying."

"How? I'm having fun!"

There was more talking between Ben and the old woman.

"She says she's afraid you'll get bit by a fish," continued Ben.

"Bit by a fish! That's crazy." I looked at her. "Fish don't bite."

"I don't understand either," yelled Ben. "But that's what she's saying."

"Fish mouths are too small!"

"Maybe you should get out now. I think I should, too. I don't know. Maybe she knows something. Let's get out."

"No way!"

"Suit yourself."

"This is too much fun," I added. Ben translated for me and the old woman shrugged, smiled, and went back to her work in the mud. Again I fell to work beside her.

I was groping around in some slime near where a little boy was splashing about when I felt a very sharp pain on my left middle finger. I let out a yelp. "Aiyyyyeeee!" Pulling my hand out from the foot-deep mud, I looked at my finger. It felt like a nail had been driven into it. Blood was streaming out of a pin-sized hole, flowing over the mud and down my hand. In a flash the old woman next to me stood bolt upright and looked at me. The features of her face, flaccid and pale before, now took on the dry dusty hue of reproach. She began berating me in overflowing carroty Lao-Isaan, pointing to my finger and up at the bank, where Ben now stood with a shot glass of whiskey in his mud-caked hands. Ben was grinning like a Cheshire cat.

"Shit, grandma," I said [in English] to the old woman, "this hurts." And it did. My finger was now throbbing in triphammer-fashion. The woman sloshed over next to me.

She grabbed my finger to inspect it and grunted. She flung the finger back. Long and tiring was the gaze of I-told-you-so she fixed on me. "I know I know," I said, humbled. Then without warning she dove down into the mud between my legs and groped around violently. Watching her, I hoped with every fiber in my being that she did not come up with a snake. Presently she pulled up a catfish. A big one. With long thick whiskers. The old matron then turned didactic. Holding the catfish up to my face, she had me know I had just been "bitten" by one of its defensive spines. Brandishing the fish at me a bit longer, for good measure, she trudged the few feet back to her basket and threw the thrashing beast in. She went back to work. I stood stupidly in the mud a while longer and bled. Everyone was watching. Many were laughing. I had no choice but to laugh as well.

Back up top with Ben, a friend of his helped me wash my "wound," just a small pin prick. But it felt like my heart was beating in just one digit of my hand. It bled continuously. This man washed my finger in paddy water and someone else tied a piece of cloth around it. In twenty minutes it had swollen to almost twice its size. I had to admit, it hurt like hell.

"Well," said Ben, smirking, "I guess that's what she meant by getting *bit* by a fish."

"Yeah, I guess so. I never thought something like this could hurt so much." I took a shot of the whiskey going around. I did not enjoy it. But in every war movie the maimed and dying always have a shot of whiskey. It's the *de rigueur* thing for Johnny Wounded.

"That's O.K. You *looked* stupid down there," Ben said. "You should have seen your face when that *yai* (grandmother) was waving that fish at you!" We both broke out laughing.

"I think there's some kind of mild poison or something in the spines," Ben continued.

"Yeah, shit, must be. It really throbs."

While the sun sank to a position more at level with the few trees surrounding, and the heat abated somewhat, we watched as the villagers pulled fewer and fewer fish from the pond. The pace had slowed dramatically. When, time and again, it seemed like all the fish had been withdrawn, and everyone would begin heading up to where the others sat, another fish would flap about and send others back into the mud in pursuit. They let nothing go. The fish were put into steel barrels. They would be taken to one man's house, where the process of sorting and divvying up would continue. They would also cook up a bunch and have a feast. Ben asked me if I wanted to go and be a part of this.

"Sure. But wouldn't we be intruding?"

He guffawed. "These are my friends. We won't be intruding."

"Still…"

"Look," replied Ben. "We helped them catch the fish, didn't we?"

"Yeah."

"So don't worry. Anyway, they would let us eat some even if we didn't help."

Ben and I were given a ride back to his place, where we bathed and changed clothes. I tried to clean out my finger and apply medicine, but it did little good; the pin-sized hole would not stop bleeding long enough. I wrapped my swollen finger with a cloth as best I could.

A half-hour later we arrived at the fish-man's house. It was a townhouse, less Thai than western, two-story with eaves. In the front yard, a few boys were busily sorting the fish. Big ones in this plastic tub, small ones in that. The steel barrels had already been dumped of their contents and cleaned. The men, meanwhile, were off in a corner of the yard on mats, drinking whiskey and singing. Their singing was hoarse and stentorian. They were celebrating. Ben's friend who had brought us to the pond rushed to meet us. He set us up with beers and found some chairs—the locals preferred mats.

The women had all the work to do, and they squatted together in the kitchen preparing the fish. I wandered in to watch them at work. Unaccountably, my eyes fixed on one woman who was pounding on the heads of fish with a wooden mallet as they were handed to her. At first I did not recognize her. But after allowing for the possibility of a bath and a bar of soap, the image clicked. It was the old woman I had worked so closely with an hour before; the woman whose stern disapprobation I had earned when I would not leave the pond. She had cleaned the layer of mud out of the cracks in her face and no longer wore a hat. But otherwise she was the same. Realizing I just now recognized her, the old woman stopped pounding on the fish heads and rolled out a regal smile. Her teeth, bruised and crooked, reflected bright vermilion in the light. I smiled back.

She stood up and wagged a finger at me, which I took to mean she wanted to know how my finger was doing. I pantomimed back that it still hurt. It was the truth—the swelling had not gone down. At this the old woman seemed to make up her mind. She put down her mallet. Saying something at the other women, she made her way over to me and stood looking up into my face. As I looked at her I realized that, out of her original mud element, she was much smaller.

Foregoing any preliminaries, the old woman plunged right in with lightening Lao-Isaan. She was tearing along at a good clip. There was no way I could understand.

"Ben! Help me out here!" I yelled, taking advantage of a pause in her soliloquy.

"Ben!" yelled the old woman, too. No doubt she had picked up on the bewildered look on my face. Seconds later Ben ambled over.

"What's up?"

"What's she saying?" I said. "She's been talking to me for a minute or so, and I have no idea what it's all about!"

They talked. From time to time she pointed to my poorly bandaged finger.

"She wants to know if it still hurts."

"Yeah, tell her it still hurts."

They talked some more.

"She says she's gonna fix your finger up for you. The old way."

"What's *the old way?*" I asked. I looked at the old woman pleadingly.

"I don't know. Lemme ask," answered Ben.

When they had finished, Ben continued: "She says she knows the right medicine."

"Yeah?"

"That's what she says. She'll fix the swelling. Look, don't worry. I know her. She won't hurt you." He went back outside to his beer and his friends.

The old woman and I looked at each other. "Well," I said, "O.K."

"O.K.!" said the woman, too. She knew that word. Leading me by the elbow she took me outside to a quiet corner of the yard. She cleared away the leaves and debris with a broom. She went to get a mat. Coming back, she motioned for me to sit down on it. I did. The rays of the sun were thinning, shadows elongated. Sunset was approaching.

For the next twenty minutes, I watched as she went back and forth from the back of the house. Apparently she was gathering the leaves of several plants, as well as a mortar and pestle. Finished with this task, she squatted next to me and began pounding the leaves into a paste. All the while she talked in a kindly, affectionate voice, aware for a certainty that I did not understand a word. Nonetheless her voice was consoling. I sat watching her prepare my "medicine," wondering just how old this "old way" really was—and if there were not perchance some "new way" in a bathroom cabinet inside the house.

After the leaves had been ground to a pulpy paste, she scraped them out of the mortar and spread them onto a banana leaf. By sign language I now understood I was supposed to allow her to apply this to my finger.

"It won't hurt, grandma, will it?" I asked in English. Of course, doing so was a waste of breath. But it felt better to say something.

"O.K.," she said.

"O.K.!" Biting my lower lip I held out my hand. She took it. Her hands were soft. Gently the old woman used a small piece of another banana leaf to apply the medicine to my finger. She put it over the entire finger, not just around the small puncture caused by the catfish spine. It hurt, but only a little. Again through sign language I was told to hold my finger up over my head. I smiled; my smile was reflected in the old woman. Guessing this was the end of the treatment process, I thanked her in Thai and got up to go. Swollen finger or no, there were people drinking beer without me.

She made me sit back down.

The next treatment involved more leaves. She went back to the lot behind the house for these. From another part of the yard, the old woman also brought back a bunch of hot coals on a piece of cookie tin and put them down in the dirt in front of me. Then, taking some of the green leaves she had just picked, she put them on the coals to create a smoky, smothered fire. The green leaves burned badly and put out an acrid smoke. And the smoke was the medicine! The woman had me kneel down beside the fire and hold my hand in the smoke. She pantomimed that I should stay that way. Then she left. Coughing and choking, I watched her walk back towards the kitchen. I was all alone.

When she finally came back and motioned for me to take my hand out of the smoke, I felt like collapsing. My hand was red hot. My lungs were on fire—even though I had tried to keep moving to stay out of the direct line of the smoke, it had proven impossible not to inhale a generous amount of it. My knees were sore. The woman had a bucket of water and doused the coals. I fell back onto the mat to rest and re-practice the breathing of fresh air. I coughed uncontrollably. I tried to rub the residue of smoke from my eyes. Cautiously certain, after a spell, that I could readjust to the way the world used to be before fish could bite people and smoke was medicine, I stood up and wiped a thick layer of sweat and ash from my forehead. Painstakingly, I also wiped away the dried paste that the woman had coated over my finger.

I looked at my finger, now clean. The swelling had disappeared. It was gone. Completely gone. *I'll be damned!* Holding the digit in front of my face I stared at it, mesmerized. My brain sent out a test-command of *wiggle*; dutifully, the finger wiggled back. "Wow, the swelling's really gone," I said aloud. I looked around, but the old woman had disappeared. With my finger still in front of my face I walked over to where Ben and his cronies were drinking beer and working their way through plates of rice and fried fish.

"Look Ben!" I said, holding the finger out at arm's length a few feet in front of him. Without realizing it I was flipping Ben a mighty bird.

"Hey! Be careful with that thing!" he joked. The Thais around us began to laugh. Although the Thais do not do it themselves, they recognize and understand "giving the finger."

"Oh, sorry." I brought my finger away from his face. "But look, there's no more swelling!"

"Lemme see." He inspected it. "Wow, I guess so. Does it still hurt?"

"No, not at all."

"Here!" Ben gave it a smart thwack with his other hand. "D'zat hurt?"

"Nope."

"Then I guess that old lady knows what she's doing after all," he went on, taking a swig of his beer. "I saw you over there, dancing around that fire."

"Yeah, I thought that old crone was gonna kill me for a while there," I joked. "I must've inhaled a gallon of smoke trying to keep my hand in that fire."

"Maybe that was her plan."

"What d'ya mean?"

"I mean, take your mind off the swelling. Think about it." He cocked his head my way, knowingly. "A man dyin' of smoke inhalation doesn't have time for a swollen finger, does he?"

"No, I guess not. Maybe you're right!"

"You see, maybe she tried to *scare* the swelling out of you!" We laughed. "You look like you need a beer."

Beer is a *topsop* in Thai. Almost as fast as Ben said the word a beer was in front of me. An unfilled glass is practically unknown to the Thais. Among its other distinctions Thailand is also the land of the magically refilling glass; drink a bit, turn your head, and when you turn back it's been refilled again by your host.

"Have you thanked her yet?" Ben asked.

"No, what's her name?"

"I don't know. Just call her *yai.*"

I went looking for her.

I found her in the kitchen, chopping up cucumbers with a wad of betel back in her mouth. She was among the same group of old women as I had seen before, all squatting and working on the floor. Knives, fish innards and vegetables were flying about. *My* old woman—for I felt somewhat proprietary towards her at this point—was in the middle of the group. I approached her and squatted down beside her. Behind me, there was the sound of a hatchet swing coming to rest in a wooden cutting board. The noise died down. Quiet settled over the room. To my embarrassment everyone had quit talking so that my fatuousness could be fully appreciated *en mass.* Holding up my finger I mumbled out the best Thai I could: "Thank you for this."

"*Mai pen rai* (never mind)" she said, as a smile played over her wrinkled visage.

I returned to the men's mats outside. Along with everyone else that night, Ben and I gorged on beer and fish. Two days later I returned to home-stay. The questions I had so keenly set out regarding my future as a Volunteer never were answered. But then I no longer cared. I knew I would figure it out eventually. And I did.

I never saw Ben or the old woman again.

Looking back, now, on the events of that afternoon, I realize how uncommon the episode of "digging for fish" really was. Even later, at my permanent village, I would not have the opportunity to repeat this experience. As to the old woman and her treatment of my "fish bite," perhaps it's best not to read too much into what took place. I know nothing about the efficacy of Isaan folk remedies. Moreover, a discussion of such things runs a delicate course between science and the intangibles of belief. Smoke as medicine? In the end the swelling in my finger did disappear. At some level I am inclined to believe the old woman had something to do with this. And for that I am thankful.

Blaine Comeaux served in Thailand from 1997-99. This story was originally published in Comeaux' memoir Two Years in the Kingdom.

ELAINE (CHRISTENSEN BAFFRY) GATES

✱

Thanks to the Turkeys

When life gives you a skinny, egg-laying turkey,
just cook up a Thanksgiving omelet.

MY FAVORITE MEMORY—AMONG MANY WONDERFUL MEMORIES—
of serving as a PCV, Pilipinas 69 (73-74), occurred at "Teachers'
Camp" in-country training in Baguio, Philippines. Arriving in
hot and sticky Manila after a cool fall season in America, we
welcomed the crisp cold air of the Philippine mountains. As
training unfolded and the holiday seasons approached, we
became more and more homesick. For many of us—young,
fresh-faced, barely out of college—this was our first time away
from our families in the States.

Though we were all growing to love the Philippines,
we were beginning to feel the strain of language acquisition
classes—so many different languages!—and the different
cultural norms we were expected to understand. As we
gathered at the dining hall one evening, pushing around food
we weren't quite used to yet, reminiscing nostalgically about
Thanksgiving and Christmas at "home," we came up with the
grand idea of buying a couple of turkeys that we could fatten
and enjoy for a real American Thanksgiving dinner.

We pooled our meager funds, and a couple of PCVs volunteered to catch the bus and ride for the sixty or so nail-biting, winding mountainous kilometers to coastal San Fernando, where we had been told we could buy "real" American-type turkeys. We waited anxiously for our friends' return, and they regaled us with the stories of the crowded, colorful, boisterous bus ride, and of their return trip with the turkeys caged in open-weave baskets poking their heads through. As they released the turkeys, these straggly birds looked absolutely nothing like any turkeys any of us had ever seen! Between the two of them, they could barely have weighed ten pounds, most of it feathers and long, long necks. We set about our plans fattening them up for Thanksgiving, saving scraps from our meals. All of us thought longingly, mouth-wateringly, of a fat roasted-bronze turkey dinner with stuffing, gravy: the works!

A funny thing derailed our plans. Our classrooms were built into the mountains, with high windows opening out onto the slopes. Each day, we struggled through our classes, eager to finally begin to master the languages we were studying. In typical Peace Corps fashion, our assignments often turned out to be nothing like we expected, and we were frantically trying to get a grasp on what we were supposed to be preparing for. As we struggled over verb conjugations, unusual inflections and pronunciations, our turkeys paraded faithfully outside our classroom windows.

They poked their long necks through open windows, pecked their long knobby beaks at the glass if the windows were closed, looked with their black beady eyes for their favorite PCVs, and gobbled incessantly through our struggling language lessons. They followed us around like puppies, and we became more and more attached to them. Our constant companions, they kept us all abuzz with "turkey drama." By the time Thanksgiving rolled around, there was no way we could sacrifice them. But neither of them had gained even a pound despite our efforts and were hardly enough to feed a couple of dozen hungry PCVs!

At Christmas, I wrote my parents: "We'll have a big holiday meal, but our Thanksgiving turkeys have again secured a reprieve by staying as scrawny as before—and goofy, too. One astonished us all as she pooched out an egg, but on the side of a steep hill. It rolled 10 feet and then dropped off a three-foot wall. Incredibly, it didn't break! This momentous event happened just before we left for some OJT (on the job training), and we returned to find her sitting on a nest of seventeen eggs and one ping-pong ball. She's a little strange.

As we headed out and settled in urban Manila and in barrios and wilderness camps throughout the Philippines on our environmental missions (leaving our Thanksgiving Turkeys behind in Teachers' Camp), we became more and more acclimated and began a lifelong love of the fascinating culture and beautiful people. We grew as men and women and began our lives as adults. But my memories, and I imagine the same holds true for my companions, include the homesick, touching, stressful, funny, intense first few months of in-country training, and how a couple of Thanksgiving Turkeys taught us about learning to adapt and enjoy life in our adopted country.

Elaine (Christensen Baffry) Gates returned to her position as a Park Ranger with the National Park Service following her Peace Corps assignment. Her PCV job as Historian with the Philippine National Park Service—doing research on World War II sites—touched her deeply because her own father had been a young American Army officer in the Philippines, captured on Bataan and held as a prisoner-of-war for three-and-a-half years. Retracing his steps was a powerful catharsis for her and forged a bond between them that lasts even beyond his passing a few years ago.

PAULINE BIRKY-KREUTZER

Willie and the Pathans

In the early 1960s the Pashtun region of northwest
Pakistan was hardly peaceful, but the Peace Corps
Volunteer who lived there was loved and admired.

WILLIE DOUGLAS NEEDED A NEW ASSIGNMENT. THAT WE KNEW,
but in Pathan country? Was it safe for a PCV to live and work
among the fiercely independent, quarrelsome, proud tribesmen
of Pakistan's northwest territory; the tribes who feud among
themselves when they aren't united to fight invaders? The
tall, blue-eyed handsome people whose history of perpetual
fighting goes back centuries to the middle seventeenth century,
when they revolted against the Moguls and annihilated an
army of forty thousand sent by Auranzeb to wipe them out?
Even though the Model Government High School for Boys
at Katlang was in desperate need of a Vocational Agriculture
teacher, and Willie Douglas was exactly the kind of person
they needed, was it safe to assign him to that remote little
village, deep in Pathan country? The safety of our Volunteers
was of utmost importance to us.

After constant phone calls and letters from the school principal, and from government officials in Mardan, the provincial
capital, as well as requests from Willie himself, we decided to

send Willie to Katlang for a few weeks to check out the assignment. Two weeks had passed since Willie, his round black face covered with a big smile, had boarded a bus in Peshawar for Mardan, where he would take a village taxi to Katlang. Ferocious, feuding Pathans bothered Willie not one whit, and he was ready for a big adventure.

Willie's face was almost always creased by a broad smile. He kept his curly hair clipped short, and his narrow mustache was always neatly trimmed as well. But in spite of the smile, I knew that underneath his outside bravado Willie hid scars from childhood trauma.

"Willie," I asked once, "how did you ever make up your mind to go through college? I know your family had financial problems."

"It was my high school Voc Ag teacher. He convinced me I could do it, and he helped me get a scholarship. It wasn't easy."

I followed Willie's progress closely. A call to the principal, Sahib A.C. Khan, told us that Willie had arrived and had been given a room at the home of the principal's brother, Taj Mohammad Khan. Willie, Sahib Khan told me, was *bahut achaha* (very good), and the school wanted him to stay. A note or two arrived from Willie assuring us that he was great, everything was great and we didn't need to worry about him.

These notes were soon followed by a phone call asking when someone was coming to visit him and how soon could a final decision be made assigning him to Katlang? He wanted that assignment, no question about it.

I had a scheduled visit to Peshawar coming up soon, and a visit to Katlang would be no problem. Taffy Payne, a PCV teaching in Peshawar, had several days off during the Moharram days of mourning and wanted to go see Willie also. This was a bonus for me, since Taffy's Urdu was very good and my two months' study of the language had provided me

with a very limited vocabulary. Early in the morning, armed
with a jug of drinking water and sandwiches, which the cook
sent along for our lunch, Taffy and I squeezed into a crowded
Government Transport bus in Peshawar. Two hours plus two
tea stops later, we arrived in Mardan, a frontier district town
of about 10,000 population. The streets were already crowded
with stalwart men dressed in earth-colored *shalwar* and chemise, with flat brown wool rolled brim hats perched jauntily
above fair-skinned faces.

"Pathans!" I whispered to Taffy.

"Sure," she replied. "We see them in Peshawar all the time.
Aren't they handsome? Be careful not to look them in the eyes
nor smile at them, though. They are real ladies' men."

Taffy's Urdu helped us take a horse-drawn *tonga* to the taxi
stand from which the cars left for Katlang. The taxi was filled
with village men when we arrived, but the two in the front
seat crowded into the back with about a dozen others, making
room for us, while the driver carefully spread a greasy cloth
over the holes in the front seat for us.

I doubt if a Pakistani driver could operate his vehicle if
his brass horn with its black rubber bulb, mounted outside
the window, stopped "hooting." Hooting, by the way, is a
most appropriate description of the raucous noise made by the
horns, and signs in front of hospitals say, "No Hooting," both
in English and in Urdu. Our driver used his "hooter" constantly as we wove in and out among bullock carts and bicycles
and pedestrians, and past donkeys so covered with enormous
loads of straw that only four tiny legs could be seen trotting
along under a moving straw stack.

The trip to Katlang took forty-five minutes, although
we had only twelve miles to cover and made no village
stops along the way. A new road to the village was being
built, and making our way around piles of broken roadbed

stone, across ditches, and through dense clouds of dust was time-consuming.

At Katlang, Taffy told the driver we wanted to go to the Model Government High School for Boys.

"You come to see the *siah Americai* (black American)?" he asked her in Urdu.

"That's right. We've come to see Willie." she replied.

"*Siah Americai* is very good. People of Katlang want him to stay here," the driver assured us, with a happy smile. So we knew that Willie was already making a name for himself.

The Model School, situated at the edge of the village, consisted of an attractive group of white-walled, one-storied buildings, surrounded by a white compound wall and built around a center plot of blooming roses, peonies and green grass. Very neat and clean, I thought to myself—a model school, indeed.

Principal A.C. Khan, a tall dark-haired man dressed in a white shirt and dark suit, hurried out of a door marked "Office" and greeted us in English.

"You must be Mrs. Birky. Willie speaks of you very often. We knew you were coming, but Willie said it would be three days from now," he said. "Willie has just now gone to Mardan on an errand. Please come. We will find him soon."

I introduced Sahib Khan to Taffy, and we were walking toward the office when a twin to our taxi drove up and Willie and several tall Pathans got out of it. Apparently we had just passed through Mardan when the word was flashed to Willie that two American ladies were headed for Katlang. Americans are a scarce commodity in this tribal area. Willie introduced us to his Pathan friends, to Taj Mohammad Khan, a brother of the Vice-Principal, to a member of the local Basic Democracies, and to a Katlang merchant. All of them told us, to paraphrase their words, "Any friend of Willie's is a friend of mine."

The Pathans, as I mentioned before, are a tall people with blue eyes. The Khan brothers, of whom we met several that day, were all six feet and over. They spoke English to a certain degree, and it was obvious that they came from a prosperous family. I remembered the warning to avoid looking these men directly in the eyes and looked down at the ground when I replied to their greetings. They certainly didn't look very war-like, I thought. Maybe the stories we had been told were old wives' tales. I soon learned, however, that the stories were all too true.

Taj Mohammad Khan took us to his house, where Willie was living in his guest room. The guest room was built outside of the wall that surrounded the family living quarters. Inside the wall lived the family of Mohammad Khan: his wife, his seven children, and his unmarried sister. The women lived in *purdah*, and Willie had never seen them, except enveloped in their white burkahs. Taj Mohammad Khan insisted that we must be his guests for lunch, so the cook's carefully prepared sandwiches went untouched. Instead we ate curried chicken floating in ghee, a kind of liquid butter made from water buffalo milk, and a soup, all with the help of our fingers and *chapatis*, a local flat bread.

Sahib Khan asked Taffy and me if we would do him the honor of visiting his home and meeting his family. This was exactly what we had been hoping to do. His wife was a small, frail-looking woman, possibly thirty years of age but looking much older, while his sister was a tall husky woman resembling her brothers. Taj Mohammad asked if I would take a photo of him and his family, and send him a copy. I was delighted to do this. I promised to send him the photo and to never publish it in a magazine.

"Please, Memsahibs, I would be honored to also show you a part of my farm," our host told us. We followed him through a four-acre citrus orchard and a vegetable garden, past fields of sugar cane, wheat stubble and cotton. In the citrus orchard, under the shade of orange trees, a large water buffalo cow was lying contentedly while the smaller children cooled her off with water from a well. Nearby stood a wobbly young donkey, obviously born that day, and his protective mama who kicked out her heels at any one venturing near her furry, long-eared young one.

Back at the school we took a tour of the buildings, the students' garden plots, and the new building under construction, which I admired.

"Thank you, Memsahib, but it is you we must thank for this new building. Without your help it is not possible. It is with American aid that we were able to build it. Americans are our friends. I must tell you now that we want Willie to live and work in our village and teach in our school. Everyone likes Willie, and we need him."

The Vice-Principal then outlined in detail his plans for Willie—teaching Vocational Agriculture, supervising the students' garden plots at the school, helping the boys with projects at home, setting up a poultry flock at the school and teaching the care of poultry, in addition to assisting with sports and physical education. I wondered how one PCV could handle the work plan the Vice-Principal outlined, but decided that we would leave that up to Willie. I had already seen enough to know that I was going to recommend Willie's assignment to the Model School. Willie Alfredo Douglas was going to conquer the Pathans, of that I was certain!

"Mrs. Birky, we had better get started on our visits, or you will miss your bus." Willie told me.

"What visits are these, Willie?" I asked.

"Village custom says we have to visit all the village elders, or head men, including the Maulvi, the Muslim religious leader. And we can't miss even one of them, or they will be very insulted."

We were quite an entourage as we loaded into the taxi: Willie, Taffy and me, the two Khans, the driver, the man who cranked the car, and two other men whose functions I never learned. The taxi responded to the first cranking, and we took off without even a push. It was obvious wherever we went that we were expected; the village grapevine had been very busy. Crowds came out to meet us at every village, and we "salaamed" countless men and boys. We were specially introduced to Willie's future students, and I observed that he knew them all and that they were very fond of him. Children crowded around Taffy and me, curious and friendly. Women were conspicuous by their absence.

We were expected to eat or drink something wherever we went. And this presented quite a problem. We drank the tea, hoping the water had been boiled long enough to kill the dysentery bacteria to which we Westerners are so susceptible, but when, at one village, we insisted that we could not drink any more tea nor eat any more of the boiled eggs, which are always served with tea, then a glass of murky water was offered to me.

I was about to refuse when one of the Khans whispered, "Take it and only hold it or they will be angry." I took the glass quickly and warned Taffy to do the same. I had no desire to anger a Pathan. Suddenly I had a happy thought. I asked if I could take photos of the son of the owner of the village, another Khan brother, and the boy's demonstration plot. The Khan enthusiastically received this idea, and I was able to get rid of the glass of water.

Time was running out. Everywhere we went we had to stay longer than planned. But although we were running much too close to the time when the last bus left Mardan for Peshawar,

Willie insisted that we had to visit the Maulvi even if we missed the bus!

At the Maulvi's village we were received royally. The village elders greeted us, along with Willie's students, and took us to the *derah*, the men's sitting place and teahouse. It was an outdoor area protected from the sun by a roof of branches supported on poles, and furnished with *charpis* (rope beds) dressed up for the occasion with bright coverings. There were chairs for us, as guests of honor, and small tables.

After we were all seated, the Maulvi made his entrance. I had no doubt that it was a well-planned one. He came striding down the village path, a well-built, middle-aged six-foot tall man with rosy cheeks, a graying hennaed beard, and twinkling blue eyes. Everyone rose to greet him, and he shook hands all the way round. Except with Willie, that is: he embraced Willie and said slowly in English, "This is my good friend." He spoke a little English, thinking carefully about each word before he spoke, but it was obvious that he understood more than he could speak. Taffy and Willie talked with him in Urdu, and he was delighted. He wore the traditional *shalwar* and chemise, white and new looking, and a gold turban wrapped with a starched white scarf that ended pointing up toward the sky—the *pagree*. The long red beard gave him the proper look of reverence and a real splash of color.

In no way did he fit the stereotype of the somewhat forbidding, sometimes fanatic religious Maulvis one reads about, hating Christians and turning his people against Westerners. He joked with Willie and said that since everyone else in the area was named Khan that they were going to christen him "Willie Khan," and then he laughed uproariously at his joke, with everyone else in the crowd joining in, as he expected them to do.

Maulvi Khan (he was the Khan brothers' uncle) asked Taffy and me whether we would go with him to his house, and of course we were delighted to do so. It was obvious that we were expected at the house also, since the women and children were dressed in what must have been their best colorful flowered chemises and bright *shalwars*. Iaulvi Khan introduced us to his three wives and to innumerable other women and older girls. Children were everywhere, quietly crowding up to get a better look at the strange Memsahibs. We asked the Maulvi how many children he had, and he answered, "Twelve boys and twelve girls." I had the feeling that he wasn't quite sure of the number himself. Later Mohammad Khan told me that the Maulvi had other wives in addition to the three we met. Being a Maulvi seemed to bring many privileges with it.

Back at the *derah* we found more food. There was curried chicken again, swimming in the usual fat, charcoal-broiled chicken gritty with ashes, *chapatis* fried in deep fat, sliced onions, hard-boiled eggs, tea and several other dishes with which I was not familiar. I knew that such feasts are rare among the village people, and I appreciated the sacrifice they had made for us. Their hospitality was almost embarrassing, but most genuine. We ate with great difficulty, but the Maulvi was watching us with the eyes of a hawk and kept insisting that we didn't like his food or we would eat more.

The Khan brothers, realizing our bus deadline, finally helped us get away. Walking down the street to the taxi, I asked the Maulvi for permission to take his picture with Willie. With a twinkle in his blue eyes the old man snatched Willie's sun helmet off and put it on his own head, while at the same time putting his gold turban with its tall starched *pagree* fan on Willie. "Now," he said, "take the photo." And I did. Then he took my arm, and Taffy's, put one of us on each side of him, with his arms about our shoulders, and told Willie to take our photo. That photo is one of my treasures, helping me to remember an exciting and memorable day.

For two years, Willie Douglas lived and worked in Pathan country, (mostly) avoiding the intricate feuds that define life there. I never really knew how or why, near the end of his service, Willie fell off the fence he was straddling in Katlang. I could only make educated guesses, and I decided it was better to keep those to myself, especially since everyone came out of Pathan country in one piece. One thing I knew for certain: Peace Corps Volunteer Willie left behind many, many positive images of Americans in that remote part of the world, and I would make a bet that even today—in the teahouses of Pakistan's wild and wooly Northwest territory—tales are being told about their legendary friend, the *siah Americai,* Willie Douglas Khan.

Pauline Birky-Kreutzer, to whom this book is dedicated, was co-author of New Frontiers for American Youth *(1961), the feasibility study that outlined the shape of the Peace Corps. She served as director of the Pak 1, trained Volunteers in Colorado, and directed two programs in Afghanistan. Pauline died in 2008 at the age of 92. This story is excerpted, with her kind permission, from her memoir* Peace Corps Pioneer.

✳

Durga Sadhu

*She is called the "One who can redeem in
situations of utmost distress."*

CROSSROADS—UNRULY PLACES ON THE OUTSKIRTS OF TOWNS—
need guardians. Crossroads loosen the rules and make space for
transformations.

Where the north-south Sirsaud road meets the two-lane
highway that runs across the top of the state of Madyha
Pradesh sat a *chai* stand. The junction looked for all the world
like a T-intersection. But I am pretty sure it was a crossroad.
Why else would the Durga Sadhu have built his shrine kitty-
corner from the lonely *chai* stand if not to anchor its other
side? Besides, if India can mark the exact convergence of
three sacred rivers, the Ganges, the Yumana, and the Saraswati
(which just happens to be invisible), then it is easy to imagine
that our Sadhu felt there was a need to protect an intersection
where the county road addressed the highway.

Maggie, my site mate, and I first got acquainted with the
bus stop *chai* stand on our village rounds starting in 1967, when
there was nothing on the other side of the road except more
rough countryside that looked exactly like West Texas. The

terrain vexed Maggie who came from the seaside and perfect climate of San Diego. It just looked like home to me.

We had gotten to know this bus stop spot because we were part of India 45's female contingent. Originally, our whole group was assigned to village level food production. But then, for no apparent reason, we became a poultry production group, and then—when someone decided that girls do not do chickens in India—we morphed into a gender divided group: guys did chickens and lived in cities (with electricity and running water); we did applied nutrition and worked in villages far, far away from those cities. Maggie and I lived in Karera, a small town in the northern part of the state with eccentric electricity and no running water, not even the dream of it. Our water came from the town well, carried in buckets by Ramcha, a poor share-cropper from a nearby village who had been conscripted (we never knew how) to serve as our chief cook and water bearer for two years. His caste, high enough for government work, gave him the necessary cultural permission to prepare and serve tea to our co-workers when they came to visit. No proper person would have touched anything we cooked.

If the amenities in Karera were minimal, our living quarters were not. The House of the Kashi Ram Major, our official address, was huge. The long entranceway, a step up from the bazaar, led into a small courtyard with a small tree in the middle. Straight ahead were two small rooms: one with a cement floor (where we ate and sat in the evening) and one with dirt (where we slept). To the right were three doors. Behind Door Number One was nothing except a bare stone room where we heated up water for bathing in a big bucket on our little kerosene stove. Behind Door Number Two was a set of steps that led to the hole that was our toilet. It was to Door Number Three that the untouchable Sweeper—the *Bhungi*—came (almost) every day to clean it all out.

Upstairs on the roof was another open space, off of which was the kitchen: a bare room with a *chula*, a small wood burning open stove built into the floor. There Ramcha boiled up our tea (composed of fresh water buffalo milk, tea, water and sugar), prepared our scrambled eggs, rolled out our *chapattis*, and fried up our onion *pakoras*. Besides the kitchen room, there was another whole big living space that overlooked the bullock-cart-wide street below and a set of steps that went up to a small shrine, inhabited by spiders. A pretty *pukka* place it was, one that might easily have housed an extended family of twenty.

Save for roughly six weeks of vacation, we were home with the door locked well before dusk for two years. In the first few months of living there, we had plenty of time to wonder how in the hell we were going to make it out to the villages where we were supposed to be promoting sound nutritional practices (plus a little birth control and nursery schools) instead of sitting around in the *duftar*, the office, drinking tea with the town dignitaries, all men, doing squat.

We arrived in Karera in early September; by November, we were fried. I was pretty sure that I was going to have a complete nervous breakdown and have to be medevaced home to Dallas in total humiliation. I couldn't carry on an adult conversation in Hindi; I didn't know how to tell a sari suitable for my station from one that our coworkers wouldn't be caught dead in; I did not catch the cultural cues that left the people in our town wondering what impolite planet we had dropped out of; and I was sick and damned tired of having otherwise sweet and lovely village women crush and bruise my un-supple American hands as they pushed yet another set of glass bangles over my thumb joints onto my wrists so that I could look like a *Hindustani aurat. Aacha! Churion buhut sundar häi!* (which is to say, I would look like an Indian woman. Good! Bangles are very beautiful!)

To prevent a total mental meltdown, because the shame of an early return held no appeal, I decided to figure it all out. I started reading books of Indian folk tales alongside *Femina* ("for all the women you are"), an English language, bi-weekly women's magazine. Interestingly, the themes regarding women were sort of the same: obey your parents, be lovely, obey your grandparents, defer to your husband when you marry, lower your eyes, and keep your head covered for heaven's sake. We knew from our first visits to our five assigned villages that the village women we met thought us strange. But based on the evidence I collected from folk tales and *Femina*, I realized we were beyond strange: we were aliens.

We made absolutely no sense to the village women we were supposed to educate. Pushing on those bangles—the most lustrous and democratic of adornments—may have made our wrists, at least, seem more familiar. All Hindu women, rich or poor, wear glass bangles. Unlike those made of gold, a married woman's personal wealth, glass bangles are both cheap and beautiful. They capture every color in the lush and opulent pallet that rose from the princely kingdoms of India's history. Not a single blue, but a dozen blues; not just red, but magenta, crimson and scarlet, splashed with highlights of gold. A *bangle-waalaa* in the smallest bazaar always attracted crowds of women and girls, all going though the hundreds of slender bracelets, picking the color combinations that when worn together would catch both the eye and the ear in glints of light and sound. Perhaps the village women hoped that our wearing bangles would break the alien spell and make us one of them

Folktales and *Femina* were light fare that seemed sweet, quaint, and flexible enough to yield to my own superior ideas of how life might best be lived and enjoyed. I imagined I was beginning to understand; I could work with this. Maybe even improve the self-esteem of village women. I pushed on to the epics. The *Ramayana* and the *Bhagavad Gita*—cosmic, penetrating treatments of duty, relationships, and how ideal humans behave—pushed back. They said, not so fast, *wideshi lurki,* foreign girl.

I read and reread them. By the time we watched the Durga Sadhu build his little shrine at the crossroads, the epics had already confirmed my darkest thoughts about the culture: there was no compassion here. Krishna tells Arjuna to kill off his kinsmen because he is the best warrior and it is his duty. Rama banishes the faithful Sita because his duty as king overrides his duty to his wife. Brother. Paradox at that level does not rest easy on the Western mind.

It was a cold thing to operate with relative comfort in a culture that I believed was missing its heart. By that second fall, we had found a rhythm in our work, liberating small packets of UNICEF vegetable seeds and big boxes of CARE gardening tools from the *duftar,* cadging a fifty-kilo bag of dehydrated milk marked for Alliance for Progress with instructions in Spanish from the regional hospital, and conducting a kitchen garden raising contest among the schoolboys in Sirsaud, using those UNICEF seeds, which quite miraculously grew.

We had learned to wrap our saris quick as a wink and to settle into the packed existence of the Third Class Ladies' Car on the Punjab Mail or the Dakshin Express and sleep all the way to New Delhi. I had given up on declining the gift of bangles and the urge to lunge at the next man who declared with delight that I was a *Hindustani aurat. Achaa!* I had resigned myself to the fact that no one would ever understand what a pain it was. My cultural information was just not available or even interesting to the local population. Women wore bangles, and that was that.

Of the five villages we worked in—Dinara, Kali Pahari, Surwaya, Sirsaud, and Toda Pichhore—we probably had our best success in Sirsaud. The lady extension agent, the *gram sevika*, assigned to Sirsaud and nearby Toda Pichore was funny, smart, and old enough to be respected. So over the months, we traveled there often and became a familiar presence at the *chai* stand. The *chai-waalaa* could explain the alien apparition that was us to Hindustani travelers passing through, and we could ask him, "*Kaun hai?* Who is that?" when the strikingly handsome young holy man started building his little shrine kitty-corner from where we sat.

"*Durga-kii sadhu hai*," he said.

A Durga Sadhu. Very interesting. I had read up on Durga as part of my effort to penetrate Hinduism's mysteries. She is a very, very impressive goddess. She rides a tiger, has eight arms, and no one messes with her. She takes a special interest in the affairs of women and children and is known for her fierce compassion, a quality I had yet to locate in my reading or personal experience of India. It was true that the Durga Sadhu seemed to attract a lot of children as he worked, a welcome relief for us who were the usual subjects of such interest. He fit the description of a good devotee.

So we watched him build his shrine and interact with the children it drew. And on those days when he came to the *chai* stand to share a *chillum* with his blue-robed sadhu colleague who sometimes passed that way, he observed us. We became nodding acquaintances. He was a beautiful man: dark-eyed, serene, with a cascade of long black wavy hair and even features. Life in Shivpuri District was hard and weathered its population of farmers and their families into a look of chronic middle age, going on old. Like Durga—who I had read lives in a state of *svatantrya*, independent from the universe—the Durga Sadhu seemed unperturbed by the physical effects of his environment.

On one particular day—and I do believe it was the last time we saw the Durga Sadhu, who may have set out to celebrate the Durga Puja in Bengal—we arrived at the crossroads, once again resplendent in a new set of glass bangles. We sat. Tired. It was late afternoon after a day of playing at the *balwaadi* with the children of Toda Picchore followed by the long hike back to the *chai* stand. Our Sadhu was there. He nodded and then, in an unusual move, gestured to the bangles. I was thinking, "I will kill this man if he says that now I am a real *Hindustani aurat! Achaa! Churion buhut sundar häi!*" What he did say was this:

"*Ki cota lagi hogi.* That must have hurt."

"*Haa, jii.*"

"*Ah.*"

The moment froze. I knew for an absolute certainty that there was nothing in the Durga Sadhu's cultural experience that would have led him to believe that wearing bangles was anything less than normal for a woman and certainly not painful. He could not have read anything regarding the anatomy of the American hand. I don't know that he was literate. But he observed with an open heart, he waited until the cultural fog lifted, and then when it was clear, he saw us and knew that one of the most commonplace details about living in his world hurt. And then he let us know he knew.

"*Ah.*"

Before I could think, that exchange startled these words right out of my mouth.

"*Lekin, churion buhut sundar häin, na?*" (But bangles are very beautiful, aren't they?)

"*Ah. Shabash.* Very good."

And we all laughed.

Jane Albritton served in an applied nutrition program in India from 1967-69. When she started her own writing, editing, and teaching business, she named it Tiger Enterprises. She has been assured that the goddess will not mind. Jane is the editor of this volume.

TAMARA BUSCH

✳

The Trick of the Megapode Egg

We never really know if what we thought we knew was real or just a trick that comes as part of everlasting cultural ambiguity.

I CAN ONLY TELL YOU THIS FROM MY PERSPECTIVE AND MEMORY. Even that is uncertain. And what am I but memories and the moment?

Facing backwards does not always tell you where you have been, but in a canoe in rough water, it is a sure way to get seasick. I knew this, about feeling seasick I mean, but it wasn't until I felt nauseous that I faced forward, salt water spraying over the bow. We followed the coast of the island Vella Lavella on our left. To our right, open sea. A map would tell you it was the New Georgia Sound and that if you traveled far enough northeast you would land on Choiseul Island, southeast you would land on Kolombangara Island, or far enough east on Isabel Island. But to the eye, it was open sea; so we watched the shore.

To four people used to changing seasons and daylight-saving time, it was a long afternoon in the heat of the equatorial sun. My watch was buried in my bag. We were Volunteer teachers who had passed nearly two years in the South Pacific in the

Solomon Islands. I had tried to reorient myself beneath a night sky where the Southern Cross is visible against the backdrop of stars. Two years of long afternoons. Not long because they dragged, but because time had been suspended. School was the only aspect of life dictated by a clock, and it mattered only to those who went. Classes finished at 1 P.M. Then the afternoon would pass with the traverse of the sun. If we had never come, if outsiders who measure time and distance, recorded history, and mapped the land had never come?

Time here could be spent waiting.

Waiting, the morning in a moment passed. Wait, *anga* in the Roviana language, one of the few words that we had learned, because we—Jeffrey my husband and I—lived at a boarding school. The students came from many different islands in the country, a country with ninety plus languages, so most people spoke in Pidgin English at the school. After all, English was supposed to be the official language.

The morning had nearly passed before our driver, Paul, met us with the canoe. He came on Solomon Time.

Solomon Time, the joke, especially among Volunteers and expats. The term had not originated locally; there is no translation for it in any of the island languages. Solomon Time meant that we weren't sure when or even if our driver would show up until we actually saw him. He could have been late or early, if we had actually set an hour. Morning was what we had agreed upon, Monday morning. That we were leaving from Gizo, where Westerners had come through with their watches and, yes, the promise of money, assured us that we had good odds of getting in a canoe on this day.

But I had said "morning" many times before: tomorrow morning. Many tomorrows would pass; sometimes tomorrow never came and sometimes it was yesterday, and you've missed it. This is a place without calendars or clocks or weather seasons, where there is the sun and the moon, the high tide and the low tide, and the egg-laying season of the crabs. There is no word for minute or hour; a moment is undefined. Most people have no birth certificate; they have no age and no document of their existence. Children might be raised by their biological parents or by some other relative. If the students fail on the exams required for them to continue their education, they may just change their name, and take the exam again. They have language names, English or Christian names, nicknames, and they may just give themselves a new name. We met students called Han Solo, Carefree, Mary Virgin, Kennedy, Nixon and even a Hitler. "Carefree" was my favorite; even though it was taken from chewing gum, it fit. Pieces of the outside world slipped in and became nonsense.

After two years, I got into a canoe with an outboard motor that arrived on Solomon Time; I got in and sat facing backwards. I didn't know the name of the village where we were going, and we couldn't see it from the shore. It was high above us, high enough to survive should the sea rise.

When one of our fellow Volunteers taught his students about global warming, they became very concerned. They suddenly realized that at any moment the waters could rise; everything they knew would disappear. The island Jeffrey and I lived on, less than two miles long and a little over a quarter mile wide, would be gone if the sea rose a meter. Most of the islands in the Roviana lagoon would no longer exist. This is the time of the islands; after the sea rises, there will just be the sea, without memory.

Steady on land, now I waited, slightly bent over, to see if I would throw up. No. I grabbed my bag, and we followed the switchbacks, cut through the bush, straight up the side of the hill. At the top, we came out into the village that had opened the grassy strip of highland to the sky, full of Melanesian people who had never seen white people. Still there must have been a term for us; *mane pura, tia vaka,* had been whispered, sometimes shouted, on other islands. Sometimes the term cleared the way to a standpipe, or it caused women to pull skirt waistbands up over their breasts, other times it elicited nothing more than a glance. Here I did not hear it. I am sure we were announced by the sound of our outboard engine.

They watched as we stood beneath freshwater standpipes fully clothed, rinsing the saltwater from our bodies. Children stood just beyond arms' reach, waiting to drop leis around our necks. We were in the fishbowl; we had swum in it before. We didn't change our clothes. We were drying in the sun when Principal Nelson met us.

Jen had arranged our visit with the school principal she had met through the principal of the school where she and Dave taught. The principal had wanted the villagers, especially the children, to see white people. He wanted to dispel the fear and strangeness of people with no color in their skin. Nelson had traveled beyond the island shores; the villagers had not.

The principal paraded us around the village so that our white hands could shake black hands, so that we could trace the geography that defined the village limits. We were given a tour of the school—four leaf-and-stick classrooms with black-boards and desks—and served dinner in the last room as some of the students watched. It was all about watching and seeing. We even watched each other. We smiled a lot because we did not know what to say.

It was in the last classroom that the formalities began, where the four of us sat at the table. The principal stood at the end; a few students stood at the back of the classroom holding bowls of food. Faces hovered by the windows and the door. Now, sepa-rate from the island, I do not remember specifically what was said, but we all knew the routine. The routine. It's like coming home and just knowing what bed to sleep in. In the English of those educated overseas, he began, "We want to thank you for honoring us with your visit. We hope that we have done nothing to offend you." There was always this concern about offending, at least in formal situations. I felt like we were a walking offense most of the time, but with the best of intentions.

Then it was our turn to speak our best and most gracious English. Martha, Jeffrey, and I looked to Dave; it was his wife who had organized the trip. But Dave, looking sheepish, had come for the plants and the geology. He had gotten his masters with a graduate thesis on lichens in Alaska where formal speeches were not a requirement. Plus, speaking up was not in his nature. Martha spoke. "We would like to thank you for welcoming us to your village. We feel very honored to be your guests. We hope that we will do nothing to offend you."

Nelson nodded in approval and bowed his head, "Let us pray."

I half expected Jesus clapping. Well, that's what I called it. At the primary school where I had been teaching during my second year, the morning began with singing prayers and clapping. A local woman, Millinaru, taught up to grade four in one room. One day Millinaru had interrupted a morning of singing and Jesus clapping after two of my students started clapping a counter rhythm. The counter rhythm, to me, seemed to improve a song that had grown monotonous, as had many of the morning clapping songs.

"I don't like this *krange* clapping all about," Millinaru scolded. "You no clap all same monkey. You clap all same human being."

Didn't realize that monkeys clapped interesting rhythms, I had thought smartly to myself. Didn't know Millinaru had ever seen an actual monkey, since there weren't any species endemic to the Solomons.

Then she pointed to Dean, one of the two offending counter rhythm clappers. She pointed to his hair. "What now this
one? What you do with hair belong you? You know time
before, grandparents belong you me, they wear this type hair,
they wear something in nose belong them, they mark body
belong them. They do this kind something. But you me no do
all same. You me no heathen. You me Christian now."

Nelson told us that the students had been preparing for our
visit all week, so we smiled. We followed him out of the classroom to join all the villagers sitting or standing in a ring. First we
were thanked for coming with gifts of nautilus, triton and cowry
shells. The nautilus was the most prized, so we saved it for Jen.

"I think it's illegal to take a nautilus out of the country,"
Dave had whispered.

"Well, if you don't want it, then you can have a triton and
we'll take it," Jeffrey was ready to make the trade.

"No, I think Jen will want it," Dave pulled it in closer. "It
is a gift."

It was one of those conflicts. We tried to be culturally sensi-
tive and environmentally conscious; we were supposed to be
those kinds of people. It was a gift; we had to accept it. Jeffrey
and I had been given a piece of reddish coral cut live from
the sea by our host brother during our first month in country. It was a gift; we had to accept it. To explain, right at that
moment, how it was destruction of the living reef would have
been ineffective, perhaps detrimental. Our host brother would
have been insulted, our point would be misunderstood; many
"sorries" for the offense would have followed. We had to build
a relationship, no matter how simple, before our words had
worth. This much we understood, or so we thought. So we
had accepted the coral. We had packed it carefully so that not
too many of the fragile pieces would break off.

To explain across the gap of cultural ambiguity, I had no way. So we accepted the shells, and Jen would get the prized nautilus.

Various groups, mostly of children, took turns in the dirt center singing or dancing. As the sunlight faded, fires grew. From that dark periphery, painted boys danced into the center. Drums called to the primitive soul. Jeffrey captured close-ups of the faces with Martha's camera. Smaller faces hover like spirits in the background. In a room with electric light, hovering faces have no presence.

The principal had included a second day in the white people's visit itinerary. But we would not return to the village that night, so white hands shook black hands, and we hiked down the switchbacks with our bags to the fiberglass canoe. Two additional canoes of villagers joined us for the next part of our itinerary. We followed them into a cove, where they idled their engines.

"There," one of the men in another canoe pointed, "is a taboo place." He waved our driver closer.

A small cave, more like a hollow in the rock, just above where the water lapped at the shore. The water probably had not risen much higher than that in decades; otherwise it could have moved what was in the hollow. Skulls and petrified clam bracelets, which had been used as money for things such as bride prices, lay on the ground. Then there were shelves balanced on stones with more skulls, growing moss from their headhunting days.

"Are you afraid?" asked the man who pointed. I suspected from the tone of his voice that he hoped we were.

Jeffrey leaned over the side of the canoe to take pictures with Martha's camera.

"Are you afraid?" he asked again.

We smiled. It felt like the beginning of a B movie. This would be the voodoo of location if we were here to film. But I was only afraid of offending, of being culturally insensitive. If they were still headhunters and we were traders or missionaries from an earlier period in time, if the outside world had not touched their world, if education and daylight had not chased away all the spirits, maybe I would fear this place. I wanted a quiver to run down my spine. I even tried to talk myself into it. The ancestors of these villagers, perhaps even some old men still living down in the narrow valley, decapitated their enemies. These were their skulls, and their power lay with those who took them.

Moss grew on the skulls. Were we afraid? We were still in a B movie. This was just part of the itinerary, a bit of history in the daylight. I came from the outside, and I knew what lay on the map. I knew the threat of men turning on me was more likely than a god in the heavens or spirits in the forest. I knew that in the daylight. But what you know in the light, you forget in the dark. The imagination can go wild. Then it is all about what you believe and what you fear. Belief is like that. Might I have prayed had these men turned on us with their bush knives? Words have their own power. I might have prayed, I might have cried, but I would not have found God. I have no belief in the supernatural.

"Are you afraid?"

We smiled. Then Nelson redirected the canoes out of the cove, around the northern tip of the village above, to where the Ulo River met the sea. We got out of the canoes. "Now we will see the volcano," Nelson announced. Of course we had to look at volcanoes before we left this island country; volcanoes had created the islands. Volcanoes were the source of myth and origin. "Well, not the actual big volcanoes, it is too far to walk in half a day," he added slightly sorry. Too far for the time allotted in the white people's visit itinerary.

So in all actuality, we were going to look at some hot springs and bubbling mud pools. The whole area was a geothermal hotspot. This would be as close as we would ever get to a volcano. All the people scattered from the canoes into the bush, many of them had gardens in the area. Nelson sent us following one of the men that he had designated as our volcanic guide.

As we followed along the path, the heat radiating from the ground increased and the smell of sulfur filled our nostrils. Then we began to hear the plop, plop of bubbling pools on either side of us. "You must walk careful now," our volcanic guide cautioned us. As if on cue, an old man carrying taro and megapode eggs came from the opposite direction. One of his calves was covered in white scar tissue. "Him burn'em leg belong him," our guide nodded.

We walked through this geothermic site, this alien landscape of bush and bubbling pools until it completely opened up. Two giant bubbling mud puddles, where the heat and the activity below broke through the earth's surface. Dave, who had come for plants and geology, crouched down to pick up samples of the soil in little film canisters. Martha, Jeffrey, and I stood close enough to the pools for sweat to instantly bead up, close enough that a nudge would have left scar tissue on our feet and calves.

Then we walked back into the bush. Our itinerary required us to be in the canoe with the coast of Vella Lavella on our right by late afternoon. We had only walked a few feet when we ran into an old woman carrying a megapode egg. The megapode is a bird that lays its eggs in geothermic areas, where the heat of the ground incubates them. The eggs are eaten for their large yolky centers.

The guide halted and talked to the old woman in local language. Around a turn or two, he halted again. He turned around to look at us. "This woman, hem like show'em you how now for find'em egg." So we went back.

She stood waiting by a tree, smiling. She pretended to look for the right kind of spot. She paused, bent down, pushed away some dirt, and held up an egg. It struck us as funny, the trick of the egg. We nodded and smiled at the find, like we were complicit in a deception. We had not understood the language, but did she think that we didn't know she had buried the egg? She had to send us out of sight and hide the egg like a game to fool us. How many times had we been tricked before with the "egg" and not realized it? What might we have missed and somehow not connected in two years? Who are we to be here?

Nelson handed Dave a megapode egg before we climbed into the canoe. "Send more white people," he said. He handed us all pieces of paper with the words, "Sibila Primary, Karaka Village," written down because he was worried we couldn't commit the spoken words to memory.

Years later, I searched the internet. I found the word eco-tourism associated with those words. Although I doubt many tourists make it there, it sounds less remote. It is all about images. Mine was of the edge of the world.

Tamara Busch served with her husband Jeffrey Rinderknecht in the Solomon Islands from 1996-98. In 2008, they took a year off from their jobs in the States and went to work as field assistants in Santa Rosa National Park in Costa Rica, researching the mating strategies of male white-faced capuchin monkeys.

✦

Snow in Sawankhaloke

*The imagination is a powerful tool that can release the
willing from a stifling classroom in Thailand to take
a bracing little trip with Nanook of the North.*

IT WAS THE HOT SEASON. I HAD LEFT YALA, THE CAPITAL CITY OF
the southern province of the same name, situated near the end
of the dangling elephant's trunk part of Thailand that latches
on to Malaysia. Having completed my first year as an English
teacher in a secondary school there, I had just relocated to
Sukhothai, the name for both the modern provincial capital of
the north-central province and the nearby *muang kao*, or old
city, with its ancient ruins of the original Thai capital. I was
starting over, trying to get my bearings in another part of the
country, preparing for a new assignment and a fresh cast of
teachers and students.

I had moved because at the end of the past school year,
several Volunteers and I had been offered the opportunity to
join a new project, a collaboration between the Ministry of
Education and Peace Corps. The idea was to place pairs of
volunteers, who had taught previously in secondary schools,
in three of the Ministry's Regional Supervisory Units, with
the goal of supporting and training teachers. Volunteers

selected for this assignment had three tasks: to team-teach English with a Thai counterpart in two secondary schools (teaching half the year in each school); to conduct ongoing teacher training in both schools; and to conduct intensive English language seminars during breaks. In this way, more Thai teachers and students would have the opportunity to interact with the English-speaking Volunteers, and teachers could share ideas and learn from one another. Thai 56 Volunteer Kevin Quigley and I were chosen to join the RSU based in Phitsanuloke, which served—in addition to that province—Sukhothai, Uttaradit, and Tak.

Prior to moving to Sukhothai, I had spent a few days at the Peace Corps office in Bangkok, researching and gathering what I hoped would be useful and fun materials. During that research, I discovered that Volunteers could borrow films from the U.S. consulate in Bangkok. After consulting the list of available films, I chose several, including, rather whimsically, *Nanook of the North*, an old black-and-white documentary about Inuit life in the Canadian arctic. I didn't realize that the film had no spoken dialogue. Had I known, I might have reconsidered, for my aim was to expose teachers to English via a different medium. As it turned out, the film did provide a change of pace, albeit in a somewhat eccentric, surreal sort of way.

For the first seminar, Kevin and I traveled to Sawankhaloke, a town about an hour's drive north of Sukhothai, located in an area once renowned for manufacturing beautiful pottery. Teaching teachers eight hours a day during the three-week seminar there at the height of the hot season was not unlike working inside a kiln.

I was not prepared for the Thai hot season. This reality was first impressed upon me upon arrival of our group in Bangkok when, disembarking from the plane wearing a perfectly inappropriate corduroy sports jacket, I was met full-force by a blast of heat and humidity that seemed powerful enough to send me straight back home. During my first year in Yala, I would often return to the teacher's room after an English class, my shirt sodden with perspiration, plastered to my chest, as if I had just walked through a sprinkler. Looking back on that Sawankhaloke seminar, through rippling heat waves of memory, it seems now as though its three weeks unfolded over the course of one very long and languid, unrelentingly hot, humid day.

We broke out *Nanook of the North* during the final week of the seminar. The timing seemed auspicious. With the end of the course now in sight, we were all pretty maxed out on English: we, beginning to run out of material and fresh ideas, and the Thai teachers approaching the saturation point that typically accompanies intensive study. We had all arrived at the point, beyond which there promises to be only diminishing returns.

It was two in the afternoon, with the unforgiving sun beating on our classroom, giving us one last brutal pounding before grudgingly starting its imperceptibly slow slide into late afternoon. The air in the classroom was inert, not unlike us, seriously immobile after another intense morning of English grammar, pronunciation, conversation, reading, writing, and the indolent aftermath of our recent break for lunch. The Canadian arctic was not on anyone's mind that afternoon; there were no visions of Inuit hunters dancing in our heads. Nonetheless, we pulled the shutters, trying to block out the blinding glare outside, and proceeded to project the film against a bare classroom wall.

And suddenly, in the flickering images, there it was— there *we* were—transported out of the lush, vivid, sweltering tropics into the stark, frozen, monochrome arctic. As the film unfolded, our own discomfort seemed to recede, allowing us to enter into the Inuit world of Nanook, his family and friends, and bear witness to their daily struggle for survival. There, in one scene, was Nanook engaged in a tug of war with a seal, while a group of fellow hunters were coming across the ice with their dogs. In another, Nanook and the hunters inched up upon a herd of walruses.

Clearly, this was not Thailand. A famous proverb expressed the country's natural good fortune when it came to food: "There is rice in the fields and fish in the water." Here, in this severe, barren land, the only food came from animals, which people had to hunt to survive. Nor was there wood or thatch or bamboo available for shelter. As we sat in our heavy wooden chairs behind heavy wooden desks inside our wooden-shuttered classroom, Nanook and his friends constructed an igloo, carving huge blocks of snow, stacking them in a circle, cutting out holes in the snow, and then using sheets of ice to make windows.

When, startlingly as it had begun, the film was over, we sat suspended between two worlds. The film's spell finally broken, we pushed open the shutters, our windows—glassless, iceless—opening into the sun. The sun was still there, blazing away in a hazy blue sky, the air static and sticky as ever. Looking out from our windows, the trees and flowers seemed more vibrant, resplendent, as if we were seeing them with a beginner's mind. It hadn't snowed in Sawankhaloke. Yet, in the space of that darkened classroom, we had pursued those seals and walruses through ice and snow, we had felt that igloo's icy embrace, we had breathed deeply the frozen air.

Bill Preston served as a VISTA volunteer in Yonkers, New York, from 1970-72, where he worked as a community organizer. He served as a Peace Corps volunteer in Thailand from 1977-80, where he taught English and trained teachers as a member of Thai 58. He has also taught English in Indonesia, Spain, and the United States. He is the author of A Sense of Wonder, *a multicultural literature anthology published by Pearson Longman. Since 1986, he has worked as an editor of English textbooks. He currently works at Cambridge University Press in New York City.*

PART THREE

Getting through the Days

GLEN HELLER

*
* *
*

The Namesake

*Just what it takes to be rewarded with a forever baby
name might just remain a forever mystery.*

EVERY PEACE CORPS VOLUNTEER GETS BABIES NAMED AFTER
them. Yeah, right. After eighteen months of service in the
Solomon Islands, the PCV living nearest to me was on her
third namesake, and I had yet to be picked for even a middle
name. It wasn't for lack of trying. I'd hung out all night talking with the village elders, had insects feast on me as I worked
in the gardens, and dug WHO certified pit toilets through
10,000-year-old compressed coral. Still, no one wanted my
name. It wasn't like there was a shortage of newborns either.
But it would be while returning to my site, after some Peace
Corps gathering in the capital, that I would finally get my
chance. It happened on a rust bucket of a passenger ship: the
Iuminao.

The *Iuminao* [pronounced "you-me-now"] is one of those
ships you occasionally read about in the paper: "Overloaded
pre-war ferry with no life boats sinks like a rock!" Imagine
it jammed with people, boxes, coconuts, firewood, chickens
and a shrilly-screaming pig or two, and you're getting the feel.

Throw in about a million seaworthy cockroaches, lace the air with the combined odors of diesel, urine and vomit, and sway the whole thing continuously, and you're there. It was a twenty-four-hour ride on the *Iuminao* for me whenever I traveled between my site and the capital. I always dreaded the ride, but when on board, I never felt more like a Peace Corps Volunteer. I was also never closer to my Peace Corps issued lifejacket!

Late at night, on one such return trip, old Third-namesake and I were awakened where we slept on the open metal deck and asked if we were doctors. A baby had been born below decks and it was "too small." Offering what assistance I could, I grabbed my handy Peace Corps medical kit and made my way into the bowels of the ship, all the while nervously trying to remember my Emergency Medical Technician training from years before in Los Angeles, most of which was concerned with how to handle gunshot wounds, overdoses, and the possibility of litigious action from those you were trying to help.

In the area near the ship's canteen, I found a large semicircle of men, standing and looking inward. Moving through them, I discovered a tight knot of a dozen or so old women. Two of them held up a bed sheet, which they opened, allowing me to pass. Entering the circle's center, I saw a teenaged woman lying on the rusted floor. Between her legs an old woman knelt holding a silent baby, umbilical cord uncut. Looking frightened, but otherwise conscious and alert, the new mother did not appear to require immediate medical help. The baby, who could have snugly fit into an American football, had skin the color of dirty rice paper and, tied to his mother by an umbilical cord that had ceased to pulse, gave no visible sign of breathing.

With two pieces of medical tape, I tied off the cord at two points and cut between them. Checking the infant's nose and mouth for a blockage of mucus, I rubbed at its face and hands.

The infant kicked and sputtered. It kicked and sputtered again. Then, on a third kick, he came to life. It was like starting an outboard motor on a damp morning.

Shortly afterward, the placenta was delivered—as far as I could tell—whole. Because there was no excessive bleeding, I slipped out from behind the suspended bed sheet, hands bloody and feeling the flood of an incredible adrenaline rush. The old women, knowing far more about the practical aspects of birthing than I will ever know, smoothly took over.

Behind me the newborn's cry could be heard above the throb of the ship's engines. One man stepped forward from the wall of men in front of me. Raising his arm he proclaimed, "The name of this baby shall be *Iuminao!*" to which the crowd responded with a cheer.

The last I heard, the baby had been taken to the provincial capital's hospital and had survived. They never even asked my name.

Glen Heller (AKA The Iuminao *Doctor) served in the Solomon Islands from 1995-97. He currently lives in the greater Washington, D.C., area and travels extensively in Africa and Asia primarily on USAID and UNICEF contracted work.*

RUTH ALLIBAND

✦

The Archeological Map

Searching for an ancient temple of the sun in the scrub land of Madhya Pradesh requires both a map and proper pronunciation.

I WAS A PART OF INDIA 34, WHICH BEGAN AS A GROUP OF 104 trainees assembled in Albany, New York, for training: August 15, 1966. We trained for one month on the SUNY campus and then, when the fall semester began, we were moved to a Jewish summer camp in the Heiderberg mountains just outside of East Berne, New York: Camp Orinsekwa-Sonnikwa.

We had been recruited to work with youth groups. But our trainers were recently returned Peace Corps Volunteers from the first wave of Volunteers to India, and they pointed out to the training grant designers and the Peace Corps administration that youth groups might exist on paper in the Indian government organization, but they did not exist in reality. Our assignment then became Poultry Expert, the specialty that our trainers had learned. Fine. Then some Ph.D. training adviser raised the objection that there would not be infrastructure and economic wherewithal to make poultry raising viable in truly rural villages located a distance from markets. By the end of the first month, our assignment focus had shifted for the third time: we became Community Development Specialists, which I understood to be agricultural and nutrition extension workers also practicing public health and family planning education.

Local county extension agents from the Albany area were enlisted to provide us with extension education short courses. We raised a pen of barred rock cross chickens at the lakeside camp. We were given a demonstration of non-mechanized seed sowing techniques by a retired extension agent. We were encouraged to transfer these new skills to the traditional agriculture settings to which we would be deployed. And, in recognition that this might be too great a leap of transferrence, remedial short courses were to be provided at Indian agricultural institutes, such as Pantnager (aka the GB Pant Agricultural and Technical University in Uttaranchal, Uttar Pradesh).

My husband, Terry Alliband, and I were stationed in the extreme southwestern corner of Uttar Pradesh, in Jhansi District. That district is long and narrow and in places if you travel 15 kilometers to the east or the west, you are in the state of Madhya Pradesh. From the first, we knew the district to be historic, the home of Rani Laxmibai of Jhansi, who joined the coalition of rajas and nababs who rose against British rule in 1857. The medieval stone fort of Jhansi, built in the 1400s, rose above the town.

On our weekends or holiday leave, we planned brief trips to attractions a short distance away. It was at the Gwalior fort in neighboring Madhya Pradesh that we purchased a wall poster of the archaeological sites in the state. There were over three dozen listed on this map, and many were not too far from where we lived in Jeryai village, three km down a zig-zagging dusty cart road from the Betwa Canal crossing at Cherona, just outside of Chirgaon. Before we departed India, and with the help of our poster, we had journeyed to a good many of those sites.

Some of them, even though they were enticingly close, were still difficult to reach via public transportation. We failed to make it to Deogarh, a sixth-century temple farther south in Jhansi District. When we arrived at Jhansi District's sub-administrative center of Lalitpur in the middle of the afternoon after a journey that included a cycle ride along the cart tracks from our home village and three bus transfers, we were so hot and tired that we stopped at a tea stall for a cola (probably a Pee Cola or Thumbs Up, not Coca Cola). During that brief interval, the *one* bus of the day left the motor stand bound for Deogarh, leaving us behind. Another site proved equally elusive: the sixth century sun temple at Pawaya. On the map it looked so close. But our inquiries at the motor stand at our district capitol, Jhansi City, were met with blank stares. There were busses to Mauranipur, Moth, Baragaon, Harbalpur, Datia: practically everywhere one would want to go, but apparently no busses or connections to Pawaya.

Undaunted, we continued to explore ruins. In the fall of 1967, two young Peace Corps Volunteers—Maggie and Jane from California and Texas respectively—moved into Karera, a town in Madhya Pradesh not too far from us. We made their acquaintance and visited them one weekend after traveling to the ruins of an eighth-century Buddhist monastery further down the road.

We had spent the day on the road and at the monastery, and it seemed unlikely that we would be able to get back to our market town until sundown. Not wanting to travel the cart road to the village in the dark, we stayed the night with Maggie and Jane. We began to talk about the mysterious and elusive sun temple at Pawaya. Jane stopped us and turned to Ramcha, their cook, to ask about an old temple at Pawaya. Ramcha had the same cloudy incomprehension on his face. Then it seemed as if a light bulb went on over his head: "Oh!!

You want to go to Pahwaynnnn." We should have known that
the deep, thick Bundelkundi dialect could transform that place
name. Ramcha proceeded to tell us how to get there by bus:
go to Datia and then transfer to another, local bus.

Armed with the new pronunciation and traveling instructions, we packed our cycles aboard a country bus on the
weekend of our second wedding anniversary, the last week
of February 1968. After an early start, we were let off the
Pahwaynnnn bus in the early afternoon. As it disappeared in
the distance, we looked at the dirt track heading off across
scrub jungle. There were no houses in sight. As we began to
cycle down the road, a rider came up behind us: a man with a
large turban set rakishly on his head. He was leaning forward
and grasping the neck and reins of the black camel he rode.
This country that we lived in was known throughout India at
that time to harbor *dacoits*—highwaymen. We looked at each
other and had the same thought.

As we continued down the road, it became apparent that
others besides the man on the black camel were traveling in
the same direction we were: whole families packed into bullock carts lumbering over the track. Eventually we came to a
ravine with a small brook running at the bottom. We lifted
and dragged our heavy Indian cycles down the bank through
the thorn bushes. So far there had been no signage pointing
us towards a 6ᵗʰ century sun temple. We asked a traveler, and
he pointed us straight ahead. He and the other travelers veered
off in another direction. They said they were going to a *mela*,
a country fair.

We climbed the bank and saw our destination ahead of us.
This temple was one of the oldest we had seen anywhere in
India. It was very plain—a series of ascending terraces. The
whole thing, as I recall, was not very high off the ground. I
imagined, with no documentation to substantiate this belief, a

group of worshipers gathering there—as the sun rose or set—
to perform sun salutations on the terraced platforms. I recalled
having seen another temple like it as part of the rock-cut cave
temples by the ocean at Mahabalipuram near Madras (now
Chenai) on our Christmas travels in the south of India.

I had not read of any other existing sun temples. I think
the reason is that religious practices changed and the open
terraced platforms no longer suggested a holy place. The terraces could be easily dismantled for building stone for more
elaborate structures, and perhaps some of the magnificent tenth
and twelfth-century temples and temple complexes were raised
over old sun temple platforms. This temple was in a really
remote location and, perhaps for that reason, had been spared.

From the terraces of the sun temple, we could see across the
little stream where bullock cartloads of families were still heading from all directions toward to a pair of structures. Slithering
down the unstable banks of the stream's ravine, we crossed the
brook and headed for the *mela* grounds. We found a colorful
crowd of people: village women in bright saris with the deco-
rative end of the sari cloth, the *pallav*, pulled over their heads
and faces so that only their eyes peered out, and Bundelkundi
farmers wearing ten-yard turbans piled on their heads. The
men hunkered on the ground together, communally smoking
chillams (clay pipes) or portable hookahs. The bullocks were
unharnessed and tethered near the carts. I could imagine that
a lot of business deals were going down: marriages were being
arranged and bullocks were being traded or sold.

The buildings at the center of this assembly were two-story
brick structures with a concrete facing. I believe they must
have been built to the memory of some 18th century Datia
rajahs at a time when Hindu rajahs were attempting to keep up
with neighboring Muslim rulers who built graves AND two-
story tombs above their dead. The Hindus would cremate their

dead, but then build structures to the memory of rajahs while this practice was fashionable. Terry was told that there were nautch girls—belly-dancing prostitutes—inside the structures, but he did not go to investigate.

Instead, our curiosity satisfied, we retraced our steps. We stayed overnight in one of the Indian hotels in Jhansi City and then headed out to our village in the morning. When I made my circuit through the village neighborhood, the Kachi (vegetable gardening caste) women wanted to know where I had been. I began to tell the story of what I felt (and still feel) was a unique adventure. Maya, one of my particular friends, exclaimed: "The Ghum Mela!! That was in my back yard when I was a girl growing up in my home village. I have been to the Ghum Mela sooo many times!"

Astonishing. All the time that we had searched for this sun temple, a person who had full knowledge of its existence lived a few paces from my own door. This revelation illustrated how deep into the countryside the network of intermarriage extended. Perhaps overland on cart tracks, Pahwayannn and the Ghum Mela grounds were not as distant as they seemed to someone who traveled to them by roads spoking out from the district capitol. It also illustrates that, like us, villagers also yearned to leave their homes and go on day trips across the dusty countryside and then come back to tell about their adventures.

Ruth Alliband served in India (India 34) from 1966-68. Her late husband Terry became a cultural anthropologist specializing in community development.

✦

A Thai Interpretation of Hemingway's "The Killers"

The assumptions we make even in our literary
interpretations may not cross the cultural divide.

I FIRST CAME ACROSS HEMINGWAY'S "THE KILLERS" IN A scarred, dog-eared Pocket Book that my father had dragged through World War II. I was sixteen and can still remember turning the thin, rationed pages till I came to the end and said to myself, "Something is moving under the surface of all those simple words, but dang if I know what it is." I read the story again. It wasn't my night. I felt like a cat that had spent two hours trying to chase a rat up a greased pole.

I tried to forget the story, but I always went back to it, especially when bogged down with one of Mr. Fowler's algebra problems. Reading "The Killers" became almost a religious experience. However, unlike religious experiences where emotions and gut instinct are vital, I needed the opposite. I needed a neat intellectual key. But what was I getting? A big immovable door with a sign that read: Enter if you can.

I was, therefore, elated when three years later, my English professor said, "Your next assignment is to read 'The Killers' by Ernest Hemingway. Be here prepared to discuss it in depth." Boy, was I ever ready! By now I knew it like my soul knew my acne. Nevertheless, read it I did, just to make sure.

I came away from the lecture with disappointment and satisfaction. We'd discussed a number of interpretations, including Cleaneth Brooks and Robert Penn Warren's "The Discovery of Evil: An Analysis of 'The Killers.'" Basically I agreed with Brooks and Warren. Yes, "Hemingway...focused not on the gangsters, but on the boys in the lunchroom." Yes, a gangster "lives...by a code which lifts him above questions of personal likes and personal animosities." And, yes, Nick discovers evil. Why, then, wasn't I satisfied?

I didn't find out until I was teaching the story to a class of Thai students at Thonburi Teachers College. As second-language learners, the students did indeed see "The Killers" as a gangster story with Max and Al as the protagonists. To undermine their folly, I wrote THE KILLERS in huge block letters across the board and asked: *Who are the killers?"*

The question drove the students back the rears of their chairs, a hurricane hitting a row of bamboo. I should have backed off, but the devil was upon me. I boomed, "I repeat: who are the *real* killers?" It was instinctual, felt by ESL teachers and Pentecostal ministers. Still, it was I who was in for a shock. Ratana, one of my boldest and brightest students, suddenly leaned forward, "Why all of them are, teacher."

At first I could not believe my ears.

"What was that, Ratana?"

"All of them," she said placidly. "They all killed Ole Andreson."

I could see in a flash what she was driving at, but I wanted her to say it, not me.

"Who are *they*?" I asked.

"Nick, George, and Sam," she said. "They all had a chance to save Ole Andreson, but they didn't. In a way they are worse than Max and Al."

"How's that?"

"Max and Al are brave. Nick, George, and Sam are not. They're cowards. I hate cowards."

"How is Sam a coward?"

"Sam minds his own business throughout the story. He never gets mixed up with other people. He's black. He knows what can happen to black men in America."

"And George?"

"I hate George the most. He wants to help Ole Andreson, but is too afraid to. So he sends Nick to warn Ole Andreson."

"What about Nick? Why don't you think he's brave?"

"Nick's a young man. All young men think they're brave. Nick, too, thinks he's brave—very brave. But he's not. We can see that when he goes to warn Ole. Nick does not offer to stay and fight against Max and Al. Even as he leaves, we can see how nervous and frightened he is with Mrs. Bell."

"Let us get your interpretation straight, Ratana. You think the theme of the 'The Killers' is cowardice?"

"Yes, teacher."

"Actually three types of cowardice: Sam is a coward and knows he's a coward. George is a coward who is ashamed he's a coward. And Nick is a coward who finds out he's a coward. Is that right?"

"Yes, teacher."

"O.K.," I said. "But, as both you and the class know, one of the cardinal rules of our class is that a theory must be tested out against contradictory elements in the story. For instance, if what you say is true, why does Nick state 'I'm going to get out of this town' toward the end of the story? Nick might be a coward, but he is not stupid. He knows Max and Al want to kill Ole, not him. Why then does he want to get out of Summit so fast?"

Ratana knitted her brow and averted her eyes. The class went silent as Thai classes do when a student has been shot down. I felt guilty for hurting her feelings and was about to apologize when she looked back at me and said hesitantly, "I–I think Nick is trying to run away from his guilty feelings, teacher. But he can't. Someday he'll have to stop running and face himself. We all have to do that or there is no meaning to life, is there?"

I was thunderstruck. I knew Ratana was smart, but not smarter than Cleaneth Brooks and Robert Penn Warren.

It was then that Ratana frowned.

"What's wrong?" I asked.

"Nothing, teacher. I was just wondering what kind of a coward you are."

I laughed.

"We're running out of time," I said. "So I will answer that question next time. Now here's the class assignment for next time. To further test Ratana's theory, think and decide what kind of a coward you are and come to class prepared to defend your position.

"Of course, if you are not a coward, state that. You must, however, have the courage to tell us why you are so brave. Class dismissed."

Girard (Gerry) Christmas became a frightful bore after his two tours of service in Thailand (1973-75) and Western Samoa (1976-78). He taught English for the Chinese government at the Institute of Foreign Languages in Guangzhou and at St. Joseph's International School in Yokohama, Japan. Returning to the United States with his wife and two daughters, he worked first for the Job Corps, then spent two decades in dysfunctional North Carolina middle schools. Many people live lives of quiet desperation. He has Peace Corps to thank for not being a member of that huge and despondent lot.

THALIA KWOK

*

The Cultural Palace

In China, nothing is ever quite what you expect.

TODAY, I LAZILY ROLLED OUT OF BED AT NOON AND, BLEARY-eyed, shuffled over to my bedroom window to pull back the heavy curtain and peer outside for my daily weather bulletin. The report was sunny, not a cloud in the sky. I touched the window for a temperature reading. Acceptably cool! Excited now, but not quite believing, I cracked the window open, bracing myself for a blast of hot, humid air. Instead a pleasantly cool breeze drifted in to greet me! I was fully satisfied.

That's when I knew today would be a good day to forget about the piles of work sitting around my apartment and overflowing from my inbox. Today I could explore another unknown stretch of the city. I whipped out my colorful bilingual city map and chose a destination.

After a quick ten-minute bus ride and a short walk, I arrive at my first destination. The Cultural Palace. Now, with a name like that, can you blame me for half-expecting to find a stately mausoleum filled with ancient silks, flowing calligraphy on yellowing scrolls, and displays of musical instruments like the ones in old martial arts films? I say half expecting because at this point I have been in China long enough to know that nothing is ever quite what you were expecting. I buy a ticket for 1 *kuai* and follow some children in through the main gate.

Instead of long halls of cultural artifacts, I find something else completely: a meandering park of concrete sidewalks and wide, open concrete squares. Scattered among these are clusters of tea tables, shaded by short corridors of trees or makeshift metal overhangs. Here a couple of middle-aged women wile away their Saturday afternoon gossiping over tea. At the next table an elderly man stares with rapt attention at the progression of a game of Go. I see wicker cages hanging from the tree branches. The canaries sing to one another over the heads of their keepers. A talking Myna calls out to me, "Wei! Wei!" I lean in close to make out what it's saying, but it doesn't seem to speak English. In the next area, I can hear the sound of hundreds of Mahjong tiles clicking against one another. I scan the courtyard and catch the flick of a wrist slapping away mosquitoes and the fluttering of paper fans against the rising afternoon heat.

Next to the tea areas is an even more unexpected sight: relics from wandering state fairs transported from another time to rest in another world. Here in the Cultural Palace sleep carnival rides with rusty gates and peeling, sun-bleached paint. Carousel animals stand frozen in step. A couple of curious teenaged girls wander from one to the next. The ride sputters to life, groaning and creaking. As the gears are set into motion, a festive carnival song strains out of the speakers. When the girls climb down and exit the gates, the ride returns to its quiet slumber until the next infrequent fare arrives.

I arrive in a small square and notice a surprising number of people milling about and staring at something over on one end of the square. Upon closer inspection I find they are all gathered in front of a long line of what seems at first glance to be advertisements. Papers of various shapes and sizes are strung up along a clothesline. I edge in with my camera for a closer look and to snap a few pictures. People are pointing and staring at me and my camera, but I just smile back at them and pretend I know what I am doing.

When I am finally close enough to read one of the advertisements, I am quite taken aback. One starts off: *Female, 27. Very tall, 1.58 meters....* I glance at a few more to be certain of what I'm looking at. Sure enough, next to it is an advertisement for a young man. All the way down the line, it's the same: singles ads! Mothers and fathers literally put their offspring out on a line to see who will bite. As I am processing this new information, a couple of women in their fifties suddenly pop up from under the line directly in front of me. One is pointing with great animation at a piece of paper, telling her friend how suitable this one is!

As I slowly back out of the crowd a man stops me, asking, "Are you a reporter?" *No, no! I'm not a reporter.* "You're not a reporter? Are you a (insert Chinese gibberish here)?" *Smile and nod?* He continues with some more semi-intelligible gibberish until I realize he is asking if I am looking for a boyfriend. My eyes widen in panic, and I hurriedly say, *No! No! Not that. I was just out for a walk!* He looks mildly disappointed and says, "Oh, that's too bad. Because you're very pretty." Flushed with embarrassment, I apologize and quickly take my leave.

As I am backtracking along towards the main gate, I come across a large building called the Cultural Palace Training Center. I wander into the darkened auditorium hall and see a grand piano up on stage. There are possibly ten or fifteen people seated along the first row in the otherwise empty hall, so I move down towards the front and take a seat near the edge. A young girl, perhaps sixteen, is on the stage. She plays like one of those virtuosos I would sometimes see at home on OETA, the Oklahoma Educational Television Authority. Listening to her play makes me embarrassed to admit that I took ten years of piano lessons.

An old man with unruly white tufts of hair growing around the sides of his head approaches the stage. He authoritatively addresses the members of the audience, "Each of you test the piano. If there are any problems tell us now."

I realize I've walked into a rehearsal for a piano concert that would most likely take place that evening. There are four pianists altogether; the eldest is eighteen years old and the youngest only eleven. They hail from all different parts of China: Shanghai, Nanjing, Chongqing. Sitting beside their overbearing mothers (one complains loudly to the director that there are too many mosquitoes backstage and they must buy something to take care of it), they wait patiently for their turn to test the instrument. One by one the performers take the stage and flex their fingers. Two of the girls return to the stage, together, and play a complicated classical duet, unlike anything I have ever seen or heard before. They all play with such emotion and clarity. No slurring through complicated measures, never rushing or hesitating. The strings of that grand piano bend to their wills, sounding out every thought and feeling that overflows from their minds down into their fingertips and out onto the keys. When they finish they are glowing, enraptured. Through the music they can reach enlightenment and share a small part of it with us.

My reverie is broken when a woman comes by and offers me a free bottle of water. Evidently she has mistaken me for someone important and not the vagrant that I am. I stay for a few more songs and then take my leave before anyone notices I don't belong there.

There weren't any old poems, no pagodas, nothing dating back to any dynasty. But that is culture from another time. There are museums for such things. This was a place brimming with Chinese culture of today. It's playing Chinese Chess in the park (here it's just called Chess), going for a spin on an aging amusement park ride, finding love for your son or daughter on a laundry line, and enjoying a master's piano concert series performed by teenagers. The Cultural Palace. Aptly named.

Thalia Kwok grew up in a small city in a state that many people know very little about (Tulsa, Oklahoma), then joined the Peace Corps to serve in a big city on the other side of the world that many people know very little about (Chongqing, China). When she graduated from high school, she was one of two Chinese-Americans in a graduating class of nearly eight hundred. When the opportunity came along with Peace Corps to return to the place of her neglected heritage, the place her ancestors called home, the decision was easy. She served from 2005-07.

L O I S   S C H N E I D E R

✦

Amrikans Drink
Their Water Hot

The concept of boiling water before drinking it
always lost something in translation.

IN 1965, WALKING IN THE STUDENT UNION AT NORTH DAKOTA State University in Fargo, North Dakota, I saw a table in the hallway with Peace Corps literature and someone that was probably a recruiter. I was walking with a friend, John. We both took their "nonsense language" test and went on our way. A few years later, John received an invitation and the next year, I did. Both of us served. I went to India a year after John—who was to become my husband—went to Afghanistan.

I expected carefully planned and coordinated programs and implementation when I joined the Peace Corps, but boarding the plane across the ocean after the first month of training in the U.S., I found India 57 Volunteers among scores of empty seats on the flight in July 1968. I suppose several groups were meant to be on the charter headed to India, but someone doing scheduling was probably new on the job. For us, all was well. Only India 57 going to Madras and another group training with us were on board. The result: extra food and drink and several seats to stretch out and sleep. This was the beginning of finding our own way with whatever the circumstances. No one was perfect or knew all the answers. Everyone had a lot to learn.

After the last two months of PC training in the city of Madras, I was assigned to All Saints Basic Training School in Trichy. Basic schools were based on Gandhi's principles: grow your own food, weave your own cloth, be self-sufficient. Students were primary teacher trainees from all castes. For the students, it must have been a first experience in many ways.

The safety of water was included in the teaching materials for health. Because the PL480 (that is, Public Law 480 of the United States, which is also known as the Agricultural Trade Development and Assistance Act) distributions included milk powder, my students would need to know the importance of mixing it with safe water. Two things come to mind as I remember mixing up milk.

First of all there was the matter of following directions: I think it was three parts water to one part milk powder. But once people had the milk powder, some used it 50/50. These proportions made the milk very rich and likely caused unset stomachs. Stomach problems prompted teachers not to give it to the children since it appeared to make them sick. But was it the richness of the milk or the unboiled water used to mix it up?

Of course, the idea of boiling water had its own problems. To demonstrate the proper way to boil water, I brought a small kerosene stove to class for boiling the water. I also bought a large clay pot that was placed in sand in the corner of the room so that the boiled water could be put in the pot to cool for safe drinking water. The class was lectured about the importance of boiling water. One of the days following, I came early to the classroom, only to find the students carrying the big pot out of the room and tossing the water onto the ground. Having spent a lot of money for the kerosene, I wasn't happy.

Why would the students do that? Their answer? "The water isn't hot anymore." What a lesson that was. How long had people misunderstood "boiling water"? I would never know.

I went to India with the expectation that there was a job to be done, and never once did I wish I were home or worry that the time was long in country. Once the needs were identified, I felt free to adapt to making the time and experience valuable. We appreciated the trust that was given to Volunteers.

The night the U.S. put a flag on the moon, I was on the roof of the school above where the head mistress Lily Charles lived. I had a portable radio, and it was probably the Voice of America station that reported the landing. I remember the sounds of the streets outside the school compound walls and the clip-clop of horses pulling carts. And I remember the flickering shadows of fires for warming hands on the side of the streets.

Lois Schneider served in India (India 57) from 1968-70. She taught health and nutrition at All Saints Basic Training School in Puthur, Trichy.

PAM ANDERSON

✦

A Day in My Life

*The making of a tri-annual report can be
its own exercise in translation.*

ANOTHER MORNING WAKE-UP CALL AT 5:30 A.M. BEGINS WITH
the village *pooyibaan* (village chief) announcing the day's events
and community news. The loud volume and static buzz of the
speakers make it nearly impossible for me to understand what
is being said. Long ago in my service, I determined it was not
just my limited Thai that was a deterrent to my understanding,
and I sleepily—if not cheerfully—begin the guessing game to
try to pick up the gist of what is said, recognizing a word here
and there. Some mornings it works, some mornings not; but
it is a worthwhile entertainment that takes me to my small
outdoor balcony kitchen where the hot water pot awaits its
morning jiggling of the cord to get the electricity flowing and
coffee on the way.

The community activity and colors I observe from my
"kitchen window" at this early hour have never ceased to
amaze me. The flowing orange robes of the monks walking
to the market for their morning alms (food from the women
to earn merit) along with the maroons, sky blue, and yellows

of school uniforms on the many students heading to schools together form a parade before a background of the changing greens of the rice fields that make up the landscape view behind my house.

Early morning is filled with the music of the students' laughter, the monks' chanting—as they return to the *wat*—the puttering of the small tractor motors pulling the carts of the farmers and their wives headed to the rice fields, the tinkling of the bells on the cows being herded into the small grassy area for their morning graze and, of course, the obnoxious loudspeakers on the vendor pickups announcing the morning specials. The morning composition ends with the sound of the national anthem being sung by the school children and signals that it is time for me to shake myself from this morning reverie and get about the business of being a community development Volunteer.

My first step is to run downstairs from my second floor home and cross the drive to turn on the water pump that will bring the water for my morning shower. I greet and hug the two-year old son of my dentist neighbor in our morning ritual of his invitation to eat breakfast with him. As his language abilities have advanced, he can tell me that I can take my shower first and he will turn off the water pump. As I return to my house, I hear his giggle as he anticipates how funny it will be to wait until he hears my shower running to do just exactly that: turn off the pump. I have learned that a bucket bath is worth the wonderful entertainment it provides him to "prank" me about the water.

After breakfast, it is time to hit the bike and make the trip to the neighboring village Day Care Center where forty pre-school children await some English games with their "*Yai Pam.*" I get to put down these visits as a "transfer of the skill of student-centered activities to the Day Care teachers" on my tri-annual reports, but this grandma knows that it is really about how loved she feels when three mornings a week she has another forty small children rushing out to greet her in order to be the first to give her a *wai* and then shake her hand and say hello. The benefit of the English words they learn by swimming like fish or scratching like monkeys or playing London Bridge barely rivals the benefit to the PC Volunteer of having troops of young friends greet her everywhere she goes.

Exhausted and feeling well-loved, I make my way to lunch with either co-workers at the office or the women who weave plastic straps to make hats, baskets, and boxes. The women have become my great friends. Sometimes we talk business, but our limited communication abilities make a lot of our time together about discussing the great Isan food they serve me or their pride in the weaving skills they have been able to pass on to their *farang*.

Occasionally, I can use my *"farang*-ness" to bring a Thai educator in for a business training, and so these delicious repasts and fun get-togethers can be called "relationship building" on my tri-annual report. Biking back to the Anamai to meet with my after-school English students, I am always warmed by these times spent with my new women friends and the sharing without the benefit of language that strengthens the bond we have built with each other.

Yet the highlight of the day is the time I spend with fifteen eager young grade school children who meet with me in the community room at the Anamai after a day at school. It is a highlight because they have worked so hard. After a year, their English abilities (and the Thai they have taught me) have made conversation a reality and a source of pride for all of us, not to mention the *sanuk* (fun) we have together. Seeing their confidence build and their visions of how their potential in life can expand, reminds me daily what community development— Peace Corps style—is really about. It is about the friends we make, the understanding of each other's culture that we foster, and what we learn from each other.

Their determination both to learn English and to teach me Thai as well has taught me so much besides the language. I have learned to husk a coconut, eat crickets, and cook a spicy bamboo soup. I have learned to cheer like a Thai parent at a sports day race and to mourn the loss of a grandfather at a Buddhist celebration of the passage into another lifetime. I have learned to pull the hammock slowly for a teething child, and wait patiently for the important guy to get there—*late*—before the meeting can start. I have learned the importance of planting one seed of rice, watching it sprout and moving it to a larger flooded field, trusting that the prepared ground and the cycle of rain will nurture it to another year of food for the family.

I have learned how the backaches and boredom of that work is rewarded with the smiles of children who cheerfully say *"im laew"* (I'm full) at the end of the meal. Watching the little seeds planted as an English word or sentence with my young student friends grow into conversational sprouts has taught me to trust in the cycles and the potential of future leaders in this community. As I approach the end of this time of "community development" in this community I have come to love, I realize one of the next big lessons in my life will be learning how to share these loving people and what they have taught me about themselves—and myself—with my friends and family back in the States.

Pam Anderson served as a teacher in the Philippines from 2002-05. After she returned to the States, she was called up by the Crisis Corps for the Katrina project. She worked for three months in Louisiana and then in January 2006 rejoined the Peace Corps as a Volunteer in Thailand. On completing her service there in 2008, she returned to her village in the Philippines—at the request of local officials—to direct summer English activities for the children there. The invitation provided her with an opportunity to renew old friendships, spend time in a community she had grown to love, and be the Lola Pam again to about eighty children.

✳

Living in the Land of Morning Calm

*It takes some time to learn where the sweetest
kernels of truth will grow.*

Two young American Peace Corps Volunteers, both carrying umbrellas, stroll along the ancient dirt path between
the rice paddies near Kwangju, South Korea, one Saturday in
1968. They peer closely at the fresh green shoots jutting about
a foot above the muddy water.

"I wonder where the rice kernels are," I muse to my friend,
Linna, bending down for a closer look at the neat rows of
smooth emerald shoots.

"Maybe they're hidden underneath the water," Linna
speculates as she gazes at the flooded fields.

"That makes sense. The rice grains probably grow just out
of sight beneath the surface of the water." I stand up, satisfied
with that guess. We adjust our bamboo umbrellas against the
spring sun and proceed on to the village of Wan Du Ri, where
my husband, Terry, awaited my return from a Chinese calligraphy lesson in Kwangju.

Could we have been more wrong about the rice? Why
were we clueless young American Volunteers from the Peace

Corps wandering on the rice paddy paths deep in the countryside of South Korea in 1968 in the first place? This countryside, which had not substantially changed for thousands of years, contained people who had rarely set eyes on Americans of any ilk, let alone had any real need of them. What were we thinking? Would any good come of it?

Ultimately the rice grew, the paddies dried, and truth was revealed, although it took the entire time we lived there to discover it. Our path to enlightenment was not unproblematic.

The path began a year after I graduated from college and married Terry. With brand new B.A.s in liberal arts from Berkeley, we joined the Peace Corps. We dreamed of the ways we would help humanity and the ways we would learn and benefit from the process. We dreamed of teaching English and of speaking French in a warm country in Africa. The Peace Corps had other ideas and surprised us with an invitation to serve in South Korea as rural public health workers. We were the fourth Peace Corps group to be invited to South Korea and the first group sent to live and work in the countryside. This was at the request of the Korean Health Ministry that had manpower needs in the areas of TB control, family planning, and maternal and child health.

Although we knew little about South Korea—didn't even know the Peace Corps was located there, in fact—and knew nothing about public health, we accepted the offer, and headed to New Mexico for training the following fall. And then on to Seoul, landing at Kimpo Airport in a flurry of snowflakes in mid-December of 1967. A crowd of reporters crowded around us as we stepped onto the runway and pelted us with a series of questions, the most unexpected of which was "Is the Peace Corps a front for the CIA?"

"Of course not," I told someone disdainfully as we exited the plane, "We would never have anything to do with that outfit. We are completely separate."

A moment later a man who had sat near me on the plane stepped behind me, grabbed my arm in a rough manner, and flashed his CIA badge.

"Don't you ever say anything against the CIA while you're here, young lady," he whispered angrily in my ear.

I wrenched myself away, utterly shocked. "I am an American citizen, and I have freedom of speech, and I didn't say anything wrong. Get your hands off of me. I am in the Peace Corps and have no connection with you."

He slunk off.

The snow was falling heavily as we hurried toward the building. I was freezing. Just outside the doors, a reporter holding a microphone requested that we sing a Korean song for his news station in Seoul. We had been told we would be asked to sing while in Korea, so we were prepared and quickly clustered together. With the snow sticking to our eyelashes, we sang "*Ari Rung*," the most beautiful of Korean folk songs, in Korean. Our group possessed several excellent singers, so by the end of the song, the eyes of the Korean listeners glistened with tears.

"Welcome Peace Corps Volunteers! Welcome! Thank you, thank you for coming to our country!"

I had only been in South Korea for a few minutes and already I had had to adjust my assumptions. Could the CIA operative have been using our Peace Corps group's arrival as a cover to sneak into the country, I worried? Also, I was moved to tears, and my heart still resonated with unexpected delight at the warm welcome of the Korean listeners. I had not expected so many conflicting emotions before I could even exit the airport, bound for more language training.

After two weeks in Seoul at the unbearably unheated Korean Language Institute, the time had come to set the Volunteers loose on the Korean countryside. We were divided into groups by province, and our particular group headed by train to Kwangju, in Cholla Namdo Province, located about five hours south of Seoul by train, east of the Yellow Sea. The snow had cleared by the time our train departed, and through the train windows I watched the winter wonderland of old Korea stream by.

There were small ochre-colored villages with thatched-roofed houses snuggled against treeless, snow-covered mountains; frosty rows of large brown kimchee pots tucked inside garden walls; occasional temples with handsome tiled roofs elegantly outlined against the sky; old women wearing their traditional billowing dress (*hanbok*) and rubber shoes (*komo shin*) that turned up at the toes; young women with babies tied closely to their backs with warm, brightly colored blankets; old men with long beards wearing full white robes and pointed black hats tied underneath their chins; big, black hairy pigs lashed to bicycles; men carrying impossible loads on their backs with A-frame packs; mourners dressed in white carrying white caskets with uplifted arms; and wispy white clouds in a high blue sky, the highest sky in all the world, we had been told, and so it looked. Our hearts filled up with the beauty.

Terry and I were assigned to village Neungju. Because the smallest of the rural villages had no inns, Volunteers were assigned to live with local families. We were to live in a room in the house of Station Master Cho.

Mr. Cho's house was a typical Korean house, with rooms opening onto a large porch. The porch in turn opened to the courtyard. Our room was very small, about five feet by seven feet. We were quite surprised by its miniature proportions. Terry was over six feet tall and barely had room to spare when he lay down. Our giant sized *yo*, the biggest object our host family had ever seen—besides Mr. Terry's feet—was settled into the room and constantly joked about. When the family found out how much we had paid for our bedding they shook their heads in disapproval. We not only had the most gigantic but, at a price of nearly a million wan, also the most overpriced *yo* (mattress) and *ebol* (coverlet) in all of Korea.

"Pitiful!" Station Master Cho's wife said, her hand covering her mouth in shocked dismay, her eyes laughing as she shook her head at our stupidity and gullibility.

Our first job as PCVs was to go with our coworkers—Mrs. Cho and Miss An—to villages and announce that there would be a contraceptive clinic soon at the Myun (county township) health center. Contraceptive loops would be installed. Mrs. Cho, a young mother, bellowed out this information as we walked through each tiny hamlet. Later when we were able to understand her Korean a little better, we found she was yelling: "Here are the American Peace Corps. They use contraceptives. They have been married a year and a half and they don't even have children, and they still use contraceptives! Contraceptives are wonderful!"

And so it went. At work we helped the co-workers on their rounds. Occasionally we found children who were ill, and we accompanied them to the hospital in Kwangju. A few days later the father would appear with glutinous rice candy or a chicken on a leash with which to thank us. We were becoming part of our community.

Then one night in March, Terry woke up feeling terrible, his temperature registering 104 degrees. I woke up the household. They took one look at him, and said, "*Chong tebuse.*" I knew this meant typhoid fever, and I was frightened. They told me his fever must be kept down with wet compresses and he must be fed kimchee soup. They brought in a basin of water, and the three adult women of the household, Mrs. Kim, Small Kitchen girl, and her mother, and began to sponge him off, doing so all night.

The household often laughed at me, but they never laughed at Mr. Terry. He was very dear to them, and his seriousness coupled with his intelligence and good nature was evident across the cultural divide. I was described by the Koreans as "bony and kind," while Terry-shi was described as "big and wise and highly intelligent." I told the family I needed to get to the only telephone in the village, which was located at the police station. I wanted to notify the Peace Corps doctor since I was so worried about Terry-shi's high temperature. They warned me that it was after curfew, but that if I were lucky, I would probably not be shot since I was an American.

The night was a typical howling snowy one, and I dressed warmly. Kitchen girl opened the gate, and I faced the snow-covered path, pretty much obliterated by the storm. I trudged toward the police station, a New York block away, hoping in my heart of hearts that I would not be shot. The police station was heavily sandbagged, and it possessed the one electric light in the village as well as the one phone. The light shone through the glass of the front door and illuminated the snow-flakes as I approached.

The three policemen saw me coming down the road and stepped out of the police yard, beyond the sandbags and pointed their submachine guns at me. I told them in my halting Korean that my husband might have typhoid fever and I needed to use the phone. Miraculously, they put down their guns. They could tell I wasn't a North or South Korean, not only by my height, but also by the fact that my skin was too white in the lamplight and that I wore a lace kerchief on my head in the middle of a snowstorm. I had worn it on purpose, actually, hoping that they would then recognize me as a woman despite my heavy clothes.

The Peace Corps doctor left Kwangju soon after my call and arrived within three hours, despite the curfew, the roadblocks, and the inclement weather. He took Terry to the Presbyterian Missionary Teaching Hospital in Kwangu where the Korean nurses insisted I stay in the room with Terry as his *poohoja*, or guardian. The American missionaries sent over fried chicken and mashed potatoes, and Terry gradually got well. His illness had been frightening, but his hospital stay gave us our first close Korean friend. It was there that we met Dr. Song of Chonam Tehakyo (University), the supervisor of the medical interns and residents there.

From the time I met Dr. Song until I left Korea, I relaxed. I accepted that the language was difficult, the job nearly impossible, the frustrations constant. But friendship is what ultimately sustains us and is universal.

Dr. Song had a proposal to make. He wished to attract Korean medical students to the villages of Korea. He felt sad that the students left Korea as soon as they were trained, which left the villages empty of medical personnel. He thought that if we held clinics in our village, then perhaps the medical students might be attracted to return to the countryside. After we were released from the hospital, Terry, Linna, and I met the Peace Corps doctor and Dr. Song in a teahouse in order to iron out our plans.

We decided we would teach the doctors English pronunciation of medical terms for the summer semester in return for their coming to our village to hold a skin clinic. The University would provide some medicine along with the students. Dr. Song also wanted to include a baby weighing and baby well-check clinic so he could gather statistics for his research on Korean maternal and child health. We Peace Corps Volunteers would assist Dr. Song in this endeavor, as well as teach the English pronunciation classes at the university.

By the middle of April, the snow had melted and the ground began to thaw. Blossoms appeared on the few trees and the surrounding hills began to turn green. It was time to make plans for the clinic.

To that end, we met with the mayor of Song Jong Ri one day in May to see if we could hold the *peebu pyung* (skin disease) clinic at the farmers' cooperative building. After a delicate negotiation with Dr. Song and the mayor, we were promised the use of the cooperative if we could obtain a lifetime supply of Preparation H for the mayor's hemorrhoids. That request required that we ride our bikes to the U.S. Army base near Kwangju to ask the commanding general if we could buy the medicine from the commissary, which it turned out we couldn't do since the commissary required dollars, which we didn't possess. We were paid by the Peace Corps in wan, the Korean currency, which was a closed currency.

It was a strange visit. We came to ask the Army to donate the medicine to our cause. In answer, we were first given a tour of the F-14 fighter jets, which flew from the base in Korea for war missions in Vietnam and then invited to have a drink and dinner at the officers' club.

We ate a Western meal followed by as many party drinks as we could drink. We had to walk our bikes home on that moonless night so we wouldn't fall off the railroad bridge that led to the village, or off the rice paddy path that led to Wan Du Ri (our particular hamlet). We arrived home with the Preparation H safe in our panniers. The farmer's cooperative was ours!

We felt good about this small success for many reasons. Dr. Song would finish his Korean baby-weighing project, which would fulfill his dream of developing a standard of recommended ages and weights for the Korean infant population. The medical students would receive hands-on experience handling patients and get to experience the countryside first hand, and perhaps become rural doctors instead of emigrating to another country. And we Volunteers would demonstrate how to supplement breastmilk with the WHO recipe for soybean gruel.

It was a small triumph for us, but certainly worth celebrating. Consider: with the help of the Peace Corps doctors who introduced us to Dr. Song, we had gotten the American Army, the local Mayor, the town intelligentsia, the farmers in the countryside, the mothers and children, and everyone with a boil within a fifty-kilometer radius together for the benefit of all.

We reveled in this mighty Peace Corps accomplishment for about one minute.

The doctors didn't like the countryside, had become doctors, in fact, to escape from the countryside, and did not ever want to come back to the countryside. The mayor wanted more from the army commissary than they were willing to give and would not let up in his requests, one of which included getting the Army to spray the county with DDT for free. The World Health Organization recipe translation had failed to mention that the soybeans had to be cooked before they were strained. Our gruel lesson was a bust because no self-respecting Korean farm woman has the excess time to spend mashing soy beans through a strainer, cooked or not. They laughed at our pitiful attempts to persuade them. However, Dr. Song did get his important measurements for infant development standards for the children of Korea. So in the end, we didn't feel too discouraged.

Indeed, the great gift of my tour of service in South Korea was that my bright dreams were tempered into ambient light that would illuminate the rest of my life. Butting up against Korean culture humbled and chastened me. I had not seen myself as a child of privilege and plenty. In Korea, I was forced to see myself through the eyes of others, and I paid attention to the lessons. I learned to live with contradictions. The Tiger of the East, most importantly, taught me to understand that until we humans learn to open our hearts to others, to see all others as ourselves, no peace is possible.

Our service ended in December 1969. We boarded the passenger train in Kwangju for Seoul in the morning. Yongiya, Dr. Song, Dr. Pak and several Ajumonies, boarded with us. They rode to the next town, so that they could honor us in the proper Korean form with their tearful presence and woeful goodbyes. The tears and wailing began. We were quite amazed and charmed by this send-off, as well as honored. When we arrived at the next station, other Volunteers got on the train with their entourage of Korean friends, and the weeping and wailing resumed. When the right time came for our Korean friends to leave the train to head back to Kwangju, I noticed that Terry was crying, too, a rare sight. We both laughed and cried all the way back to Seoul Station. We hugged each other. Not only had we learned to live harmoniously with the Koreans, but also with each other.

Coda

Two American Volunteers wearing *hanbok* stroll with a Korean girl and a tall, redheaded man along the rice paddy paths in the autumn of 1969. The rice is being harvested. From seedlings set in the flooded rice paddies in May, to tiny green shoots pushing up out of the water to taller green stalks, the rice stalks turned golden, the grains appeared at the very top of the stalk, like rich ripe wheat, ready for harvest in October. The paddies are now dry. Little nubs remain where the stalks have been cut, and the stalks are tied together in bundles that lie all over the fields. Nothing remains below the surface anymore. The courtyards are strewn with mats to catch any grain of rice that falls when the rice is separated from the stalks. Each grain is precious and nothing is wasted. The rice sustains the Korean people, who eat it three times a day, every day of their lives, as did we from 1967 to 1969.

Karen and Terry Boyle returned to the United States in 1969. Terry Boyle became an attorney working for the county counsel in Alameda County in California. Karen Boyle became a middle school teacher in Daly City, California. In both jobs, they put the lessons of peace and understanding they learned from their Korean experience to use every day in both concrete and subtle ways. Terry Boyle died in 1994.

✦
✶ ✶

A Non-Matrix Spouse

An Indian wedding is the most festive of occasions,
no matter who is getting married.

SONDRA AND I WERE MARRIED IN AN EXTRAORDINARY CERemony on Saturday June 13, 1970. My family couldn't be at the wedding in Musiri, Tamil Nadu, India, but Sondra and I tried to give them a detailed account. The preparations were not as harried as in America, but they presented problems. We couldn't have done it without the help of our friends both in Musiri and Trichy.

The three days of festivities began with a shower given by a Peace Corps girl in Trichy. I wasn't there, but here is how Sandy described it.

"Since a shower is a typical American custom, Indian friends here were a bit confused over Thursday's happening. However, with the help of the Peace Corps girls, it was a grand success. About ten women all sat around and talked. Women love to talk! After a while we had a 'tiffin': cake, sweets and more sweets. WOW! What great useful presents. I received beautiful linen, handloom bedspreads, a bucket and dipper (for taking Indian baths), honey and catsup (luxuries for me), a sandwich toaster, placemats, napkin holders, a scrub brush, clothespins, and more. Looks like I will be quite busy!

"The best gift of all was a beautiful silver peacock presented to 'Mr. and Mrs. Roger' by the Servites (Catholic Order of Priests in Trichy). All in all we women had a good time. It was a good experiment in cultural exchange plus a good opportunity for Roger and me to receive useful items for our new house."

While Sandy was at the shower, I was at home trying to check out wedding details. They were all left in the capable hands of my friends, Dr. and Mrs. Rajagopal in Musiri.

Saturday was the big day. Musiri had been awaiting this event with fervor. I learned just how great it was when, on my walk to see Sandy, I met a bullock cart driver who I had never seen before. He grinned at me through betel-stained teeth and spurted one word: "Marriage!" At that moment I knew it would be no ordinary wedding.

We had a rehearsal in the morning, and then we went our separate ways. Sandy was sequestered with Mrs. Rajagopal while I busied myself by entertaining the training school staff at a "bachelor lunch."

Time rolled on. Five o'clock approached. Sandy dressed at the Rajagopals admist a crowd of friends. I dressed alone in my house. At 4:30 I joined her for pictures with our best man, Frank Fairchild, and maid of honor, Susan Lane. At a little past five, we got into cars and headed for the church, where the entire town of Musiri was waiting to cheer our arrival at the gates.

The ceremony had to be held in the courtyard because the church was too small. The whole courtyard was jam-packed, and the crowds surged across the street. Even the balconies of the houses nearby were packed. We were led in by a traditional Indian band while the crowd cheered. The Mass began. After the Gospel, we exchanged wedding vows. As we exchanged rings, the church bells rang, the band sounded, and everyone cheered.

It was overwhelming! After Communion, the crowd began to surge towards us. It was like the end of a championship football game when the fans try to get on the field. I didn't think the priest would be able to finish Mass, but somehow he did. We were pelted with rice and showered with confetti. We were embraced, garlanded, and congratulated by all.

We were led to the reception hall next to the church (both the hall and the church had been decorated by the Musiri sisters and some teachers). The guests came offering gifts. We cut the wedding cake and had light tiffin. Outside, the teeming horde was entertained by the band. It was a democratic wedding. All castes and classes were represented. There were priests, doctors, an English minister, nurses, business men, shopkeepers, bankers, government officials, teachers, students, farmers, servants, *dhobis* (laundry men), bullock cart drivers, coolies, beggars, hotel owners, peons, and vendors who did a thriving business outside Sacred Heart Church. A hotel owner named Haroon, a Muslim, had come all the way from Bangalore to organize the wedding and reception.

After a while, we fought our way to a waiting car. We left for our honeymoon that night. Instead of the usual third-class train ride, we were given first-class tickets by four Peace Corps Volunteers. We slept on separate berths that night—one right above the other—holding hands.

Epilogue: In January 2004, we returned to India with our two daughters, Julia and Erica to see long-time friends in Musiri and Sacred Heart Church. Our friends there still remember us and were excited to meet our daughters. Now our whole family has experienced the richness and mystery of India, and thirty-seven years and eight trips later, we still have contact with Dr. and Mrs. Lalitha Rajagopal.

Roger LeGrand, India 79, taught English as a Second Language at a Basic Boy's Training School in Tamil Nadu. In 1968, he had to petition the Peace Corps to allow his potential wife, Sandy (Sondra) to marry him in Musiri. This process took about a year. Peace Corps officially called her a "non-matrix spouse." He is a Tax Appeals Commissioner for the State of Wisconsin, after enjoying a distinguished career of County Court Commissioner, District Attorney, and Circuit Court Judge for La Crosse County in La Crosse, Wisconsin.

Sondra LeGrand is a retired Special Education teacher in La Crosse, Wisconsin. Through the local Rotary Club, she has been involved with Tsunami relief projects serving a small fishing village called Sirkali, Tamil Nadu, India.

JOHN D. TOBIAS

Snapshots from the Graveyard of Empires

From a time when fishing and the "noon gun"
provided the most memorable pyrotechnics.

"Doctor my eyes have seen...." —Jackson Browne

MY FIRST CLEAR RECOLLECTION OF AFGHANISTAN IS A GRIM ONE.
Our group of fifty was already down to forty-nine, and we had
only been in country for about four hours.

A guy from Montana got deathly sick after drinking a bottle
of fruit juice from a Kabul vendor. He made a B-line back to
the airport after trying out a *toshnob*—an Afghani bathroom—
for the first...the second...and the third time. His four-hour
stay was probably the shortest Peace Corps commitment on
record.

On the ride from the airport, I was hit with 1,000 volts of
culture shock: donkeys, camels, sheep, turbans, veiled women,
staring eyes, dusty streets, peculiar odors, mud houses.

A small dog tiptoed along the edge of the roof of a
mud-baked house. On second glance, I realized this was
no Chihuahua, but a big, fat rat with a tail long enough to

measure legal fish in Wisconsin. I've seen big rats in Chicago, but they are mere mice compared to Mr. Kabul Rat.

The white crowned peaks of the Hindu Kush rose in the distance. I figured a place that would name its mountains "Killer of Hindus" could not be too hospitable. This country seemed the antithesis of civilized society.

We arrived at the Peace Corps compound in the Shari Nau section of Kabul. Shari Nau literally means "new city," but I could find nothing new about it. They should have named it "ancient fortress." I glanced at the strange people. They didn't look as they had in the slides we saw in the Philadelphia orientation. There were men in baggy pants, with generous beards and fiery eyes. The women were pretty, but avoided eye contact. I hadn't expected the Peace Corps staff to look like this!

The Peace Corps doctor gave us a caveat-filled medical lecture on the subtle differences between basillary dysentery, giardia, stomach flu, and your run-of-the-mill diarrhea. The rich smell of roasting kabobs tickled my nose. My stomach growled. I was afraid the doc was going to tell me I couldn't eat kabobs. That would have been heartbreaking.

He told us to drink only boiled water, never from the street vendors, and keep water out of your mouth and eyes even when showering. He laughed as he said not to worry: there aren't any showers here anyway. No one else was laughing.

He advised that we shake our shoes and clothes before dressing because scorpions like warm places. ("Is that a scorpion in your pocket, or are you just pained to see me?")

A couple of weeks later, our group was tested and failed. We became sick at a 4th of July picnic caused, I believe, by the potato salad. I lost fifteen pounds in a week. The Peace Corps doctor darted from one bed to another assuring us that this was business as usual. I wondered if the Montana guy regretted his early departure. He missed a good picnic.

"Fish, fish… fish…fish…fish, fish…. fishing" —Taj Mahal

Ben, Kathy, Betsy and I decided to head for the mountains for a camping weekend during training. City life was wearing thin. We hoped the great outdoors would renew our spirits while we got away from it all. However, it's hard to find solitude when you stick out like a sore thumb.

The Peace Corps camping equipment consisted of a small dome tent requiring an advanced degree for assembly. We had the usual pots and pans, freeze-dried meals, and a four-piece Eagle Claw fiberglass fishing rod, with a Mitchell 300 reel. I envisioned finding a virgin stream where the trout jumped out of the water. I got more than I bargained for.

We hitched a ride on a lorry that dropped us off high in the Hindu Kush, near the Salang Pass. We set up camp next to the Panshir River, near a village called Gulbahar. It was an idyllic site for camping, but we drew curious onlookers, then a few more, and finally the whole village.

Our campsite was ablaze with Afghani gazes. Ben had a bit of a temper. He was irritated by the scrutiny and yelled *"burro…Burro…BURRO!* (go, get away)" each time louder and louder to compensate for his limited Farsi vocabulary. The audience laughed. Ben retreated to the tent, searching for his dictionary, and the correct way to say, "It's impolite and rude to stare, please leave us alone."

I took a walk along the river with my Eagle Claw rod. This looked like gold medal wild trout water. I tied on a silver #2 Mepps spinner and made a couple of casts. On the third cast, I had a jolting strike, but missed the fish. An old Afghan man came and stood beside me. He smiled and asked what I was doing. I said I was fishing. I asked what he was doing. He said he was fishing, too. Must have a Popeil Pocket Fisherman, I surmised.

He challenged me to a fishing contest, Amrika versus Afwanistan, the first ever fishing Olympics. Five casts only… the most fish in five casts would be the winner. I went first and caught, to my surprise, a nice 12-inch brown trout. It was my only fish.

"Your turn. Get your cane pole and fire away," I said confidently.

He pulled a stick of dynamite from his coat, lit it, and "cast" it into the river. The ground shook as the water erupted with a *Kaboom!* Lots of fish rose to the surface. He threw a seining net into the river and retrieved his catch. I wondered what the daily limit was in Afghanistan.

I declined a rematch. I congratulated him on his casting technique. When people ask me how the fishing was in Afghanistan, I simply reply, "Dynamite!"

"I feel like I'm the best. But you're not going to get me to say that."
—Jerry Rice, football legend

I played defense on the best football team ever to play in Afghanistan. The 1970 Peace Corps team was one of a four- or five-team league that included the American High School, the American Embassy Marine Guard, and Kabul University. There might have been a world traveler/hippie team, but they could never remember game times.

We had some amazing athletes on that team, including Bob Talmedge, member of a world record sprint relay team from San Jose State that featured the legendary Lee Evans. Naturally, Bob was our wide receiver. He didn't have the greatest hands in the world, but he could run like a deer, leaving defenders to wonder if the wind had just picked up.

Our quarterback was a 6'4", nearly Big League baseball player named Bill Heinz who could throw a football seventy yards with accuracy. Ben Bradley, son of the American journalist, and a gifted writer in his own right, was the running back. Ben was a natural athlete who played hockey in college. He was fast and strong, and he didn't mind running over an occasional high school kid if necessary.

Frank Light and Shelly Pittman were also on that team. Both were quick defenders who enjoyed contact. Frank had been a Green Beret in Vietnam prior to his Peace Corps stint. I'm sure he found a little controlled violence comforting. Shelly's professorial appearance belied his fierce competitiveness. I played in my bare feet which, I believed, gave me a quick, primitive edge.

The homecoming for the American High School was a big deal. Their coach, a real gung ho type, wanted to beat us badly. They had a fast little running back who knew the trick of spinning like a whirling dervish when he was about to get his tag pulled. They had cute cheerleaders. We had one old Afghan guy who came to every game with his donkey. That was our version of a mascot.

We won that game, much to the dismay of the high school student body and the coach who refused to shake hands. Our mascot had a look of pride on his long face. We won the league that year and were awarded small trophies that read Ariana Afghan Airlines—Champs—1970 Kabul Football. It's my proudest award to date.

"What seemed so strong has been and gone." —James Blunt, 1973

Nearly four decades ago, an old man would climb a hill overlooking Kabul each noon. He'd pull out an old pocketwatch and, precisely at 12, would ignite the fuse of a cannon hauled there a century earlier by elephants. The cannon's boom could be heard throughout the city.

This keeper of the "noon gun" hadn't missed a day in many years. The cotton stuffed into his ears wasn't of much help; he was nearly deaf.

I'd like to believe an old man, perhaps his son, still trudges up the hill to announce midday to Kabul. Hopefully, the cannon's roar smothers, if only for an instant, the sound of war below.

John D. Tobias served in Afghanistan from 1970-72. He lives with his wife, two dogs, and three cats in the Chicago suburb of St. Charles. He is a Licensed Professional Counselor with a Masters Degree in Counseling, who specializes in drug and alcohol addiction. He himself has been addicted to fishing ever since Afghanistan, but no longer fishes in contests. He loves steelhead fishing, photography and running his two black labs, Lily and Yoshi. His wife Betty works in a homeless shelter. He still regards his Afghan football trophy as his most prized possession.

JENNICE FISHBURN

✶

Planes, Trains, and Bullock Carts

Learning to play chicken with carts, rickshaws, buses, cars,
and goats was just another part of the acculturation process.

I WAS A "COMMUNICATIONS TECHNICIAN" WITH THE EAST Pakistan (now Bangladesh) nutrition survey project headquartered at the University of Dacca (now Dhaka) Department of Biochemistry and Nutrition, under the auspices of three U.N. agencies (UNICEF, WHO, and FAO), the U.S. Agency for International Development, the Government of Pakistan, and the University of Dacca.

My job was to travel with the survey team to randomly selected villages in each district to be of general assistance, while educating myself about the nutritional needs and culture so I could develop relevant educational materials. Once a month, I traveled with a team of about thirty to a specific survey site, then worked on educational materials at the university for the rest of the time.

On our nutrition survey trip to the Kushtia District in December 1963, I was asked to accompany a lady doctor whose schedule didn't permit her to leave with the rest of the team. Our modes of transportation illustrated the small gap between the ancient and the modern so often found in this country. We left Dacca on a Pakistan International Airlines DC-3, went by cycle rickshaw from the airport to the railroad station, traveled a few hours on the "Calcutta Mail" train, and transferred to a scooter rickshaw that took us to the grand finale for ground transportation: a bullock cart ride, eight hours round trip.

The only way to survive in the cramped cart area was to sit cross-legged and look out for the low top, or to lie down and roll with the bumps. Not being talented in the art of sitting cross-legged for any length of time, I chose to lie down. It would have been fine if the rains hadn't come. I spent a couple of hours holding an umbrella across the back of the cart, and we still got wet. The frustrating part was that we were only traveling seven miles; everyone who was walking was passing us. However, it was necessary to travel by bullock cart because the roads were waist-deep in clay-like mud and the huge wheels of carts propelled by powerful water buffalo were the most effective means of transport. On the way back from the survey site, it was bullock cart first, then on to Dacca by train and river steamer.

Other survey trips required other modes of transportation. Travel to the Khulna District involved spending time on the river. We started out on a smelly motor launch with a very low deck that gave us bumps on the head. The next morning we transferred to a caravan of twenty-eight cycle rickshaws for a five-mile ride to the river where we found what must have been all the country boats from the area. These wonderful little inventions might compare to sampans. Again I had the choice of sitting cross-legged or lying down, and again I chose the horizontal position. Luckily, country boats are larger and smoother than bullock carts, and I enjoyed the five hours traveling the five miles to our campsite. Always traveling against the current, we became familiar with the nuances of river life.

Once we left the boats and began walking the rest of the way to the survey centers in the villages, we were faced with another challenge: one-bamboo bridges. The bridges consisted of one long log or two narrow bamboo poles fastened together. Sometimes they were equipped with a handrail that wasn't of much use since I had to lean way out to grab hold. No matter the style, they all had one important feature: they required a good sense of balance and nerves of steel. I have neither. However, by the end of the week I was casually swinging across those bridges with all the assurance of Tarzan's Jane.

As uncomfortable as "public" transportation might be, my main pain was riding to and from work on my bicycle. The riding itself was not unpleasant at all, but I flirted with death every time my pedals made a revolution. I believed that if I met my end while in the Peace Corps, it would not be because of cholera, typhoid, the plague, or tuberculosis. No indeedy, you could blame it on a bus, or rickshaw, or car, or goat, or cart. The law of the road is "might makes right," and you know where that puts the bicycle on the protocol list: only above people and goats, and they don't count because they're completely unpredictable. I've learned to play "chicken" with the best of them.

Jennice Fishburn served in East Pakistan, now Bangladesh, from 1963-65. When she returned to Dhaka in 1992, she noticed right away that traffic had made bicycles obsolete. To deal with the new realities of wild, undisciplined traffic, she simply relaxed, pulled her dupatta *over her nose and mouth, and enjoyed the sights, secure in the assumption that her driver did not want to die any more than she did. An active member of the League of Women Voters, Jennice now lives in Placitas, New Mexico, where she continues to travel and volunteer in other countries.*

ARLENE B. LIPMAN

Of Girls and Dogs and Cats

*Some of the strongest, most enduring bonds were
created between Volunteers and their "helpers."*

WHEN DAVID AND I FOUND OUT THAT WE WERE GOING TO THE
Philippines, I didn't know what to think. Where was the
Philippines? After three months of training in Vermont and
New Hampshire, we flew from New York to Manila. As we
came off the plane, a wave of superheated, moist air hit us. I
could barely breathe. September in New England is not warm.
September in Manilla is not cool!

After more training, we departed for Mindanao, the second
largest and easternmost island in the Philippines. We would be
elementary school teachers in Davao City and live in Toril,
a suburb. Host country folks had found us a bungalow: three
rooms. I thought we would be living in a bamboo-and-thatch
nipa hut! Instead, our house had two bedrooms, a closet bath,
and a "great room" with a kitchen area at one end. We even
had electricity!

We bought a bed made from fishing line strung in a web
on a bamboo frame. We hung a yellow mosquito net from
the poles on the corners. For a mattress we had a woven *banig*

mat. I tucked a sheet over the *banig*, and then we tucked in the net under the mat. The bath consisted of a room was the width of a toilet seat with just enough room to swing the door open before it hit the toilet. The shower and the faucet below it were connected to a roof-fed water tank in the back. There was only enough pressure to shower if the tank was full after a rain, and then the water was cold! We heated water to pour into the bucket, then took can showers from that.

After a few days in our house, we told a neighbor (our landlord's sister) that we were thinking about getting a *labenderra* (someone to wash the clothes). The next morning she told us that she had found us a "helper." What to do? How could we say that we hadn't decided yet? We had been told that we should have SIP—smooth interpersonal relationships—and not rock the boat. So we decided to give it a try.

In two days, Patring arrived from a barrio up the mountain. She would work for us and stay next door where her cousin was the maid. Patring was sixteen. She did the laundry in a tub behind the house using water from the tank. She also cleaned the house and did marketing and some cooking. I was happy to let her go to the market because I have a hard time buying fish that are looking at me or watching beef cut from a haunch hanging from a hook. I really don't like looking dinner in the face.

For this work, we paid Patring 30 pesos per month (about $5). This was a little more than average for a "helper." She used some of her earnings to pay tuition at the high school she attended in the evenings.

After a month, her cousin was no longer working next door, and so Patring asked if she could move into our other bedroom because going home up the mountain after school was sometimes a problem. She moved in and stayed. During the two years we lived there, the next-door neighbor went through probably eighteen maids, but Patring lived with us for three-and-a-half years. She was the one who brought Pocahontas into our home to guard it.

"*Ang polo ni sir*! (David's shirt!)," she kept saying. Someone had climbed over the fence in the back of our house and taken two shirts from the clothesline. She was certain that she would get fired for allowing that to happen. So that weekend Patring went home and came back the next day with a "watch dog," the runt of the litter. We decided to name her Pocahontas, Pokie for short.

"Pokie" was an unfortunate nickname. In the local slang, *pokie* was term used to describe a very private part of the female anatomy! A cowry shell is also called *pokie* for its resemblance to the same part. By the time we discovered our error, it was too late. Pokie knew her name. But Patring said that we pronounced the word with the accent on a different syllable; Pokie stayed and soon grew up to a fine-looking dog, about the size of a terrier. People called her an "American" dog because she was so healthy.

Pokie guarded our house, and Tabian the cat kept it free from mice. Tabian seemed to own our house, so when she had kittens, we kept one—Aswan, the "witch"—and distributed the rest to neighbors who also needed mousers. Tabian and Aswan amused themselves by playing hockey on the kitchen floor with giant cockroaches. Nothing would kill the cockroaches, not even a direct spray with Raid!

We taught for our two years in Toril; but when we heard that there weren't enough Volunteers for the requests they had in the new education group, we asked Peace Corps if we could extend into one of the new spots. The regional rep told us about several places that wanted two Volunteers in math and science, so we decided to extend our stay in Bohol, a Cebuano-speaking island to the north of Mindanao. We told Patring's father that if she wanted to come with us, we would like to have her. He was originally from Bohol, so she had an uncle and cousins there. Patring said yes. When we moved by boat, packing up our stuff into a shipping crate that was made for us, we had Patring, Pokie, and Aswan with us. Tabian, after all, owned the house so she stayed with it.

We stayed in Bohol for eighteen months until our project was done. We had given one-week seminars to all of the elementary teachers in the province. Then it was time to go home. Patring told us that she wanted to take Pokie home to her barrio in Davao, but she had one question.

"Is there birth control for dogs?" she asked.

She knew that barrio dogs would have litter after litter and would end up skinny with dragging tits, not a pretty picture. She knew that we were using birth control because people would ask us why we didn't have kids yet and that is the answer we would give. It cost us 100 pesos to get Pokie spayed, but worth it. Patring had become not just a helper, but a friend, almost like a younger sister.

After we left, Patring finished high school and took a course in tailoring. That wasn't what she wanted, so she went to a two-year college in agriculture. Then she decided to study to become a midwife. Pokie lived out her life in the barrio with Patring's family. Visiting Toril after twenty-eight years, we found Patring living with her husband and child, a shingle hanging out in front, "Laying In—Patricia Igono—Midwife." A photo of the three of us was in her front room! She said, "Mam Arlene, you didn't forget me" as we hugged.

Arlene B. Lipman spent three-and-a-half years as a Peace Corps Volunteer in the Philippines with her husband David. They were education Volunteers assigned to bring modern methods of teaching math and science to elementary school teachers, first in Toril, Davao City, and then in Tagbilaran City, Bohol.

RON BARBUR

*
* *
*

Night Passages

For most Westerners, a visit to Mother Ganges requires a willing
suspension of disbelief that such a place could possess such power.

As we were slowly rocked and cradled in the belly of the
beast, my slumber was shaken by one intense arrhythmic jerk
as the train followed the track around a sharp corner. The
rhythm, having forgotten this interruption, fell back into its
swaying to-and-fro, as did I, hoping to release my conscious
mind into a deeper sleep.

But I knew that was not going to happen. A deep, lapis
lazuli-colored emergency light penetrated my eyelids and
washed over the forms in the compartment. Eyes opened, I
looked down on those bodies lying in the eerie cool blue:
silent, except for the occasional cough, the perfect echo of
a Henry Moore sketch of sleeping figures taking shelter in
the tubes during The War. Wrapped in Kashmiri scarves like
quiet mummies, the sleepers were removed from the noise
outside. Warm air whisked past the half-opened, barred windows carrying ash and firefly-like glowing embers along the
side of the slow, undulating snake that followed the straining
steam engine.

As if awakening again, I remembered that we were on an overnight milk train heading northwest to Benares! Some journeys are meant to be taken. There was no reason for it, no souls to be set free, no absolution of my sins, or help in attaining salvation, just the curiosity of the mysterious and morbid happening that occurred on the banks of Mother Ganga: the Ganges. I leaned out over the edge of the metal overhead luggage rack to see if Peter was awake in his lofty perch of the luggage rack across from mine. He laid on his side in an enviably peaceful sleep. He barely stirred.

Third-class train travel in India is a world unto itself. It begins as an egalitarian experiment and ends in a free-for-all with every passenger for himself. It was cheap transport, though, so everyone allowed for the minor inconveniences of being intimately wedged up against strangers you would normally have crossed the street to miss. In fact, this intimacy made the adventure all the more appealing, rubbing elbows with the working classes of India. I kept this thought close to me as I tried to figure out the source of the spicy *biriani* and *bidi* cigarette smells that perfumed the air.

Our journey to the famous burning/cremation ghats of Benares started in Calcutta, now Kolkata, and wound 680 kilometers to the banks of the Ganges. We started and stopped from one train station to the next throughout the night. At each station, we would gradually begin a slow descent of speed as arc lights illuminated a station's platform gliding past our portal. The train slowed down by degrees of clickety-clack tempos ending in a lurching stop. Looking down through the window, I could see people asleep on the platform, dogs stirring, and glimpses of torsos and legs getting on board. A chorus of vendors hawking fruit and tea cut through the silent night. These sellers had expressive and practiced voices, combining deep froggy sounds and pathos that said, "Give me a chance!"

"*Or-angee, Or-angee,*" called the salesmen stretching the word out while walking the length of the car. "*Chai, chai, chai,*" shouted a disembodied voice offering hot sweet tea and milk served in unfired sun-baked pottery. These cups were clean, smooth, hygienic and completely recyclable. They left me wondering why our advanced society couldn't come up with simple solutions like this. After a drink, you toss the cup on the shards pile, add water and make new cups. Marvelous!

Two stops from Benares, now Varanasi on the train schedules, I awoke to hear a cacophony of noise entering the rail car. Hundreds of people were filling the third-class section climbing over the tops of sleeping passengers already in the train corridor. Women and children with baskets and bedrolls pushed into the compartment space as they crammed and complained their way up against the walls and wooden seats, doubling the occupants on the floors. It was a nightmare of bodies that I think even those used to the mobs of India couldn't fathom. The next crowd found space where there was none, and soon there were people hanging on to my luggage rack, feet barely on the seats below, trying to climb up. I felt the temperature rising in the compartment as body heat and close proximity added to a suffocating lack of air.

I panicked and shouted to Peter, "Let's get out of here!"

But we had no escape route through the corridor and out the door as even more tried to push into the car. I pushed some heads aside from the edge of the rack and swung my feet over the side and partially out the top of the window, hanging onto the rack I shimmied—first my legs, then my body—through the narrow opening. Peter passed our bags through the window and went head first out the window into my arms. The night air, though warm, was so much cooler than the inside of the compartment. I felt alive and whole on the platform as I watched people hanging out the doors and flattened up to the window bars where we just were.

Immediately the train started to move. We ran forward to the second-class cars, where a businessman standing at an open door, having seen the whole affair, helped us onboard. He quickly closed the door and locked it as more of the mob running along side of us tried to board the second-class car. He explained there was a local festival and these people who weren't paying any fares were simply hitching a ride to the next stop from the night's festivities. We settled back into the relatively empty car enjoying the padded seats and warm glances. At the next stop the entire crowd emptied out of the third-class section, but we decided to stay on in second class until Varanasi.

We arrived at about 11 at night. Most of the streets were quiet, except for the tea stalls lit brightly with strings of bulbs, while Bollywood cinema music blared into the night. Bugs circled around attracted to the light that distracted them for a moment from bothering us as we had a snack. We stopped at a stall and ordered *koppee* and a *vadai*, hot street food. We watched as the Indian barista poured hot, milky Nescafe in a long stream from one cup back and forth to the other mixing the sugar into a frothy rich stimulant.

Finishing this snack, we walked across the road to an auto-rickshaw and gently nudged the driver, asleep on the back seat. He stirred and yawned, getting slowly to his feet. After a stretch or two, he seemed willing to drive us near the river. We drove east on Shri Ramakrishna road and, through a number of shortcuts, ended up in walking distance of the ghats. We were high on coffee and still groggy from the train ride, which added to the otherworldliness of what we saw. Wandering tiredly down a narrow alley crowded with cloth shops closed for the night, we followed the corridor as it made its meandering way to the top of some steps.

By now a fog from the river had assumed a pea soup density. Only the diffused glow of lights bobbing on boats in the river differentiated the land from the water. We tentatively put one foot in front of the other descending the steps until we got near the sound of lapping water. We squatted on the steps and looked out into nothingness. In time our eyes adjusted to the darkness and looking back up the ghat we saw the glow of window lights illuminating hundreds of bodies. Some had come to die, but mostly to sleep near the comfort of their Mother. We laid our bodies down on the steps that night and dreamt of moving trains and silent water.

Ron Barbur served in India from 1970-72. He and his wife Shirley met and fell in love in the Nilgiri Hills of Tamil Nadu in 1971 and have never looked back. They reside in Portland, Oregon, where he has been consummately interested in art, photography, gardening and ceramics, which he taught in a local high school, along with ESL, English, and Art for twenty-three years. He hopes to join the Crisis Corps to be of use when needed and to have another adventure.

KRISTINA ENGSTROM,
PATRICIA G. MITTENDORFF,
MARGERY AFFLECK, LYNN LAFROTH

Now the Eyes of My Eyes are Opened

Slowly, Volunteers learn to see what a casual glance always misses in Afghanistan.

KRISTINA ENGSTROM: HAIDERDEAN AND HIS SON ZAHIR SHAH—named after the King—came from Herat to live with me in Kabul. The Volunteers in Herat thought he was just the person to help me since I lived alone and didn't have the time or desire to shop for food in the bazaar every day, or wash the clothes, or keep the stove going all day and night in winter.

So Haiderdean and Zahir Shah traveled across the country with a small bundle of clothes and set up housekeeping, sleeping in the living room/dining room on the thin mattresses I had for furniture instead of chairs. Zahir Shah went off to school and, with Volunteer friends' help, Haiderdean figured out how to operate in the city. He was always lovely company, albeit no English from him and no Dari from me. But when I'd had a particularly unpleasant day, Haiderdean would make us tea and would just sit with me for a while in the living room.

It wasn't long, however, before Haiderdean started to get sick. He couldn't eat, and his whole digestive tract was messed up. The Peace Corps doctor made a house call. An assistant

259

of the neighborhood mullah came by with prayers. And Haiderdean just got worse.

We didn't know if he was dying, and no one knew what else to do. So we decided, over Haiderdean's protests, that he should go home to his family in Herat. The night before he left, four or five Volunteers and I lay down on mattresses on the living room floor, raising our heads like prairie dogs at every sound Haiderdean made. We had hired a taxi to take Haiderdean, Zahir Shah, and one of the Volunteers to Herat, and when they left, we all cried—those inside the cab and those outside, too.

We heard from friends traveling from Herat that Haiderdean had gotten better after only a few days. He was happy to be back home with his wife and his other four children. Although he didn't know it and we didn't know it at the time, homesickness almost killed our Haiderdean.

Patricia G. Mittendorff: I received a phone call from an old Peace Corps friend several years ago saying that she had read an advertisement in "Friends of Afghanistan" written by an Afghan, asking my whereabouts. His name was Abdul Wazi, a rather common Afghan name. I had taught English as a second language in Herat for a time, and during this adventure I took up the challenge of attempting to get American Field Service (AFS) scholarships for good students who were not from Kabul, the capital.

We organized seminar classes after school for tenth graders who were good students and interested in applying. The class was full, but a ninth grader kept coming to the class, begging entrance. He was too young, his English skills were not all that good, and I said no. But Abdul Wazi was extremely persistent, showed up for every class, and asked the same question: "Please can I join this class?"

He wore me down, and I finally relented and let him in. That year, seven AFS scholarships went to Herat students, and we considered our project a huge success. Abdul Wazi was not among them because he was too young to apply. But the following year, after I had gone home, he applied and was given a scholarship to the United States. That was the last I heard of him. What I didn't know was that there was a much greater success yet to unfold.

As the Russians invaded Afghanistan and coerced all young males to join the army, Abdul Wazi and his family saw the "writing on the wall" and decided to make a break for Pakistan. Their entire family, including aunts, uncles, and cousins, made it over the border safely. Once in Pakistan, Abdul Wazi offered his services as a translator to the consulate in Peshawar. Having spent a year sharpening his English in America with the AFS scholarship, Wazi's English was good enough to land the job, and he was able to support his family. With his connections at the consulate, he was able to get visas for every member of his family. No one was left behind, and the entire family immigrated to California, where they all currently live and continue to raise their families. Abdul Wazi sent in the advertisement because he wanted to find me to say "thank you" for helping him gain the skill to get his family to safety. One lesson I learned was that we don't always know how our actions help change lives, even in spite of ourselves!

Through Our Eyes

Lynn LaFroth: A Kuchi caravan wound slowly through the valley. Turbaned nomadic men with rifles slung over their shoulders herded camels, horses, and donkeys, plus fat-tailed sheep, to drink from the icy-cold mountain stream below. My trip to Bamian to see the Giant Buddhas coincided with the nomads' semi-annual trek.

Traditional Muslim women, veiled in head-to-toe tent-like *chadris* of bright purple, red, green, or blue, floated through the throng. One veiled woman balanced a caged goldfinch perfectly atop her head while gliding lithely as if she were walking in a park with no one around. Men in knee-length shirts worn over baggy trousers walked arm-in-arm, pink roses stuck in their turbans. These were happier, more peaceful days in Afghanistan.

Smells of dung fires and unleavened bread baking mingled with odors of ripening fruits and urine from back alleyways. In the cloth market, multicolored cotton and silk scarves from India flew like flags. I remember passing teahouses emitting fragrances of hashish smoke and cardamom tea. Vendors selling pistachios, walnuts, and wild almonds called from their stalls to come and buy.

I loved Bamian's jewelry bazaar where Kuchi women wearing forehead amulets made out of agates and tin, fingered pieces of lapis lazuli. It was the Kuchi women I admired because of their freedom of expression—wearing bright multicolored dresses in seemingly untamed colors of reds and oranges, blues, and purples with no *chadris* to cover their faces—wild, bold, and confident as they walked in this world of men.

Margery Affleck: One day, I took a walk through some of the back streets of Kabul. As I walked, it seemed like a whole new world, an experience to be had:

Seeing a man shoveling waste from the street into his donkey cart, and saying to myself, "Best fertilizer in Afghanistan and it's free at that."

A child carefully sorting out garbage, hoping for a tasty morsel or some useful item. She uncovers a dilapidated flower and, smiling, scampers to receive admiration from her playmates in the garbage next door.

From head to toe, I feel the unclothing stares from men in the street. I hear the humming from the soldiers softly chanting *khorigee inja bien*—"foreigner come here." I feel rock and sand being thrown at my feet. A rather dignified Afghan possessing a full white beard says in accented English, "Hello, mister, come to my house." A young man slowly emerges from behind, pinches my bottom, and walks on with an air of satisfaction.

As I gaze ahead, I find I am witnessing a grand procession of three magnificent, majestic, noble beasts. Nonchalantly chewing and drooling, parading with an imperturbable gait, their skins looking shaggy and well worn. One lone lump seems to be floating rhythmically in the breeze—long protruding necks swaying proudly. The proud turbaned Afghan leading this parade seems to be saying, "These are my beautiful camels."

Smells here seem indistinguishable—I catch the faintly sizzling aroma of kabob meat from a nearby *chai hona* (teahouse); is that fresh hot bread I also smell out of the dirt ovens? I smell goats, waste, dung, people. They all form a stagnant aroma hemmed in by compound walls.

But I only had to walk a block to find my escape onto a busy Kabul street with familiar odors of buses and taxis. The smell of perspiration wafts around those jamming themselves into an overcrowded bus. I smell the heat penetrating a woman in *chadri*. A city has a million faces; no two look alike or know what another is thinking. This was my ten-minute walk into the bowels of Kabul.

Kristina Engstrom, Patricia G. Mittendorff, Margery Affleck, and Lynn LaFroth served in Afghan 15 from 1969-70 as part of the smallpox vaccinator team of all-female Volunteers. Other parts of their collective story appear in "Taking Out Smallpox."

JAMES JOUPPI

A Spillway for Nong Bua

Building a spillway for a dam in a time of war and insurgency can be risky business that makes rabbit snares look like explosive trip wires.

WHILE ON VACATION IN 2007, MY WIFE AND I RENTED A TAXI and took the road to Nong Bua.

"This used to be communist country," the driver told us as we cruised along paved Thai Route 2276.

We stopped at a village store where an old woman told my wife Phoorita that there'd once been a *farawng* named Jim who'd helped them build a spillway years ago.

And it was many years ago. We in Group 38 had been trained to build the best concrete spillways in rural Thailand. We even used steel reinforcement. Our goal was to help Thai villagers capture water during their four-month rainy season, which could then be used as fish habitat for the following eight months when their rivers would all run dry.

In 1970 and again in 1971, all Community Development Department Peace Corps trainees in Thailand congregated for training projects near the Air Base in my province, Nakohn Panome, and the Air Force's Civic Action had used their bull-dozers to build large earthen dams while Peace Corps trainees and Thai villagers worked side by side to build concrete spill-ways to pass water over these dams.

On arriving in Thailand, I'd worked with other trainees on the 1971 project. Later, after being permanently stationed in Nakohn Panome, I'd gone to the nearby Air Base and cajoled a major there to complete the earthen dam part of our trainee project. And yet, in all, it didn't seem right that I should need to grovel for assistance from a major at the Air Base just in order to do my job, even though our Thai department had very little funding.

There were no new CD trainees sent to Thailand in '72; nor did I continue the cozy relationship with the Air Force my predecessor—known as Santee, meaning "peace" in Thai—had established. Instead I solicited funding from women's clubs in Bangkok, three of them in fact.

My second year Peace Corp project, which for the most part was funded by the women of Bangkok, was located in Nong Bua. *Nong Bua* means "Lotus Pond" in Thai, but there were no lotus ponds there. In fact their well was running dry. Nong Bua was located just down the dirt road that went past our training project for which the Air Force had sent their bulldozer drivers to help us out. It was on our very first workday on that project that we'd heard a blast in the jungle from down this very road. The next day a truckload of Thai Army troops had arrived to guard us as we worked. When we inquired why they were needed, we were told that down the road a Thai policeman had been killed and that that was the blast we'd all heard.

"But don't worry," our Peace Corps trainers told us. "You aren't in any danger, but our Thai language instructors with us might be in danger just because they're with us."

Understandably, when I arrived in Nong Bua to live and work, I asked the village headman whose name was Kong Paeng about safety along this road.

"I wouldn't travel down that road," Kong Paeng advised me. "There's no villages along that road, and so there's probably ghosts out there. Of course I don't know that for a fact because I've never been down that road. I always take the *rot song teo* (shuttle bus) which goes the long way around."

But the long way around was much longer, and I wasn't afraid of ghosts.

Kong Paeng was anxious to use me. For years his villagers had been building a large earthen dam, but they'd never had the expertise to build a concrete spillway for the dam with the materials the government would sometimes drop at his house. They'd tried to build spillways before, but the river would run around them, and so their dam wouldn't hold back water.

I had little knowledge of the history of this place, and I'd been taken by surprise when Michael, a foreign service employee of the American Consulate in Northeast Thailand, had arrived to talk to our governor late in 1972, just days before I was set to start work on four spillways in Na Kaa District. I learned from a Peace Corps coworker that Michael had told the governor that he didn't want Americans in Na Kaa. We were given Michael's consulate number, and we called him from the crank telephone in our government office building to ask what the problem was. He told me over the static that I'd probably be safe out in Na Kaa, but that my that my presence on the Na Kaa projects would lend credence to communist propaganda in that area that Thailand was a lackey state of America.

"We don't know about conditions in that area," Michael told me later, "so if I were you I wouldn't go down that road. Of course you can do what you like. I have no authority to tell you what to do."

When I realized Michael had no more information than I did, I decided it would be paranoid for me to stop using my shortcut through the road to Nong Bua. But I had another problem with the project: Kong Paeng, Nong Bua's headman, didn't even want the project I'd drawn because it made no use of the earthen dam his villagers had been working on for years. The problem was that there simply weren't enough materials in front of his house to build a spillway other than one in a steam bed, which would capture perhaps a meter of streambed water.

And Kong Paeng didn't want that. No. He wanted the whole enchilada. He wanted the earthen dam his villagers had built to function as a barrier, which would dam up water for a couple of kilometers upstream. I knew it would be impossible to build what he wanted with just the couple hundred dollars worth of cement, steel, gravel, and sand that was sitting in front of his house for us to use. His spillway would cost more than a thousand dollars.

I told Kong Paeng I'd go home and draw a plan more in tune with what he wanted and then try my best to get enough money to build what he had in mind. When I returned a week later with my new plan, I saw he already had village children busy burying a washed out spillway in preparation for the spillway I would help them build. And yet I had no funding to build what Kong Paeng wanted. All I had was the knowledge that a recent Peace Corps newsletter had suggested the American Women's Club in Bangkok as a possible source of funding. But time was hardly on our side. I knew that by this time, we had less than four months to work and that every day that passed was bringing us closer to the rainy season. Still Kong Paeng obviously believed that his project would come to fruition, and so I took a trip to Bangkok to see if I could get enough money to help him.

It seemed that there were two realities in play with this project. There was Kong Paeng's reality of hope, which seemed naïve. There was also a political and/or military reality, which seemed more based on fear. This second reality, I came to feel, was being monitored from above. And although I didn't consider that Kong Paeng's project in Nong Bua could possibly seem like a threat to anyone, I have to admit that the 1,000-cubic-meter excavation dug by hand by Kong Paeng, his villagers, and me in early '73 might well have looked suspicious from the air.

The digging was very hard work because construction methods on the Nong Bua project didn't involve any United States Air Force Civic Action bulldozers. Quite to the contrary, our project progressed more like in the movie *Bridge Over River Kwai* where the excavation quota was a yard and a half per day per soldier. Villagers, of course, have more freedom than do soldiers, and Kong Paeng was unable to rally more than a few of his charges to work in the heat of the day.

But that didn't stop Kong Paeng. He called a village meeting to set down new guidelines, and after that he and Wang, his assistant, began to rise long before dawn to measure chunks of excavation. With each household then digging a cubic meter of excavation every fourth day in the cool of the morning, we saw steady progress.

I grew to respect Kong Paeng. He had boundless energy and enthusiasm and thought about the welfare of his village day and night. He was overjoyed that a *farawng* such as myself would be willing to work in his village, live with his family, and supervise the construction of a spillway to give them a dry season source of water. He'd only had one test to see if I could be there. The first day I saw him, he gave me a *kiat*, which looked something like a small white frog. He said that if I could eat the *kiat*, it would prove to him that I could stay and work in his village.

I ate Kong Paeng's *kiat* that day, but I never ate another. If it weren't for the fact that the villagers ate so many *kiat*, I might have never felt the need to go back and forth along the primitive road to Nong Bua to shop for food quite as frequently as I did. And I might never have had my encounter with a trip wire.

Because our progress on the ground could also be seen from the air, and Nong Bua was situated a mile beyond a ten mile radius surrounding the American Air Base, which was their pacification area, American Intelligence may well have considered me to be something of a loose canon. In any case, just as our excavation was nearing completion, but before we could pour our concrete, all Volunteers in Northeast Thailand received a memo from our country director. His memo designated twelve Thai districts "red."

"While it is difficult to assess the real risk in any given area or situation," he wrote in his memo, "it would be prudent of Volunteers to avoid the red districts whenever possible. There is also a longer list of blue districts, which could be hazardous. The recommendation here is that you check with the consulate regarding these areas."

And then just a week or two later he came to pay a visit, and together we traveled down the road to Nong Bua: the country director, his driver, two more senior Volunteers and myself. But we only went a half-kilometer down the road to visit the completed trainee project. Our director showed no interest in traveling further down the road to view the excavation in Nong Bua or to talk through his driver/interpreter to Kong Paeng or the people there. He also made no mention of the memo he'd just sent us. He didn't say much at all other that that he was very tired from his long jeep ride from Bangkok. I didn't want to talk to him that day about security issues for fear he'd shut my project down. We'd just about completed our excavation, and I felt that I ought to finish what I'd started. This was my job, and I didn't think it was all that rebellious of me to travel on the road to Nong Bua.

The first half-kilometer of the road, that went as far as the trainee project, was actually pretty good. But beyond that point, the road was in bad repair. There were three or four bridges, and all of them were out.

The bridgeless road, of course, wasn't very well traveled, and it was little more than a two-track as it crossed through chopped-over jungle. This wasn't high canopy virgin jungle, nor were there rice fields or villages for a seven-kilometer stretch right after the trainee project. The first village after that was the village of Coke Glang, perhaps a kilometer before Nong Bua, and just before Coke Glang, there was a clearly visible bunker with white sand bags a hundred meters east of the road. I learned that headman Kong Paeng and his assistant Wang were among a group of volunteer soldiers who, for five dollars a month, stayed as guards behind these sandbagged bunkers ten nights each month.

And surely there was more to it than that. They probably patrolled the surrounding jungle. For me to believe that there were no insurgents in this area would have been naïve, but it seemed like a cat and mouse game which had little do with me.

But then there was that morning I almost hit the tripwire. When I came upon that tripwire, I felt on the one hand foolish for even traveling on that road, but I also felt very fortunate to have been able to stop my Hodaka motorcycle just a foot or two before I would have hit it. I carefully got off the Hodaka. I inspected the contraption, and I saw the circular wires that were hanging from a horizontal wire, which was stretched tautly across the road from one side clear to the other.

Arriving at that tripwire became, I realized later, my moment of truth. Already before the Peace Corps, I'd been persuaded to believe that the Vietnam War had nothing to do with me. I'd applied for conscientious objector status with my draft board before enlisting in the Peace Corps. And yet I knew I couldn't deny that the wire was there. I knew I couldn't just go around it the way I'd been going around the bridges. I knew I needed to abandon my personal politics, bite the bullet, and do the right thing.

I decided my best course of action would be to go back down the road to Nong Ya Sai and talk to the headman there. He knew who I was, and his village was the closest. I decided to tell him straight up about the trip wire and ask him to send a few villagers on their bicycles to make sure that no one tripped it while I went by myself to the Air Base.

We were, at that time, doing excavation work very early in the morning before the heat of the day. I found the headman in Nong Ya Sai had just woken up when I arrived to talk to him. He sensed the urgency of the matter as he wiped the sleep from his eyes, and within a minute or two he began to beat the wooden gong in front of his house to summon his villagers to an emergency meeting.

The villagers began to arrive; some on bicycles; some just walking; most not dressed but for the *pakamas* around their waists. As they started to arrive, the headman questioned me further, and I explained to him once more just what I'd seen. He grew pensive for a moment, and then he pointed to a wire contraption hanging on the side of his house.

"Is THAT what you saw?" he asked me.

I looked at the wire contraption. I had no idea what it was, but when I saw it I realized I'd probably seen something that was not what I'd thought it was.

"Yes," I said. "That's what I saw."

"That's a rabbit trap," he said softly.

And that would have been the end of it right there. It could have been a little joke between the Nong Ya Sai headman and me; something we might have kept between ourselves, or something he could have talked to his villagers about later after I'd left. But it couldn't be that way because he'd already hit his gong, and the villagers were already hurrying to his house because they knew there must be some very important news for them to be summoned to a meeting so early in the morning.

"A rabbit trap? The *farawng* saw a rabbit trap?"

I watched as the first arriving villagers began to repeat what the headman had told me, but the villagers weren't talking quite so softly about my encounter with the rabbit trap as had their headman.

"What's this meeting about?" the new arrivals asked the villagers who'd come first, the ones who'd seen me admit to the headman that I'd seen a wire contraption just like the one which was hanging from a nail on the side of his house.

"It's about a rabbit trap," they answered.

No one seemed inclined to leave, because the gong the headman had hit was the gong used to announce a village meeting, and all the villagers knew the headman wouldn't tell them more until a representative from each household in the village was present to hear what he had to say.

I decided I didn't want to be around when they had their emergency rabbit trap meeting in the village of Nong Ya Sai, and I left as most of the villagers were still arriving. Instead of going to the Air Base to fetch the bomb squad, I went back down the road toward my spillway project in Nong Bua.

I felt I'd been set up. We'd never been told anything in training about these rabbit trap trip wires; nor had Kong Paeng been of much assistance when I'd asked him if the road to his village was safe to travel. He'd warned me how I might be harassed by ghosts, but he hadn't said one word about rabbit traps. When I arrived once again at the trap, I encountered a boy I recognized. He was a fourteen-year-old who'd been undermining our work team early on by providing his friends with marijuana joints. They'd take a toke or two, then work very rapidly, but only for a short time before collapsing in the shade in fits of laughter to watch the rest of us work. And there he was again. He'd just arrived on his bicycle to dismantle his trap as I returned.

"Did you catch any rabbits today," I asked the boy.

"No luck today," he smiled. "I set six traps all along this road last night, but I didn't catch even one rabbit."

By this time the monsoon season was rapidly approaching. We'd yet to lay our steel or pour our concrete, and even my Thai co-worker (*patanagawn*) seemed to have turned against me. Kong Paeng told me he'd paid a visit on a day when we weren't working, which might well have been the day we were hosting our Peace Corps director. He said he had looked at the size of our excavation and told him we couldn't possibly finish pouring the concrete before the rains would come and wash everything away.

"I told him I didn't know if we'd finish in time or not," Kong Paeng told me, "but I told him we would try."

We actually poured the last of our concrete on April 23rd, a full three weeks before the monsoons were due to arrive. We celebrated our accomplishment on Kong Paeng's porch: the villagers, the Thai soldiers, the *ni ampur* (district officer), the local *patanagawn*, me, and even one GI. All the politics for that one day seemed to fade away.

James Jouppi served in Thailand from 1971-73. He is one of many Americans using their education to make sure that each and every

American receives his mail every single day (except on Sundays and postal holidays, of course). He was the only member of his family born in New York and was driving a taxi in Manhattan just before the Peace Corps. He was naïve at the time and also naïve in the Peace Corps. Most people think he still is. "A Spillway for Nong Bua" *is part of an unpublished work entitled* War of Hearts and Minds, an American Memoir.

LORI ENGELMANN ROBINSON

✳

Chasing Gulls,
Chasing Dreams

Oh, the shark he, has such teeth, babe, and
he makes some dreams come true.

I LAY MY HEAD BACK ON THE SEAT OF THE BUS, A SMILE SPREADING
across my face. I was living out my dream right here and now,
and it was amazing. This had been the kind of day I dreamed
of after receiving my invitation from the Peace Corps in 1994,
over a year ago. I was not bothered by the stench of sweat and
fish in the overcrowded bus. Nor was I bothered by the whispers and mutters of the locals in reference to the *"I-Matang"*
who was clearly a bit crazy. I felt crazy alive. Like I had just
won the lottery!

When my acceptance letter arrived from Peace Corps telling me my assignment was to The Republic of Kiribati in the
Central Pacific, my fantasies began. I fantasized about all the
exotic places I would visit. I would swim in turquoise lagoons,
swing under coconut trees in my hammock, and walk barefoot
on beaches in an island paradise.

My first year as a Volunteer proved to be quite the opposite
of what I expected. Going anywhere alone was quite inappropriate for young women. Hanging a hammock under a

coconut tree? Well, that was just asking for a nut on the noggin! The beaches and lagoons? They serve more as latrines than local swimming hot spots.

I spent a lot of time the first year trying to live out some of my dreams. I'd been laughed at for wanting to *go fishing,* when in Kiribati women *cook* the fish. In one early attempt, I approached a fisherman and asked to join him, only to end up walking home, perplexed, with his entire catch. Apparently he thought I was starving. It had been a tough culture to crack, but this day proved I was making progress.

On a visit to Tarawa, the capital, my host family there had agreed to take me out fishing. I was told to show up bright and early for the morning's launch. Now as I bounced back home on the bus, I closed my eyes and reviewed my day.

It had dawned bright and hot, as does every day in the equatorial doldrums. I had peeled my already sweaty self off my mat and dressed. I filled my fanny pack with bus fare, sunscreen and sunglasses. I slung a large bottle of smoky (but boiled-for-three-minutes water) over my shoulder and hopped the bus. My family greeted me with a meal. Local custom demanded that any guest entering the house be fed. So at about 8 A.M., I worked down some fish, rice, and taro. Believe me, it took about four cups of tea to wash it all down.

Finally it was time to leave. As I waded to the boat, I thought the aura of excitement around me was probably visible. I swigged my water, put my face to the sky and said a silent thanks for the day. We had not been out long, when a rain cloud moved in. My thoughts of ignorant dismissal towards this pesky cloud turned to concern as I observed the three men securing a compass to the floor. "Just in case the island is lost when the rain stops" Ah, come again? The rain cloud overtook us, and the island disappeared. I held on to an amazing amount of composure, mainly by exercising some deep breathing and trying not to envision my parents reading: "Peace Corps Volunteer Missing in Pacific."

Thankfully, the sky cleared; I sighed with relief as I spotted the island. Then—and this is the truth—a rainbow arched across the sky and slid into an emerald ocean. The water began to ripple. The ripples spread all around the boat as though they were alive. They were. The dolphins leapt up, dancing all around our boat. I laughed as free as the wind. I laughed like a three year old at the circus. Even the three grown men in the boat smiled in awe. We waited and watched this enchanting spectacle until the curtain dropped, and the sea was still again.

The show over, we began chasing the gulls in our effort to find tuna. A movement caught my eye. I glanced overboard and gasped. A four-foot-long shark was circling our boat. "*Te bakua!*" I yelled.

The men jumped into action. I was banished to sit on the bow of the boat and told to keep my feet up. They sliced up a small tuna we had already caught, attached a chunk to a hook, and threw it overboard. They all seemed to know what to do next. One man produced a club, which I had failed to notice before, and stood with it poised over his head. The other two manned the line.

After taking the bait, the shark seemed surprised as his lunch hauled him out of the water into the bottom of the boat. As soon as he landed all feet were off the floor! The guy with the club took care of business. Once the shark was still, I found myself enduring some backslapping for spotting the shark. Apparently that made it mine. We headed in to tell the story.

Then came the bus ride home. As I sat bumping closer to home, I looked down at my lap and laughed. There rested about a third of my shark. The men wanted me to take the entire thing, but I bartered my way down. My hair was stuck to my face; my clothes smelled of shark, salt water and

B.O.; and I was about the happiest I had ever been. The bus screeched to a halt. I stood, hefting the shark up, hugging it with bare arms, struggling for a grip. I descended the stairs of the bus feeling the stares and whispers behind me. My laughter became uncontrollable as I tried to imagine what I looked like. I staggered home, laughing the whole way.

I was still laughing as I ate shark for dinner. I didn't find shark for breakfast quite as humorous.

Lori Engelmann Robinson served in Kiribati from 1995-97 as a TESL Trainer on the Island of Nikunau. Lori grew up in the Northeast Kingdom of Vermont. She currently resides in Maine with her husband and two daughters. Lori teaches Special Education in her community.

PART FOUR

Close Encounters

A Loss of Innocence

*The first Volunteers to answer JFK's call were
in the field when he was assassinated.*

Saturday morning, November 23, 1963, Calingapatnam, Andhra Pradesh, India.

"Rossgaru, Rossgaru, Mrs. Kennedy shot! Mrs. Kennedy shot!"

Ramamurthy had scrambled the news heard over the Voice of America broadcast from Colombo, Ceylon. Some other teachers and students and I squatted by the short-wave radio in the high school library to hear the even more shocking news. The headmaster K. Krishnarao offered to cancel the half-day of school, in memory of President Kennedy. We settled on having several minutes of silence at the flag raising that morning.

Saturday afternoon I bicycled the flat eighteen miles to meet with three other Peace Corps Volunteers and share our grief. JFK was not just our President; he had promoted the idea of a "peace corps" early in his 1960 Presidential campaign, and he instituted it by an executive order the following year. Moreover, Kennedy truly inspired hope among the poor and disadvantaged of the world. They felt that he, and America,

281

cared. I was often reminded of this, such as when two years after the assassination I stopped to eat at a small café in an Iranian village on the Caspian Sea. There were displayed only two portraits on the bare mud walls—a mandatory one of the Shah and a larger one of President Kennedy.

Of course, JFK was far from the saint portrayed by the media in the early 1960s. But when I meet with former Peace Corps Volunteers from that era, we sometimes wonder what the world would have been like if Kennedy had lived. And now every year when November 22 comes, I feel a certain sadness for the loss of vision he gave and the optimism he aroused. Are these gone forever?

Peter Ross served in India 4 from 1963-65. He was assigned to teach science and math at a secondary school in the village of Calingapatnamin in southern India at a time when India was the poorest country in the world, with a life expectancy of thirty-eight years. Because his students had no electricity, they studied on his porch in the evenings. Still teaching, he is a senior lecturer in math at Santa Clara University.

MICHAEL SCHMICKER

The Mosquito Bar

*Who could argue with foreign aid paid directly to the neediest
with language lessons thrown in for good measure?*

THE MOSQUITO BAR WAS THE END OF THE LINE FOR A BANGKOK
prostitute back in 1969. It was a two-story, concrete, dockside
dive dumped on the banks of the Chao Phraya River south of
the humid Thai capital, surrounded by the notorious Klong
Toey slum.

Pretty girls started out servicing *farangs* at the big tourist and business hotels like the Siam Intercontinental and
Montien, making several thousand baht a trick. When their
looks and boobs slipped, they moved on to Patpong Road
where they danced and drank with well-heeled local expats
and American G.I.s on R&R from Vietnam, still making good
money. Eventually the booze and drugs wasted them, and
they slipped down the ladder to work off-Patpong haunts like
the Grace, servicing Thai men out for a night on the town
for a hundred baht or less. Eventually, when they couldn't
find another home, their careers nearly over, they ended up
sharing nightmares with psychotic tramp steamer sailors at
the Mosquito. The Baa Phii—the "ghost bar" as the girls

called it—got the troublemakers, the deranged and disfigured, worn-out women hustling for nothing more than bus fare back home to their village.

I taught TEFL at Wat Bovornives School during the day and spent my nights at the Mosquito—I have no idea what the place looked like in daylight—drinking beer and scribbling notes for my Great American Novel. I fancied myself a writer and idolized Hemingway. Back in college, I read all his books and dreamed of living his romantic life: drinking in cafés and arguing politics; romancing beautiful, doomed women; chasing wars.

I needed something dramatic to happen to the hero, like an encounter with a prostitute. Prostitutes didn't live the constricted, boring lives most of us did. They were outlaws, they shunned society's rules, did forbidden things, suffered hard lives that ended in tragedy. They fascinated readers, so writers included them in their books: the streetwalker Georgette in Hemingway's *The Sun Also Rises*, the saintly Sofya Semyonova in Dostoevsky's *Crime and Punishment*, Salinger's Sunny in *The Catcher in the Rye*. Shakespeare had a bordello full in his plays.

The alienated hero in my story wouldn't go to bed with a prostitute, simply because I never had that experience (thank you, Doctor Ron, for that graphic lecture on VD). Instead, the two outlaws would lead parallel lives of anomie, friends but not lovers, melodramatically meeting on occasion as the narrator moped existentially through the demi-monde.

My first night at the Mosquito, I was nursing a beer upstairs just off the dance floor when an Aussie at the next table picked up a Mekhong bottle and clocked his friend over the head. Why? I don't know, but I knocked over my table getting the hell out of there. The two of them fell to the floor, rolling around on the shattered glass and punching each other.

The bar girls didn't join me in a race to the wall. They headed straight for the entertainment, and threw in a few kicks of their own before the bar's no-neck bouncers waded in. The Mosquito knew its clientele. The owner hired *nak-lang*—real gangsters—mean and efficient in a fight. They shoved spectators out of the way and locked choke holds on the combatants. "Good-Day-Mate" struggled frantically for a few seconds, gasping for breath, then slumped against the bouncer. Both brawlers were quickly dragged downstairs. Folding metal chairs and tables righted, the band launched into the Shondell's "Mony Mony," and the girls returned to the dance floor. After that, I always chose a table at the back of the room, near the exit.

I spotted Maa ("horse": high tone in Thai) the first night I drank there. I don't know how she picked up her nickname. Maybe it was her loud, braying laugh. I called her Maa ("dog": rising tone) by mistake and she sourpussed me. She was the feisty, in-your-face leader of the pack, and she did what she pleased. She did her peeing in the men's room and toyed with the boys, even other girls' boys. You entertained her at your peril. One night she was rejected by a drunk after flirting him up through several Singha *yai*, wasting her precious time. When he abandoned her and started dancing alone on the floor in a boozy stupor, she grabbed a long strip of toilet paper, stuffed it in the seat of his pants and lit it with a match. He waltzed around the floor with a flaming tail until his jeans scorched and friends doused his butt with beer.

It didn't pay to get Thai girls too mad. Crimes of passion were common. One woman two-timed by her boyfriend cut off his cock while he slept and tossed it out the window where it was eaten by a duck.

The first time Maa came over to hustle me, I told her I didn't have any money. That should have sent her running, but the *farang* spoke Thai. Surprised, she sat down and bombarded me with questions. Where did I learn Thai? What was I doing in Thailand? Did I have a girlfriend already? I explained the Peace Corps to her.

"*Phuut Thai geng maak!*" You speak Thai so well!, she squealed. I was prepared for that inevitable line.

"*Baak waan,*" I replied. She broke out in a laugh. Literally, it means "sweet mouth," a neat Thai colloquialism for "you flatter me."

She grabbed my crotch and looked me in the eye. She told me she had a customer, but she would return before the night was over. Promise. Two A.M., she stopped by for a swig of my beer before she left, towing her trick who waited impatiently, scowling at me and wondering who the hell I was. Then she was gone.

But Maa could also be kind. She strolled over to my table one night with another girl, hoping I was in the market. I still wasn't, but I noticed something odd about the girl; she was subdued, quiet, looked down at the floor. Maa raised the girl's chin, brushed back her hair and pointed to the girl's eyes.

"*Dtaa baawt,*" Maa explained. The girl was blind.

I didn't even know they had blind prostitutes. I watched Maa as she worked the room for the girl, using bait and switch. Maa got the table of guys excited, then dragged the girl over. The girl made Maa work. She drank stiffly, laughed too little, snuggled badly. But Maa pulled it off. She sold them both. The two of them left that night with paid boyfriends.

Another evening, despite her best efforts, Maa struck out. She came over to my table, mad as hell. She would have to do a two-for-the-price-of-one with some guy, and they would end up splitting the money. She drank my beer and gave a karmic sigh before brightening up again, bumming a cigarette and going back to work.

After that, I was always good for a few baht, plus I found a way to repay her for her steady kindness to Miss Baawt.

Peace Corps encouraged us to continue studying Thai while in country. If we chose an AUA-certified Thai language teacher, Peace Corps reimbursed them 40 baht, $2 an hour. If we couldn't find a certified instructor, we could hire any Thai for 20 baht an hour to help us build our vocabulary. Maa became my personal, dollar-an-hour Thai language tutor.

Every time I dropped into the Ba Phii, we talked. At the end of the evening, I looked at my watch, toted up the hours, paid her, presented her with the reimbursement slip, which she proudly signed, and turned it in to the Peace Corps. It was the least I could do for Peace Corps critic Congressman Otto Passman who hated wasting U.S. taxpayers' dollars. My foreign aid program operated on minimal overhead, went straight to the neediest, and made Maa a lifelong friend of America. I learned a notebook full of streetwise words Peace Corps forgot to teach us during training. How could you argue with that?

Maa rarely left the bar without a trick, but one dead evening she uncharacteristically struck out. She didn't have the cab fare, so I gave her a lift home on my motorcycle. It was almost 3 A.M. The docks were dark and deserted, no streetlights, a few dogs snuffling through garbage outside a shuttered *raan ahaan*. She directed me through a confusing maze of narrow alleys until we finally crossed over a small stream—an open sewer— and stopped. Ahead, amid a jumble of wooden shacks, a light bulb shone through the slit of a shuttered window. Did I want to come in, she asked. I wasn't buying, but I was curious to see how she lived.

I followed her across some algae-slick planks spanning more foul-smelling water and stepped inside. Her one-room box was surprisingly neat and clean, the walls decorated with photos of Thai movie stars and a portrait of King Bhumibol. She immediately went over to a small Buddhist shrine tucked in the corner, clasped her hands and performed a *wai*. A small wooden cabinet beside her bed held the tools of her trade: cosmetics, powders, lotions and an enamel wash basin she filled each morning from a community spigot. A wire strung across the room served as a clothes closet. I didn't see a bathroom. She slept alone in a narrow, hard bed. Not scoring that night meant more than just a loss of money. Tricks came complete with a big, soft hotel bed and a private bathroom with running water, hot shower and a flush toilet. I tried to cheer her up. Tomorrow might bring a ship full of high-spending Brits, or a slumming embassy staffer.

"Go home," she said, and went off to fetch her toothbrush.

When I left, I got hopelessly lost and drove around in circles for a half-hour before finally running across a street I recognized, which eventually led me home.

The following weekend, Maa dragged over to my table a knock-out friend in a push-up bra who clutched a thin blue aerogramme. They sat down beside me and the girl, Dang, handed me the letter, written in English, from some moon-struck sailor in South Africa.

"What does it say?" Maa demanded. I translated it into Thai.

David had mailed it from Durban. His ship was headed for Tokyo, with a stop in Bangkok. He couldn't wait to see her. Maa grinned and poked Dang in the ribs. Dang beamed with delight. They scrunched closer, all ears. David declared he had never stopped thinking about Dang from the night they first met, three months before. Other girls no longer interested him. David had finally found the girl of his dreams, and it was Dang. He was returning with a special present, something for her *niu*, finger. That sparked wild *hoo-haas* from Maa who pretended to model a big rock on her left hand, which broke Dang up. He would be docking in Bangkok on October 18th and promised to be at the bar that evening looking for his little honey-bunny.

Dang had to seize the opportunity, Maa told her breath-lessly. Write a letter back, immediately, before his ardor waned.

"Maitri will write the letter for you, in English," she announced. I had a pen, and a notebook. I could compose it, then copy it onto an aerogramme and mail it for Dang. I would do that for Dang, wouldn't I?

Feeling like a Yiddish matchmaker, I asked Dang what she wanted to say to David, her one true love. She thought for a second.

"*Thii rahk,*" "Sweetheart," she started. Good, good, nodded Maa. I dutifully wrote it down.

Long pause, then "*Chan rahk khun,*" "I love you."

Dang looked at Maa. How was she doing? Great, great, replied Maa.

I waited. They fiddled with the beer bottles, trying to come up with something more. A crew-cut *farang* walked by unwrapping a pack of smokes and Dang gave him a swat on the butt and a hundred-watt smile. He laughed and pointed to his table on the other side of the room. Dang turned back to the job at hand.

Sudden inspiration.

"*Khit theung maak!*" I think of you a lot!" She smiled trium-phantly, like someone who had correctly answered a million dollar question. No, no, something better, interjected Maa, bouncing on her seat.

"*Khit theung maak MAAK!*" I think of you a WHOLE lot!" They fell into each others arms giggling.

Dang walked over to crew cut's table, sat on his lap, and pulled the cigarette out of his mouth. A little grind in pay-ment, and she returned to our table with her smoke. She was getting bored. Maa was also getting distracted. A knot of new customers made their noisy entrance. The band launched into the Archies' "Sugar Sugar." It was going to be a race to get to them first, and other girls were already peeling off and zoom-ing in. Dang jumped up, smoothed her miniskirt over her hips, pushed up her boobs and set off for the boys, Maa right behind her.

I only had three sentences. I yelled at Maa that I needed something more. She waved her hand dismissively.

"Finish it up for us," she laughed. "You're a writer."

Michael Schmicker served in Thailand from 1969-72. He is a journal-ist and author living in Hawaii. His website is www.booksbymichael. com. He and his fellow Thai 27 RPCVs congregate at www.thai27. com. This incident is excerpted from a Peace Corps autobiography he is working on entitled Land of Smiles.

USHA ALEXANDER

✳

At the Foot of Mount Yasur

*Walking in the darkness to the edge of the abyss is best done
in the company of wise children and an intuitive friend.*

I AM 600 MILES EAST OF THE GREAT BARRIER REEF IN THE
archipelago of Vanuatu—or, as they say in Vanuatu, the "*ni-
Vanuatu*" archipelago—home to nine active volcanoes. One,
Mount Yasur on the southern island of Tanna, is said to be
the most easily accessible live volcano in the world. Anyone
can walk right up and peer down into its fiery belly. A real
volcano: fire and brimstone and flying ash.

It is late in the dry season when I get to Tanna with my
friend Michael. The days are crisp and warm, the nights cool
enough to require long pants and a sweatshirt, a departure from
the perpetual warmth of Ambae, an island famously known as
Michener's "Bali Hai," the more northerly island, just shy of the
equator. I have lived and worked for eight months as a Peace
Corps science teacher. We plan to spend three days at Port
Resolution and then head up to Ienemaha, the village closest
to the crater, where Michael's tenth-grade student, David, lives.
David adores Michael as his teacher and as a living soccer mae-
stro, so his family graciously asked us to be their guests.

We climb onto a flatbed truck near Lenakal, the tiny capital of Tanna, alongside a half-dozen Tannese, and jostle and bounce the dirt road distance across the island to Port Resolution. As teachers and foreigners, we always feel that we are the objects of special attention, especially from the children. In animated Bislama, the local *lingua franca*, they ask about us and are eager to tell stories along the drive. As we cross the ash flats that flank Mount Yasur, its black cone smoking above us, they provide details about the mountain's random acts of carnage. Three years ago, a tourist and her *ni*-Vanuatu guide were both burned alive near the crater's lip when gobs of molten lava rained down on them. After that, the *ni*-Vanuatu government shut down tourist access to the volcano for two years. With animated gestures and vivid language, the children describe further particulars: how half of the guide's body was found, the right side of it burned away; how the woman, well, had lost her head; how, more recently, a local village boy felled by a blob of brimstone lived long enough to be carried back to his village, his one leg burned away below the knee. He did not last much longer, lacking access to more advanced medicine than his village could provide.

I look at Michael with fresh trepidation, and I can see he shares my thoughts.

Oblivious to our fears, a fine-faced boy brightens up and asks me, "Have you heard the good news?" I have heard this before from *ni*-Vanuatu children; the first time, it stumped me, but I learned that it is always followed by, "Do you know about Jesus?" I evade the question. "Yes," I reply with a smile, "I've heard it."

Until the latter years of the nineteenth century, the islanders themselves had never heard the Good News. But when missionaries arrived to help colonize the islands in the nineteenth century, a veneer of Christianity spread rapidly over the indigenous animism. And, for the most part, the *ni*-Vanuatu still practice a Christianity that seems to have changed little in a century. To sit on decaying benches in an unlit, unadorned, square wooden church, surrounded by the steamy breath of vivid green forest, to hear old Anglican hymns sung in the spontaneous, nasalized harmonies that characterize the traditional vocal style, one imagines a fervent, sweating missionary might at any moment swagger to the front of the assembly.

But things have changed. Bibles are now printed in Bislama, and the islanders have made this religion their own. Alongside this ardent devotion to Jesus, the indigenous ideas persist, still regulating life and social power in communities. In times of social crisis, people commune with the spirits of the dead; misfortune and antisocial behavior are attributed to supernatural forces. Nor is such belief in *tabu*, magic, and all manner of spirits seen as being at odds with Christian practice. While Jesus' presence is abstract, spirits and demons are manifest around us, giving context and sense to everyday life, providing limits and contrast to our humanity.

At Port Resolution Guest House, we are shown to our round bungalow. Spacious, with latticed strips of wood for walls under a thatched roof, it contains only two beds and a small table. Accustomed as we are to the lack of electricity and heated water, the bungalow feels luxurious for the mosquito netting covering the beds. Out front lean two wooden lounge chairs overlooking Port Resolution Bay, a circular body of placid, azure seawater, ringed by a mango-colored ridge that once demarked a volcanic crater.

Had I just arrived at this place from the United States, I might have imagined it the most picturesque and serene spot on Earth. *Paradise.* But I came from Ambae—likewise a "paradise," surrounded by the clearest water in the world, swarming with vibrantly colored creatures that inhabit and hunt in its offshore reefs—and I already know the limits of this metaphor. Already I had learned to watch out for cone shells and sea snakes near the beaches, to guard vigilantly against malaria, and to lock my door at night.

Lounging in the sun, we hear the far away booming of Mount Yasur. But for the present, we focus on the tranquil beauty of the bay and wonder about the resident *dugong*—a large, marine mammal, cousin to the manatee—who is said to enjoy playing with swimmers. "You notice, the local people don't get in there to swim," Michael observes one afternoon. "It's only the tourists who talk about it."

It is true. We have met a dozen tourists at the guesthouse— French, Australian, Kiwi, American—who speak excitedly about their attempts to flush out the *dugong*. We watch them swim around the bay in large circles, in search of the elusive creature. We hear them clap and slap the water, following the example of their *ni*-Vanuatu guides, to rouse the old guy. Still, though the guides happily demonstrate how to "call" the *dugong*, they never venture into the water themselves. Children never wander in above their waistlines. Fishermen stay in their canoes. Only the tourists swim here, to whose chagrin, the *dugong* does not appear.

In the guesthouse book, we read of past encounters with the *dugong* and the wistful regrets of tourists who missed him. Some have seen him from a distance or even turned a few delighted circles with him. Others give warnings explicitly or implicitly couched in their tales: keep your distance; do not attempt to touch him; get out of the water if he swims straight toward you. One marine biologist emphasized his point with capitals: REMEMBER THAT THIS IS A LARGE, WILD ANIMAL. HE IS NOT TAME. HE IS NOT PLAYING WITH YOU.

I am increasingly convinced that an encounter with the *dugong* is not to be taken lightly, any more so than an encounter with a wild elephant. Listening to more tourists eager to jump in, I am struck by how blithely we pass through here, as though this really is a paradise: a benign and thrilling place, here to serve our wishes. But the Western dream of a clean, safe, ordered world is not more well met here in Vanuatu than it is in most of the world.

In the guesthouse, we also hear stories from those who have climbed the volcano. They went up by jeep at night, when the fiery glow is most stunning. They hiked the last ten minutes to the top and stood around for a few minutes, waiting for something to happen. But Mount Yasur has been quiet lately, so there are few tales of spewing lava. One couple says they laid out their bags and slept overnight a few feet from the crater. When I ask if they had been scared, imagining clumps of molten rock raining down on them in their sleep, singeing holes through their bags then their flesh, as the high-tech, synthetic materials ignite, they laugh dismissively as though I am naïve. Bad things will not happen to them; they are Westerners on holiday.

It is our last morning at Port Resolution when a young couple arrives with a pack of local men who had promised to show them the *dugong*. They clap and slap and out of nowhere a fat, grey body slides into view under the perfectly transparent skin of the water. He looks about the size of a rhinoceros. Clearly, the young man considers this opportunity a highlight of his life, given the gusto with which he dives in behind the creature.

At first the *dugong* shows little interest in him, so the young man—an athletic swimmer—draws up behind him. But the *dugong*, at home in his element, casually evades the swimmer, who laughs and keeps up the chase. Within minutes, however, the game has changed, and it is the *dugong* chasing the swimmer. He laughs until the dugong makes contact, ramming him in the gut and rushing him backwards through the water.

When the *dugong* moves off, the swimmer appears stunned at his unexpected loss of control, at the unexpected aggression of the *dugong*. He moves back toward the shore, but before he reaches it, the dugong is upon him again, having circled round to his front, shoving him forcefully and speedily backwards. The girlfriend on shore looks frightened. When the *dugong* releases him and he recovers his breath, the boyfriend swims as fast as he can for the rocks. The *dugong* comes at him a third time, and the man flails awkwardly, yelling wildly for help. His girlfriend is at a loss, dropping to her knees at the water's edge, and his *ni*-Vanuatu guides, until now clustered on shore, talking amongst themselves, take notice of their man's situation and chuckle nervously. No one, though, is ready to jump in, not even his girlfriend.

I expect the *dugong* has never killed or seriously injured anyone. He is, after all, a vegetarian. But he makes a clear point that he is nobody's pet and no human is in control here. This place is not paradise, for paradise is a human creation, and this place yet exceeds our human imagination.

A fisherman glides by in his outrigger canoe, and the men on shore coax him to pick up the panicked swimmer. The fisherman complies without speaking, his eyelids fluttering with annoyance. As soon as it comes within range, the swimmer grabs the narrow front of the canoe and desperately tries to pull himself aboard. This move capsizes the small craft, and swimmer, fisherman, morning's catch, and fishing gear are plunged into the clear brine. The fisherman sighs as the swimmer still scrabbles with mad futility to mount the upturned hull. By now the *dugong* has swum off, and the men ashore are roaring with laughter. I am relieved the man is not hurt, but I wonder what stories this couple will tell their friends back home.

Later this same morning, David arrives with his father, sisters, and some friends. We head on foot across the island to

Ienemaha. For two hours we hike up and down narrow, forested ridges, between stands of ferns thick and tall as trees. And as we move toward the volcano, we hear more of its clamor. By the time we reach Ienemaha, we smell sulfur lightly on the breeze. The muted rumbling of the volcano blends with the rustle of leaves, the call of birds, and the voices of playing children, occasionally giving way to a fierce, guttural blast.

I converse with the children in Bislama until they become incoherent with giggles. Then they whisper to each other in their local language, which is completely opaque to me. Before the missionaries and blackbirders and colonists came to these islands, before the populations were decimated, these islands were populated with nearly a million people speaking over a thousand different languages. The fractionation of languages is attributed to the rugged terrain and the surprising fact that, in this land of natural abundance, the traditional cultures were extremely warlike. Apparently, the combined onslaught of Christianity, blackbirding—kidnapping youngsters for the slave trade—colonization, and population decline subdued this aspect of their culture, but most of the original languages have died out. Yet even today, the *ni*-Vanuatu archipelago is home to one of the highest ratios of languages to people in the world. Some 170,000 people speak over a hundred surviving languages.

I learn that David's father is a baker. This means that most days he rises early and mixes up a huge batch of plain, basic bread dough (the only kind of bread one can get on the islands). He cuts and divides it among his two dozen aluminum bread pans, then bakes it in his homemade oven. As the sun rises, the bread is done, and he stacks some of it in the back of a hired truck for delivery to a small market; the rest he sells to his neighbors. In this way, David's family has some cash flow, which is used to send David to school on faraway Epi, and to buy the few foreign goods that have become staples of life here, like the cheap Western-style clothing—produced in China—that is now worn almost everywhere on the islands. The rest of the time, David's father does what village men do: visit with neighbors and take care of whatever needs doing in the home and community.

Like nearly all *ni*-Vanuatu, David's family subsists primarily on traditional horticulture. The garden plots take a fair amount of tending, which is women's work, but the gardens are probably smaller than they traditionally were, since now the table is supplemented with foreign foods such as rice, tinned beef, and Top Ramen, more cosmopolitan cuisine than the staples of taro, manioc, yams, plantains, and the enormous variety of local fruits, vegetables, greens, and seafood. The most prized food is the occasional pig or cow that gets slaughtered for special occasions.

In preparation for our morning walk to the foot of the volcano, I steal a moment to dash fifty meters down the path to the local store for film. Like most island stores in Vanuatu, this is a square wooden shack with mostly empty shelves built onto the walls. Luckily, this one has a few boxes of film for the volcano tourists, like me.

After dinner, David's father takes Michael away to drink kava. Michael does not relish it, but, being a man, he is expected to go. As I settle down with a book and a hurricane lamp, David's mother knocks and steps in for a chat. She entreats me not to run off by myself again.

"I have two daughters, and there is a whole village full of girls. Just ask one of them to come with you if you want to go somewhere." She stresses that they do not want me to get hurt, not to fall, for instance. And then she reminds me of the devils in the forest.

I have heard this before. On Ambae I am warned often that I should not leave the village alone, that I should be cautious of *ol devils* who inhabit the surrounds. This is an injunction I routinely ignore; I walk by myself nearly every day. Still, I have become more hesitant about it. In this culture, a lone woman is fair prey to any group of young men who might wish to exert their will over her. Already I had been chased and grabbed a number of times in various situations, but never when I was alone in the forest. Listening to David's mother's sincere concern, it occurs to me that groups of roguish boys might be the very "devils" that the women are trying to warn me about.

David's mother also talks about the ancestors who live in the volcano. They sleep in there most of the time, she says. Sometimes they wake up, and that is when the real pyrotechnics begin. She cautions me to be quiet when we ascend the volcano, so as not to disturb *ol bubu*.

I cannot sleep in the cool night air. After months on Ambae, Tannese nights are too cold. When Michael returns, we lie awake in the darkness, listening to the rumbling of the island below and around us.

"Are you sure you want to go up there?" he asks. "It's kind of crazy. We don't have to go."

I am scared, I tell him, but also certain. At his suggestion, we make a pact: If either one of us gets too scared to go all the way up, for any reason, at any point, we will both turn around and come back down together.

The next day the children take us to the ash flats, a wide, treeless space, a surreal landscape of orange, red, black, and grey, rolling here and jagged there around the edges. The ash cone called Mount Yasur peaks sharply above the plane; to one side, a large pond reflects the bare branches of long-dead trees that reach up from its stillness in supplicant poses. Above us, a steady cloud of light gray smoke issues from the crater. I take in what I can, knowing that when we return in the immaculate darkness of the *ni*-Vanuatu night, I will see none of this.

Beneath the stark landscape, the earth rumbles; the volcano's power is inescapable. It is impossible not to feel small.

I watch the children chasing the ball with Michael, laughing and playing; they look up now and then, glance at Yasur's smouldering crown. Fire is like life, disembodied. And a fascination for volcanoes is ancient and universal among those who live around them. They are touch points with the divine, the dwelling places of gods and spirits. The goddess Péle of the Hawai'ian islands, the Roman god Vulcanus, and *ol bubu* of Mount Yasur are only a few among them.

After soccer, the children run into the stagnant pool and swim before the bone white branches of the trees. Perhaps these children already understand something of death. I sense it is not alien to them, not separate. These girls and boys will not be blindsided by the apprehension of their mortality one fine day in midlife, as we are in the West, witnessing the death of a parent or friend, feeling our bodies dry up. Here, life and death surround them. Their lives—the life of their whole community—are poised in between, at the mercy of spirits, magic, and other mysterious powers. Neither will these children grow up to share our illusions of safety, of dominion, of control. Every day tells them that they are only human, small compared to what lies around them, and strength lies in numbers, in community. In the West, we expect the opposite: that strength lies in our individuality, that we are at the top of all things.

It is too soon after dinner that we start back to the volcano that evening. My stomach is overfull with our hosts' generosity. I bring my flashlight, but one of the older children commandeers it for the walk. They grew up in these long, black nights, and can see in the darkness far better than we can. They walk easily and flick on the torch only for a microsecond if something large is in the path.

Emerging from the forest onto the ash plain, no feature of the landscape is visible to me in the moonless night. Only

Yasur's luminous, amber halo looms in the sky above us, Venus and Saturn standing as sentinels to each side. It is alive, a breath of fire from blackness.

We make our way across the rough ground. The ascent starts immediately and steeply. The children stop us after a few feet, reminding us to be quiet as we walk: no laughing. And then the way grows steeper, though we follow a path of sharp switchbacks. We are ascending the "backside" of the volcano. This is the way the locals go up, not the trucks carrying tourists. On the other side of the volcano, the truck path goes nearly to the top. But we have a long climb ahead of us.

Maybe it is twenty-five minutes, but it feels like forever, walking blind up a sharp incline, beneath us the ash sliding down from our footsteps into nothingness. The cone is so steep, that tipping to one side, I could sit against it; leaning away from it will send me tumbling to oblivion. But we do not rest on the ascent. My rugged sandals are a liability in the deep ash, so I remove them and sink to my ankles in its warmth. As we climb higher, more chunks of dried lava litter our invisible path, and the hillside heats up beneath my feet. The crust is thinner near the top.

The slope ends abruptly, and we are standing on the crater's flat lip. A few feet in front of us yawns its cavernous mouth, nearly a perfect circle. The inner walls are illuminated by the glow of lava somewhere deep below. We approach the mouth cautiously until the children tell us to stop. Standing three feet from the edge, I lean over. Anxiously, children grab each of my hands and lean back. I am contained, held by them.

It is magnificent. Some distance below me—I cannot say how far down—a churning sea of iridescent orange. Above it tiny fairies careen, shimmer and dance, as though in slow motion; whirling drops of radiant lava wheel toward us and then fall back to their source. I am looking back through time, past myself, through the ancestors, and into the eye of God. I have no sense of safety or danger or self-preservation: arched over the mouth of the volcano, I stand outside of time.

Michael interrupts my meditations. "I have a bad feeling about being here," he says. "Let's go."

For the sake of the promise, I follow him. Our descent is rapid. Following the children, we slide and skid haphazardly through the loose ash, running blindly down the cone, like falling. When we hit the flat, we keep moving without words, swimming through the darkness to the edge of the forest. And there we sit on a craggy stone, looking back at Yasur's halo.

We are not seated more than a few seconds when the volcano lets out a momentous boom. Great, glowing whirls of lava explode from its mouth. We watch them twist skyward, searing light and dark as their surfaces cool and break open again. The largest of the globs veers leftward and thuds finally down on the crater's lip, the very spot where only minutes before we were standing. No one says anything as we watch the lava cool and darken until it is invisible in the night.

Elation comes over me. Awe. Wonder. I am completely alive within the bounds of my pressing mortality. Around me, the children share my secret of life in death. And this binds us, binds all people, I know then.

Michael looks at me somberly. "Good call," I whisper. He nods.

Usha Alexander was born to Indian immigrants who came to the United States in the 1950s and settled in Pocatello, Idaho. After studying chemistry and anthropology, she joined the Peace Corps, where she served as a science teacher in Vanuatu from 1997-98. Her first novel was Only the Eyes Are Mine. *She and her partner divide their time between India and Northern California, where she's currently working on a second novel.*

✳
✳

Handsin's Story

The grief that comes from the loss of one who dies
too young transcends all cultural boundaries.

N NA URINGA. I WILL REMEMBER.

The tide seems still now. I'm not sure when it will turn. It's the moon's first quarter, so the changes are gentle. I've come to the beach because my spirit needs gentling. There's someone on my mind, something I must understand.

Handsin was the last of the three boys to be born, seven years younger than Retiire, who became a seaman. His sister, Eute, wrote to him occasionally from Fiji, where she was a student at the University of the South Pacific. She had been paying Handsin's school fees when she had a job, but now everyone in the family had been scraping together whatever they could so that Handsin could graduate from Hiram Bingham High School. Some terms, there just wasn't enough money soon enough, and he would have to stay out of school with his guardians in the nearby village, missing classes, until the next $135 could be found, somehow.

He was sixteen, the youngest in the Form 5 class, slight and small compared to some of the older guys. Still, he was a

member of the island's champion soccer team and a good run-
ner. His light frame made him an agile toddy-cutter high in
the coconut trees, a swift spear-fisherman on the reef, and he
could crawl around rafters following electrical lines with grace
and ease.

Though he was the house commander for his 50 dormitory
members, a job requiring leadership and toughness, it was his
command of *things*, mechanical and electrical, that fascinated
and delighted him. He had been taking things apart for as long
as he could remember, and he often fixed the hopelessly unfix-
able. Curious, persistent, imaginative, and able to improvise,
he definitely had a knack. He wanted to learn, and he was
hungry for information and hands-on experience.

He was a good Christian at our church school, but not a
perfect one. He told a few lies, was acquisitive and a bit nosey,
occasionally cheeky, but never really rude. He had few friends,
and his piety covered some regular, serious rule breaking. But
he had a dream, a big one.

In tiny Kiribati, with a national airline fleet of three planes
(total passenger capacity of sixty), he wanted to be the first
native mechanic/avionics repair person to be trained and hired
to replace the New Zealander currently employed. He came to
me, his Peace Corps Volunteer English teacher, hoping I could
help him figure out how to do it. I was willing, but I hadn't a
clue where to start.

I saw an ad for Queensland Aerospace College in Australia,
but the tuition seemed astronomical and the coursework
too theoretical. Then a magazine appeared on the school's
staff room table, meant for a former teacher, unopened
and unwanted. Missionary Aviation Fellowship, it said—a
Christian flying service in Australia, New Zealand, and Papua
New Guinea—with a small mechanics' training program for
local young men in the interior of PNG. Perfect for an i-Kiribati boy who'd been as far as Nauru, but not beyond.

And so began a delightful correspondence with various leaders of what must be the world's friendliest airline. Encouragement and enthusiasm, hopefulness and helpfulness, all flowed from the minds and hearts of these men. But there were difficulties with eligibility and immigration, ultimately, the doors at MAF seemed reluctantly closed to Handsin.

Next we tried a community college in New Zealand. But after three months, I still had no reply of any sort. Patience, we thought. When this term's exams were over and grades recorded, I'd write again. Graduation was still five months away and, during the term holidays, I was returning to America for my daughter's wedding. There I could gather some information and grab some magazines that might lead us in some new directions.

Two months later, and several days after Laurie's marriage, I was returning to the small airport in my hometown in the USA to begin my trip back to my Peace Corps site. On that day, Handsin was lying semiconscious on the floor of Air Kiribati's 30-seat plane, being evacuated from our remote atoll to the country's only hospital on the capital island of Tarawa. He had been ill with a fever for a week, and he'd lost a lot of weight. He died two days later, probably of hepatitis, though none of us here would ever know that for sure. I returned to Beru Island and Hiram Bingham High School on September 8, 1992. That fall I kept waiting for him to show up in class, or at my front door with a question, or with an offer to help me in some way.

Then a letter came from one of those wonderful men at Missionary Aviation Fellowship. He had convinced the Papua New Guinea government people that an i-Kiribati boy wouldn't eliminate a local applicant; MAF would just expand the program by one. The door was suddenly open wide, the dream was coming true. My tears blurred the next words.

I remember my thoughts on that day as the tide was quietly going out going out and I watched the reef herons and the terns as they fished and bathed and napped in the last of today's sunlight. There was no trace of mankind, only the curling crash on the reef, and the gentle lap-lap on the beach. "Am I meant to understand, or only to accept?"

N na uringa teuaei. I will remember him.

Epilogue: In January 2004, I stood at Handsin's grave with his father, Itamaeri, and his sister Eute. I laid the traditional offering, a brightly colored, tropically designed length of cotton cloth, with which we covered the gravelly surface between the large flat rocks forming the border of the grave. We stood in silence, I reliving Handsin's presence at my little concrete house at Hiram Bingham High School, they with thoughts I could only imagine. I-Kiribati have no easy access to their feelings of sadness, so Itamaeri had only a vaguely melancoly demeanor and clasped hands.

Later, over plastic cups of tea mixed with coconut toddy, Itamaeri said he had been reminded today of the intensity of his sadness on Handsin's death. He wanted to exhume the bones and move them to Aranuka, the home island, to keep him close to his grandparents' gravesite. He said he was glad I had come, for now we could all celebrate the young man Handsin was and the part he continues to play in all our lives. I cannot begin to describe my own, long-delayed farewell to the student who continues to teach me almost every day.

Havard Bauer has managed or directed seventeen pre-service trainings for more than 400 Peace Corps trainees in Armenia, Kiribati, Mongolia, Namibia, the Republic of Georgia, Ukraine, Uzbekistan and the Solomon, Marshall and Gilbert islands. She served in the Philippines in 1990 and taught English as a foreign language in Kiribati from 1990-1992. She lives in rural Oregon where a west-flowing mountain creek behind her house sends its waters toward Beru Island.

FARRAR ATKINSON

* ✷ *

The Boarding House

*Some culturally accepted behaviors are so disturbing
they defy reconciliation with the deep affection
Volunteers feel for the places they serve.*

OF MORE THAN EIGHT THOUSAND VOLUNTEERS ASSIGNED TO THE
Philippines since 1961, I may be the only one who departed
the country with a duck on her lap, deliciously roasted and
wrapped in banana leaves. My benefactors prepared it in the
dark of night and rode many kilometers on a Rabbit bus (the
major mode of transportation to and from the provinces) to
join some of my co-teachers, the principal, and former students
at the Manila airport. Their unexpected effort touched my
heavy heart, for I had met them only once when their daughter, a fellow teacher at Manila High, took me to visit them. I
had praised the roast duck they served on that occasion. Thus
they made the long trek to Manila for their farewell.

Hours later, I ate the duck with great relish at the hotel restaurant in Hong Kong, where it cost as much to heat and serve
with rice and vegetables as it would have cost if I had ordered
the whole dinner from their menu.

The view of my wonderful host country through the air-
plane window brought tears, for I believed this was the last

time I would see the warm, generous people. My tenure as a biology teacher at Manila High School, from the fall of 1962 until my departure in May of 1964, was at an end. And while I eagerly anticipated the next three months of travel through the Far East, Middle East and Europe, and would welcome an eventual return home to my biological family in Georgia, I felt great sadness that May morning.

Little did I dream I would make five *babaliks* (return trips) through the years: in 1978 (with my ten-year-old daughter Stefanie) for the baptism of my goddaughter, the daughter of a former student; in 1986 and 1996 with other RPCVs, aided by arrangements through the Minister of Tourism and Peace Corps; one in 2000, and the last one in 2004 when the graduating class of 1964 honored me at their first high school reunion. It seems to some that I might be considered the longest-serving Volunteer, although forty-four of those years have not been in an official capacity.

In 1962, I was a lone assignee to Manila High School, the other two members of my team having been sent to schools in the provinces. Housing was a problem; after a month of temporary accommodations at PC headquarters and at the home of the high school principal, I settled into a boarding house, a female household with the exception of our landlady's nephew, seven-year-old Pedro. My two roommates were older than I: a college professor (part owner of the boardinghouse) and a high school science teacher. Other boarders were college students. The landlady's sisters did the cleaning, laundry, shopping, and food preparation.

While I adjusted early to not having hot water for bathing, unless it was heated, dipped and poured, physical adjustments to climate and diet took their toll. In a few months, I had lost the twelve pounds I had gained during ten weeks of training at San Francisco State. This caused *hiya* (shame) to my landlady who was chided that she was not feeding me well. She remedied that by serving me milkshakes of canned PET milk, raw eggs and sugar, as well as adding bread to my diet of rice, fish and vegetables.

Diet wasn't the only cause of my distress. I came home one day to the screams of Pedro. I rushed into the house and found the boy stripped to the waist, bent over his cot while his aunt Belena whipped him with a belt. She was so enraged, she paid no attention to my hand on her shoulder or my plea to stop. I could not bear such brutality and ran to a neighbor's place. They advised me not to interfere. Belena must have good reason to discipline the boy. Later, one of my roommates told me it was due to a tussle with a classmate, which soiled his uniform. Nothing was said, and Pedro silently went about his business as if nothing happened.

A few months later, emotions again erupted when Belena found her twenty-six-year-old sister at the movies holding hands with her boyfriend. Our irate landlady decreed Tita would be shipped back to the provinces in disgrace, to work in the rice paddies. Tita, with bruised arms and tear-swollen eyes, vowed she would jump off the boat and drown herself. My roommate intervened. The youngest, actually a half-sister, could not possibly do all chores necessary to keep the household running, especially since the poor girl was trying to attend college herself.

Tensions tightened, especially at mealtime. Belena's grim face dared anyone to question or defy her.

Some weeks later we came home and found the half-sister with a black eye and bruises, cowering in her lower bunk. The cause of that abuse was her spending ten centavos too much for a half head of cabbage.

These incidents aggravated my digestive system, so I visited our Peace Corps physician. He recommended I eat nothing but baby food for three weeks. Not funny, but I did as directed.

Months passed before the next catastrophe. I was spared what transpired between Belena and Pedro when she discovered he had been stealing. His cache of purloined centavos in a little hole in the wall near his cot may have been his effort to save enough for passage home to his mother. We had not missed the coins. All the boarders felt pity for the little boy who was never permitted to join other kids out in the street— they might teach him to play cards and gamble. He perched behind the bars of the bedroom window while he wistfully watched other kids play below.

All these events prompted me to talk with our Filipino Peace Corps psychiatrist. Baby food had not relieved my abdominal distress. Having been a psychology major, I guessed the stress of my living conditions contributed to my physical malady and consequent weight loss.

After discussing why Belena was so dictatorial and controlling, I realized several things. She did not measure up to expectations of herself and tried to appease her psyche by finding fault with others and by attempting to control their actions. I had learned several things from my roommate: Her mother came from a wealthy family that disowned her when she ran away with the Japanese chauffeur. Belena and her siblings were raised in poverty, so she determined to better herself. She had broken off her long engagement after her fiancé failed his bar exam three times.

Her behavior was unlikely to change, so I needed to seek other accommodations. It had to be done with delicacy so as not to cause Belena *hiya*.

That summer, our group had a training seminar at the University of the Philippines. Despite my living close enough to commute by bus, PC staff agreed I needed to be on campus with the other Volunteers. In the meantime, Joan, another lone Volunteer, had been assigned to a high school in Manila.

Before classes began, I retrieved my belongings and joined Joan in our move to an apartment house across town. Some Filipino acquaintances asked if the government was paying us extra to live together, for Joan was black and I, Caucasian.

The second year, my health problems disappeared. The time passed swiftly. Our last few weeks in Manila were filled with *despedidas* (farewell parties) and visitors with *pasalubong* (gifts). The guidance counselor at my high school brought a large box of mangoes—my favorite. "Eat enough to make yourself sick. Then you won't miss them so much," she advised. The home economics teachers got together and made a gorgeous peach colored *terno,* the formal dress of Filipinas. They sewed tiny seed pearls on the gold embossed flowers adorning the delicate pineapple fiber material. The big stiff butterfly sleeves were detachable so the dress could be worn without them.

My seamstress made another *terno* with material purchased by her son, one of my students. They felt *utang* (obligated), for the boy came to me one day in great pain with a tiny fleck of metal in his eye. They had no money, the note said, so I rushed him to my Filipino ophthalmologist who removed the fragment just in time to prevent blindness in that eye. Before I left Manila, I shipped their beautiful teal *terno* and the peach one to my home in Georgia in a trunk full of *pasalubong.* Those still hang in my closet, too small to fit my current figure, but they look great on my granddaughter.

Epilogue: In most disturbing stories, one wonders what became of some characters.

During the 2000 *babalik,* Imelda—a former student and my hostess on all return trips—arranged a visit to a teacher's retirement community where Belena lived with her younger sister. Tita still filled the role of maid. I asked about Pedro and was told he was *mataba* (fat) and had a family of his own.

Then, on a recent March night, my telephone rang at 12:30 A.M. Imelda was visiting her oldest daughter in San Francisco and had forgotten the three-hour time difference between there and Georgia.

"Oh, *Ate* Far, (*ate* is a Filipino term for "older sister," by which all my former students address me), Sheina called from home to tell me that 'Mum' Belena died. The maids found her in the comfort room with a head injury. She was dead before the ambulance reached the hospital."

Imelda called again several days later. "Mum, it was no accidental fall or health problem. Belena was murdered! Her two young maids had chicken pox, so when someone knocked on the door that night, Mum Belena ordered the girls to stay in their room. She admitted the visitors herself. The maids heard loud voices, gunshots and were terrified. After the visitors left, they found Belena unconscious and called the ambulance."

Both Imelda and I believe Belena knew her assailants. I wonder if the killers were boyfriends of the maids, who might have been forbidden to call on the girls. Had a mistreated family member sought revenge?

Some mysteries are never solved, but if this one is, I shall probably hear of it although I am half way around the world. My former students and I remain as close as my computer or the telephone.

Farrar Atkinson served in the Philippines, Group V, from 1962-64. A "perpetual PCV," she remains in contact with more than thirty of her students. Half a dozen have visited her in Georgia. She gets emails or Facebook messages almost daily and attends special celebrations with Filipinos who live near her.

MICHAEL LEVY

*

Parmesan and Politics

What would Marx have to say about "eating bitterness"?

I WENT ON A CHEESE-BUYING EXPEDITION WITH A CHINESE friend yesterday. Teacher Ma—a colleague in the English department of Guizhou University—is one of the few people I know with a palate for Western food. She's been asking me for months to teach her to cook pizza. I have an oven (purchased from one of the only other foreigners in this city of 2 million), olive oil (available at the local Wal-Mart), and can easily find flour and vegetables. The cheese, however, is a bit of a problem. Ma assured me we could find some, and with her help, I ended up buying a two-foot long, twenty-five pound log of frozen Parmesan at a restaurant supply store—enough cheese for a year.

As we rode the minibus back to campus, I started reading. Reading is a little difficult on Chinese buses, because you often have someone sitting on your lap. But I was engrossed in Cornel West's *The Ethical Dimensions of Marxism* and wanted to finish, no matter how nauseous I felt.

Ma did not have a seat, so she was squatting to my side. She saw the title of the book, and was clearly taken aback. "Do you believe in Marx?"

I am never really sure how to parse that question, though I've been asked dozens of times by Chinese friends. What, exactly, does it mean to "believe" in Marx? Since this was no time for ontology, I went for a simple answer: "Yes, I do."

Ma was shocked. Her eyes opened wide and her jaw dropped. "So you do not believe in God?"

This was not the follow-up question I was expecting, and I paused to ponder the implications. As I pondered, the bus swerved to miss a man carrying a pig carcass on his back.

"Um…I am Jewish, so I don't really have to believe in God." I can't imagine why those were the words I chose, but the statement was more or less true, and that's what popped out. I continued: "But this author is an interesting man. He is black, and Christian, and also a socialist."

"How can he believe in Marx and be a Christian?" Ma was tossed into my lap by another swerve of the bus, and blushed a bit before she regained her balance.

"Hmmm." I scratched my chin as I pondered an answer. "I think he believes that Marx guides his head, and God guides his heart." That seemed to be a reasonable summary.

"That is an interesting belief," Ma said while nodding. "In China, we have to study Marx. I remember when I wanted to go get a Ph.D. I took the entrance examination for that degree and scored well on four of the sections, but my politics score was one point too low. So I failed."

Ma said all of this without emotion. She was *chi ku*—eating bitterness—a common practice for Chinese women. "What," I asked, "does politics have to do with your abilities as an English doctoral student?"

"Nothing. It is stupid. But I scored 59 on the Marxism section, so I could not apply for a doctor's degree."

The bus swerved again, this time so the doorman could haul an old man in a Mao suit onboard. Each minibus has a driver who tries his best never to come to a complete stop, and a doorman who tries to round up business. After making sure the old man was reasonably safe, he leaned out of the open door and screamed "HUAXI! HUAXI!" He was letting everyone know where we were going.

I didn't want Ma to feel too depressed about the inanity of the testing system in China, so I tried to draw a parallel: "Americans must also study their government. We call it 'civics' class."

"But do you need to pass an exam on civics to go to college?"

"No."

"Are you forced to study civics every year from elementary school through graduate school?"

I shook my head. My attempt to cheer her up had obviously failed.

A jolt, a screech of metal-on-metal, and an increase in G-forces as the bus shimmies to a halt. I grab Ma by the elbow to keep her from flying into the windshield. All bus rides in China are adventurous, but this was something new. Our bus had nearly collided with another: its rear-view mirror sheared off.

The bus drivers and doormen hopped out and had a quiet *tête-à-tête*. They were haggling over the price of the broken mirror. It was a typically hot day, and all four hagglers rolled their pants up to their knees and pulled their shirts up above their nipples, two common ways that local men cooled off under a hot sun. I wondered who would pay whom? The accident seemed to be the fault of the other bus, but I couldn't understand what the two men were saying during their bargaining session.

I looked at Ma. Her face was blank. She continued: "The second time I took the exam, I cheated. All of the students cheat. The teachers usually allow it."

I wonder what she meant by "cheat." Was I in a moment of cultural misunderstanding? A few months ago I would have been shocked to hear a teacher say she cheated her way into graduate school. Now I am not the least bit surprised. "Well," I said, "if the test is stupid, perhaps it is smart to cheat."

"Yes." Ma was now staring with me at the four men standing outside of the bus. They were exchanging money, their dispute resolved. "Most Chinese students are very good at cheating. I also cheated in gym class and in our military class. All students in China must learn the names of all of the weapons, and how large the army is, and the things it has done. And we must learn to march. But we always cheat. No one really cares."

Our driver returned and was quickly asked who won in the bargain. He smiled a gap-toothed smile, and started the engine. "I think if I had to take a class on marching, I would also cheat. But do students cheat on more important tests?"

Ma turned to me and raised her eyebrows. "Here in our China, there is no shame in cheating. I have heard that in America, if a student cheats, the other students will scorn him and make him feel shame. This does not happen here."

The bus began moving again. I was finding this conversation a little bit depressing. Ma continued:

"I caught a student cheating last weekend on the national English exam. I was a proctor. She was getting the answers through her cell phone." Ma was looking directly at me, speaking slowly. "The student looked at the phone and I asked her why. She said she was looking at the time. I told her I would tell her the time, and I took her phone. When I looked at it, it had a text message with all of the answers. She probably paid three or four thousand kuai for this information. But she is not very bright. This was the final exam of her college career, and now she will be expelled."

This was a surprise! I had never heard of any consequence for cheating in China other than having to take the test again, and often not even that. But perhaps for the national exams it is a different story.

"I am sorry you were put in that situation. That sounds stressful."

"Yes," Ma says, looking down at her shoes. "My mother told me I was foolish for turning the student in because she will hate me forever. There is another teacher in our department who had the same situation, but he did not turn in the student because the student begged him. If I hated this teacher, I would tell the department, and he would be in trouble. But cheating is the Chinese way."

We were finally nearing the University. I put away my book and got ready for the mad push to the door that I knew would begin when we got within about twenty yards of the school gate. I held the frozen log of cheese against my chest as a battering ram. Ma and I smashed our way forward as the bus door opened to expel those of us who had reached our destination. We barely reached the pavement before the bus barreled off again. "HUAXI! HUAXI!" barked the doorman.

Ma patted dust off of her blouse. "Perhaps I can read your book someday, though it is probably very boring. Marx is very boring." Most Chinese think Marx is boring because they've never read anything he wrote. All they've read are the sanitized summaries approved by the government.

I decide to take a risk: "Tell you what: if you can get me invited to the next Party meeting, I will lend you my book." I had always wanted to go to a Communist Party meeting, and this seemed like a good chance.

"Why would you want to come to a Party meeting? They are also so very boring."

"Well, I read in *The New York Times* that Party members are being asked to study Marxism more closely and to self-criticize. I would like to see this for myself."

As we approach the door to my apartment, Ma agreed to call me for the next meeting. "I think you will not enjoy it. But I think you can attend."

What I had read in the *Times* was that China's Communist Party is using a Mao style "ideology campaign" to try to stem corruption and reinvigorate itself. All Party members were apparently being forced to spend hours in study groups, memorizing slogans. The campaign was being called *bao xian* ("protecting the progress"). Jim Yardley, one of the China reporters for the *Times*, wrote that "for fourteen months and counting, the party's 70 million rank-and-file members have been ordered to read speeches by Mao and Deng Xiaoping, as well as the numbing treatise of 17,000-plus words that is the party constitution. Mandatory meetings include sessions where cadres must offer self-criticisms and also criticize everyone else."

Would this help stem the tide of cheating Ma saw as so pervasive? Doubtful. But I knew it would be interesting to see what a *bao xian* session was actually like. Foreigners are technically not allowed at Party meetings, since we're not Party members, but out here in the boonies Beijing's rules are often ignored. With luck, I would be able to attend.

The rest of the afternoon was spent cooking pizza. Chinese politics seemed far away as we broke bread.

Michael Levy is a writer and teacher currently living in Northampton, Massachusetts, with his lovely wife Becca and his fish, Bartholomew. Before moving to Northampton, he and Becca served as PCVs in western China where they taught English at Guizhou University. Mike wishes he could live behind home plate at Wrigley Field, eating deep-dish pizza every day.

MARSHA MARTIN WEST

The Week of the Jackal

A protective ceremony by a local healer required the
animal's fur; until then, a doctor would have to do.

THE DOCTOR SET THE NEEDLE BESIDE THE SPOOL OF PLAIN BLACK
sewing thread. Suddenly, my head was spinning and the lights
seemed to dim. As I started to faint, the doctor caught me
and set me down in a chair. It embarrassed me to display such
weakness after he had done me such a great favor. He left me
to recuperate in a darkened examination room. He dismissed
the patient to the lobby to wait for me.

That morning I had been working in the community
demonstration garden as I had done most mornings for the past
year or so. As I was hoeing between rows of okra and eggplant,
a group of tribal women—Adivasi—approached at a distance.

The Adivasis, we had learned in training, are the native
people of the area, while the Hindus and Muslims arrived
much later. They are darker, taller and slimmer than the people
who live in the valleys. They have stronger teeth and bones
than other groups in India because—at least partially—they
eat both the bones of the animals they kill and a native grain
ground on a sandstone high in calcium. Although they have

adopted many practices of the dominant Hindu culture, they continue to worship turtles and other animal totems along with Krishna, Ram, and the other Hindu gods. Their life expectancy is only in the forties, however, because they live a hard and precarious life.

I saw them as they climbed down the hill and crossed the dry, rocky streambed. I then lost sight of them as they walked the mile and a half to the garden near my home. This group lived on land owned by a local farmer. They built houses of mud and sticks and would stay as long as he would let them. They could hunt and gather enough to eat. Some Adivasis wandered over quite an area, but this tribe had pretty much settled on the outskirts of Warandh.

When I was completing a nutritional survey of the 300 families in the area, I went into the Adivasi *wadi* with its thirty shacks and inadvertently stirred up a controversy there. I tried not to take a stand, but had to admit when asked that I didn't eat rats. The Adivasi proceeded to debate whether eating rats was acceptable. In the end, they pretty much agreed to disagree. Some ate them and some didn't. The consensus was that the two groups shouldn't intermarry, but they could all live in the same village.

A few of the strong Adivasis would earn a coin or two harvesting rice. They would glean the fields after harvest, the biggest part of their pay. They swept up the rice that fell off the shaft during harvesting, using brooms they made of reeds that grew by the river. That rice they got to keep.

I had never seen Adivasis come to the garden before, and thought perhaps it was a good sign that they now wanted to participate in my program. I knew they were about to tell me to cut off the handles of my hoes and shovels. The local tools all required people to squat to work in the fields. Standing up seemed unnatural to them, although far more comfortable and efficient to me. I thought if they'd just give it a try they would come to see the advantages.

"Marshatai," they called me, meaning Marsha-little-sister.

I looked up and knew something was wrong. I saw Shantabai, an Adivasi mother whose two children attended my preschool—*balwadi*—and feeding program, holding her mouth while blood dripped to the ground. My stomach contracted and my saliva turned bitter in my mouth. Shantabai is a Hindu name meaning Peaceful Woman: *Shanta* means "peace" and *bai* is a respectful way of addressing a woman. Shantabai and I seemed to have a special connection because the name for my position, Peace Corps Volunteer, is *shanti duth* from the same word stem.

I ran over to Shantabai and could see her mouth was torn from the bottom lip half way down her neck. She could not put her hand down because the blood would gush instead of drip. She tried to tell me what had happened, but it was difficult for her to talk. Her friend Godabai explained that because the rains were late, they had to walk many miles to get water. As Shantabai walked to a distant river, she had been attacked by a jackal.

I knew a jackal that attacked a human almost had to be rabid. Normally, they are far too cautious to approach people. The chance of contracting rabies from a rabid jackal bite are better than 50-50. The local doctor, Doctor Garge, with a only Bachelor's of Medicine and Bachelor's of Surgery, could not treat this woman. There was no electricity and no refrigeration in Warandh, so there could be no rabies vaccine. Shantabai had never been to any doctor in her life. Although she had wandered in the jungle, she had never been to a city. She had never ridden in a bus. How could I get her in a bus, fourteen miles away, to Mahad, to the doctor? The only bus to Mahad today would be leaving in less than an hour.

I was glad this hadn't happened when I first got to Warandh, over a year and a half before. I could not have begun to explain what was needed, would not have had a shot of convincing her to go. The Adivasis explained to me that if they could find the jackal that attacked her, they could kill it and give the fur to the healer. He would perform a ceremony that would protect her. Their concern was that the jackal hadn't been located. I didn't argue with their logic, but just encouraged treatment by the doctor in Mahad. At the end of my talk, they agreed that Shantabai would go to Mahad with me.

I washed the wound at my house with cooled water that had been filtered and boiled twenty minutes to kill all the parasites. Shantabai was very brave and did not make a sound. I applied antiseptic ointment and a temporary bandage. The wound was so large that Shantabai still had to hold it closed even with the multiple gauze pads taped in place.

We walked the length of ten blocks to the bus stop on the one paved road through Warandh. The bus is called an S.T., even in Marathi "Ess Tee," for State Transport. Shantabai was stoic, although she had to be in great pain. I wish I had thought to give her an aspirin at the house, although I'm not sure she could have swallowed it with all the blood. She squatted barefoot in the shade of the bus station with fifteen other people waiting. She was the only one clothed in dirty, torn rags. She was the only person waiting whose hair was matted with dirt, leaves and twigs. But, then, she was the only Adivasi waiting for the bus. My greater concern: she was the only one bleeding. The bandage had bled through. But as my concern grew, the blood started to dry. The flow had almost stopped.

As we waited, I really looked at Shantabai. Her eyes were so dark brown I couldn't distinguish her iris from her pupil. She had lovely, high cheekbones. Her nose and ears seemed small for her head. I'd guess she was seventeen years old.

She was one of the tallest women in the village, almost five-foot-two. With very slim shoulders and hips, she probably weighed eighty pounds. In the nutrition survey, I'd weighed many Adivasis. Many adults were less than sixty five pounds. Shantabai's teeth were large for her mouth, straight, and very white. Her skin was the color of a Nestlé chocolate bar. She had calluses on her elbows and knees, and some insect bites on her chest. The muscles in her arms, in her legs, even on her abdomen, looked compact and strong.

Despite her obvious lack of hygiene, I detected no body odor. Several people started complaining that the S.T. was late again. Shantabai said softly to me that it would come soon enough. The idea of getting on the bus scared her more than going to the doctor. I was used to seeing Shantabai with a scrap of material on her head as she carried a clay pot of water there and one child on her hip. She always smiled big. I hoped she would get that smile back soon and would survive to care for her children.

The S.T. arrived. It had been bright red the last time it was washed, but the dusty roads made it a red-gray. The driver took my money for two seats. Shantabai looked at my change. It was probably more money than she had ever touched in her life. Many Adivasis did not participate in the cash economy at all. As the bus loaded, some people tried to crawl in the windows so they wouldn't have to pay, but other riders would not let them in. Passengers were yelling at each other and yelling goodbyes and last-minute instructions to those outside the bus. I tried to protect Shantabai's mouth from elbows, luggage, and crates. She stayed right with me. The metal seats were hard. Brown-red *areconut* juice stained the floor where passengers had chewed and spit. There was an odor of dirty humans and diesel exhaust in the air. The bus rocked in the ruts, but then pulled out. The passengers finally settled down.

Shantabai said nothing, but rode with her eyes closed. I tried to get her to open her eyes to see the sights on the way. I suspect it was all too much for her and decided to give her her peace.

We walked the twelve blocks to the government health clinic in Mahad, passing shops, street vendors, and bakeries, Shantabai still holding the flesh over her jaw. The clinic was closed for an in-service training. Refusing to be discouraged, I asked directions and took Shantabai to a private physician. We must have been a sight, the white woman in native dress, leading a bleeding Adivasi.

The doctor took us in immediately. He admired the job I had done in cleaning the wound. I felt proud. He explained that he didn't have any anti-rabies serum, but it would not be too late to start that treatment tomorrow at the government clinic that would be open. It would take fourteen daily shots. He then asked me to hold Shantabai down on the exam table. The nurse held her legs. The doctor took a plain sewing needle and plain black sewing thread. I held her arms tightly. She squirmed as the doctor sewed up the horrible wound with nothing to dull the pain. Just when I was no longer needed, I passed out. The doctor never charged me.

Shantabai did come back to Mahad with me the following day. The government nurse pinched the tiny amount of flesh available above Shantabai's belly button and injected the serum. We returned to Mahad about nine times. Then the jackal was caught. The healer with the jackal hairs performed his ceremony, and the Adivasi tribe members saw no reason for Shantabai to continue a pilgrimage to Mahad.

When I left Warandh for good about four months later, I saw Shantabai smiling. I hope the smile continued. The incubation period for rabies had not yet passed.

Marsha Martin West (then Marsha Privee) served in the village of Warandh, Taluka Mahad, Jilla Kolaba, in the state of Maharashtra, India, during her Peace Corps service from 1971-74. She currently lives in Highland City in central Florida and runs a small non-profit agency.

* ★ *

A Different Kind of House Guest

*It doesn't matter who you were or when you
died; in Samoa your bones are sacred.*

WHEN I FOUND I WOULD BE LIVING IN A TROPICAL PARADISE, I
had visions of warm sun, gentle breezes, and white sand beaches
rolling into brilliant aquamarine waters teeming with an array of
life forms not seen in the cold waters of the Pacific Northwest.
I did not have visions of spending a night with the bones of a
long deceased Samoan girl in the room next to mine.

I was posted to a small village of just forty-three families,
and as the honored *pisikoa,* I lived in the home of the village
High Chief from which I had an oceanside view of the vast
South Pacific. The dock where fishing boats, doubling as ferry
boats, brought people to and took them away from our island
was just a few hundred yards from my living room. The waves
lapped on the seawall just outside my bedroom window, and
at high tide sometimes were uncomfortably close. But this was
paradise, so no worries. It was an idyllic setting: exactly what I
expected a South Sea island village to be.

Living in the High Chief's home had its perks like running
water, flush toilet, and electricity. It also had disadvantages, as

I found when the former High Chief died. There was to be a funeral with burial to follow in the family plot in front of the house. A long time ago, Samoans buried their dead in cemeteries much as we do. However, when the Spanish flu decimated the population in 1918, so many people died that the cemeteries filled up. With nowhere else to put them, families took their loved ones home and buried them in front of their homes, placing large cement slabs and elaborate monuments over their cement-lined graves. This burial system has become the norm, and thus it was to be with our former chief. There were preparations to be made, a grave to be dug, and arrangements to be made to accommodate all the visitors who would stay at least one night. There was food to be prepared for the feast that would follow. The family compound was buzzing with people.

In the middle of all this activity, a young village boy arrived with a message that I was wanted on the telephone. Even the High Chief does not have a phone in the house, so I walked back with the boy across the village square to use the community phone located in the Women's Center. I finished my call, and then walked back to the compound with a message for one of the women who was working on the burial arrangements. I found her in the family meetinghouse adjacent to the residence.

As I approached, I noticed that she and another woman were sitting on the floor with a pile of something in front of them. They appeared to be washing those things in an infant bathtub, wiping them dry, and putting them in another pile. It wasn't until I was directly in front of them that I realized what they were washing. It was human bones. I cannot say I was shocked, appalled, or horrified, but I was certainly surprised. I attempted to behave nonchalantly, delivered my message, and retired to the main house where I was free to indulge my curiosity about what I had just witnessed.

A family member told me that when they were digging the new grave, they came upon the remains of a girl, a poor unfortunate soul from the time of the flu who had not had sufficient family status to warrant a cement crypt or even a marker, but who had simply been buried in the ground next to another grave. A lack of status then did not, however, lessen an enduring cultural imperative: the bones of the deceased are sacred and must be treated with respect. So they were gently collected, lovingly washed and dried, and then placed on a ceremonial mat and wrapped into a bundle, which was carried into the house and placed respectfully on a table in the room next to mine. When the burial of the High Chief was completed the next day, a new small grave was dug, and the Samoan girl returned to her permanent resting place, this time covered by a proper cement slab.

At first I found the experience a bit bizarre, wondering in an arrogantly Western way, "Where is the coroner when you really need one?" But then I began to appreciate the hands-on love and respect that was bestowed upon this girl many decades after her death by people who never knew her. I realized that perhaps the efficiency and sterility of our world could use some humanizing.

Lili Yocom served in Samoa from 2006-07 as part of the Village-Based Development program to convert an unused building into a health center and to renovate and acquire books for the elementary school library. She is currently enjoying retirement and volunteering with a therapeutic riding program and with a WSU Extension program called Beach Watchers.

L E L A   L A N T Z

The River at My Door

In a land where monsoonal floods and storm surges routinely fill homes with water, a mere four inches on the floor amounts to a puddle.

It was Saturday night and a neighbor in my town of Sunamganj knocked on my window to tell me to put all of my things up high. The water was coming. It had been raining incessantly for days, and the river had been steadily rising, coming close to crawling over the edge of its boundary line. That night the river overflowed and started moving up the street. I was ready to move to my new house the next day, but I hadn't been able to move for the last two days because no *tel-agari* (a large wagon pulled by a human) could work in a monsoon downpour, so I just had to wait until the rain stopped.

Early in the morning it was raining lightly. When I opened the front gate leading to the street, I just stared unbelievingly at a river before me! I thought that I was really stuck, that I wouldn't be able to move anywhere. Then I realized that the water at my gate couldn't be more than a foot deep. I would just have to wade through it to take my things to the new house.

I filled up a plastic bucket with possessions, put the lid on it to keep out rain, put on my bright red poncho, rolled up my pants, put the hood of the poncho over my head, made sure the lid was snuggly attached to the bucket, tucked it safely under my poncho and slowly made my way through the river and up the street.

I must have looked silly. Several people watched me wade and some asked if the water had entered my home. No, my house was not flooded. I was moving. Certain that the water was rising and going to enter the old house within a day or two, I tried to move my things quickly. Using only my plastic bucket, I made 70 trips to my new house! The *telagari* owner would move my big furniture later.

Not even a full week after the water level of the first flood decreased, the river swelled again and rose feet within hours. By night it was up to the main street. The whole town was on the watch. This was going to be a major flood! That night at 11, I took one last look at the water level, and it was just three inches away from the door of my new house, threatening to come in. At 1 A.M., I made sure everything was off the floor except my alarm clock and my shoes. I spread the last of the ant killer on a bunch of tiny intruders near my bed, put up my mosquito net, hoping it would help keep out the ants, and went to bed with the light on.

I slept very little, dreaming about ants in my bed, then woke up with an urgent need to use the bathroom. Pushing aside my mosquito net, I put my hand on the floor in search of my sandals. Instead, my fingers found water. Water had entered the house! Since the electricity had gone out, I couldn't assess the situation. By my bed, the water wasn't more than an inch deep, but the floor was uneven, so I didn't know how much water was really there, or if there were any snakes in the water. And stupid me had left the candle on the table across the room. I tried to make sense of the situation with the light of the frequent lightening bolts. I considered urinating over the end of the bed, but decided not to since I didn't want to smell the stench all night nor in the morning.

Finally I recalled going to two other houses that had been inundated in the previous flood and remembered that there had been no danger in walking around in those houses. So I bit the bullet, put on my sandals, and carefully made my way in the dark through the deepening water to the bathroom. I had to feel my way to the toilet and hoped I would not fall into my low Bangladeshi commode. Once I relieved myself, I found the candle and matches and, not wanting to stand in the water longer than I had to, hurried back to my bed. There were no snakes or bugs in sight: a relief.

A strange sensation did come over me. As I sat there inside the protection of the mosquito net holding my lit candle, I had flashbacks to my childhood camping trips. I once again felt that I was safe in my tent.

As I sat for a few minutes on my bed comforted by the little candle, I could hear rain coming down in white sheets outside. The rain no longer sounded like cats and dogs. It had graduated to elephants and dinosaurs! I couldn't imagine what the rain must be like in the mountains just north of us. I had never witnessed so much rain and water in my life. Right now the deepest water in my room was three or four inches. I wondered how much more the water would rise before morning.

Nearby I could hear voices and occasional yelling. I was surprised they had so much energy in the middle of the night. Although I didn't realize it at the time, the next morning I was to find out that all those voices were from the traffic in the street of people abandoning their homes, looking for higher shelter as the water level persistently rose. When I was finally ready to sleep again, I lay down next to my burning candle and let it tuck me safe and sound into bed and wish me sweet dreams. Then I blew it out and held onto it while the lasting sensation of its peace finally led me to sleep.

Bright and early in the morning, I opened the door to greet my friend whose newly opened computer shop was beginning to flood. As he walked through my house, he assessed my situation. I was happy to have someone to talk to. He reminded me to take all precautions for flooding and power outages. We boiled water for drinking and stored normal water in buckets. We left the stove gas turned on very slightly to avoid cut-off from the water.

I went to the second floor to stand on the veranda and observe the situation on the street. Some people were carrying their belongings and going to shelters. Other people were simply taking walks in the water, looking at the worst flood the town had experienced in over seventy years. There were rickshaws carrying passengers and fighting their way through the strong waters. I even saw a few boats transporting people. In amazement, I took some pictures and returned to my room to get ready for work.

My friend told me I was crazy for going to work. I told him that the microfinance workers of my NGO go out in all kinds of weather. If they had to continue to work, so did I. I put on the bright red poncho my thoughtful mother had sent me and my bright yellow fluffy flip-flops. I put my bag over my shoulder and started my trek through the river.

Everyone stared at me. "Who is that?" "What is she wearing?" "Look at those shoes!" I ignored all the comments and kept trekking. On most of the road to work, the water was ankle deep. I assumed the situation would improve once I hit the main road of the town.

Boy was I wrong! The main road in town was lying under a full foot of water. Everybody thought I was out looking at the flood, when actually I was on my way to work. A few people I knew stopped me in the street, and after I told them I was going to work, they reminded me all offices were closed.

"Mine's not. My office never closes!" I exclaimed.

They told me I wouldn't even be able to get there. There was too much water. So I decided to go to a friend's house on the way and call from there. That road was covered in thigh-high water. Good heavens! When I called the office, my colleague told me not to come. "You won't be able to come! The water will be up to your neck!"

On my way home again, I stocked up on what little food, candles, and matches I could find in the market, passed several people who were now using boats for transportation instead of the usual rickshaws, and ignored comments about my unusual outfit. I was extremely lucky. I was cautious about how much water I used; but my building still had some water stored in the tank, so I was not yet in an emergency situation. My gas had not yet been cut off, so I was still able to cook, although with difficulty. And since there were only four inches of water in my house, it was still livable.

My friends, and most of the town's people for that matter, were not so lucky. Except for four or five houses in the entire town, everything was flooded, and most of those houses flooded to the extent that people had to temporarily relocate to buildings with second and third floors. Some of my friends had waist- or neck-high water in their houses. Good grief!

After a couple of days of touring the drowned city and realizing the horrors of the reality, I was finally able to return to my office. There, to my pleasant surprise, staff members were engaged in making tortillas and solid molasses and putting them in relief packages with candles and matches to be distributed to poor people out in the villages. This was the beginning of a long process of able people reaching out and attempting to minimize the suffering of those poor, less fortunate people who were the real victims of this terrible flood.

Lela Lantz served in Bangladesh from 2000-01. After completing her service as an English teacher in Sunamganj, a small town located near the Indian border, she remained in Bangladesh, working with several development projects and facilitating educational visits between the U.S. and Bangladesh. After September 11, 2001, her group was evacuated in advance of the politically volatile parliamentary elections.

LISA McCALLUM

Foreigner! Forever

The safety net of the home village is rarely torn
by children who point and shout.

I LIVE IN A COUNTRY WHERE PEOPLE USED TO EAT EACH OTHER. Besides tree bark and weeds, the flesh of dogs and fellow villagers helped them survive. This occurred not during some long-ago era of cavemen; it was about forty years ago, but I am not sure when it ceased. Perhaps people still eat each other, in one way or another, to go on living here. I believe they do; I have seen signs of it.

Today I feel a tingle in my legs of excitement and nervousness and the need to walk. I need to get out in this one day of blue sky and white puffy clouds streaking above on my balcony. Feeling the cool breeze through my long-sleeved t-shirt, I turn back inside and head for my tennis shoes.

Shoes on, headphones in ears, I walk across concrete stairs and past tall firs, little patches of grass, huge bushes of lavender blooms, to the front gate. Outside, the road is all mud dragged over from the construction going on at the river, eventually to be turned into another Chinese dam. I try to pick through the mud for a minute to head out on the road to the peasants' fields of vegetables and pigsties, the usual path out the front gate, but today I can't cope with the mud. I turn back, through the gate at the left side, past the gatekeeper's hut, and up the hill, across the campus of the college where I teach, and out the back gate. I finally begin my walk.

The road here goes from my village—with open shops, quiet games of roadside mahjong, and sellers of peaches and watermelons—past a high school. Nearby are several more schools, so children always run around the road and play games around the schoolyards. Today is a Sunday, so there are several children. I picked today to walk because it is Sunday; I always think about the day and time before I walk. If it is a weekday or a busy time, when children are running around, when people are eating, I forego my walk. I can't walk at those times.

There are always people. I let this sentence slip out once to my students. Giving an oral test for a final exam, we walked around campus and stopped at three places before I finished giving everyone the test. There are always people who want to listen to what I have to say, even though they can't understand it. I speak a form of gibberish to them, yet they stand fascinated, ear cocked near me, stopping all action and conversation to hear my words.

Today I walk down the road past more shops filled with the same goods as in my village, the same goods as in town, the same goods as in every small Chinese town in every province. Soy sauce, instant noodles, rotting candy, stale crackers, old cookies, soda, beer. The necessities. People look at me, then walk past. They stop what they are doing, look up, look at me, look at my shoes and in my eyes and at my chest, as I walk past. They take in every movement. They drink in my existence without knowing my name or country of origin. They all look at me. Sometimes I look back.

I often look at others, the ones who don't look at me or who do look, but then look away, as we Americans have been taught to do. They are the polite ones, the ones I make uncomfortable with my presence. Even they want to look at me, desperately, but they know it is wrong somehow. I look at the old man who eats his noodles by the side of the road and turns the other way after glancing at me. He is not at all interested in my movements. I am amazed. Of course, he is the only one of everyone I happen to meet today who does this; all the others find some reason or way to look at me.

I am violated in my every pore. If it were socially acceptable, I would live in a glass house so they could look at me. That would be best; they could watch me eat and sleep and shit. They would like that, just to see if I am really human. I do these things like they do, but I suppose they think I don't. I suppose to them I am like a panda, a freak of nature with strange colors and habits. They have decided, by my shoes and chest and eyes and hair: I am not human. I don't look human. Real people have black hair and yellow skin, they think. I look like those people who live far, far away who produce movies for them to copy illegally. That's who I am. I am one of those. I don't have a name or a country of origin.

"What the hell are you looking at? Can't you see I'm just a person like you? I'm just a person, goddammit. And stop staring at my shoes!" This is my inner monologue, of course. I can't just scream at these people. While my heart races and I try to decide in a split second whether to stare back or pretend to ignore them and read my magazine or look out the window, I begin to sweat under my five shirts and sweaters. They make me nervous; they do, with all those dark black eyes looking me up and down. As if I don't have a right to be here. In their country.

I want to tell them, all the people in my village, college, and town, that I promise I won't interbreed with their beloved race. I promise I'll just teach and come straight on home afterwards without trying to make social contacts. I promise to keep to myself and not ask too many questions about the wretched parts of their history that would make them uncomfortable. Actually, I can't really make these promises because I truly want to find out more. But I do promise, truly and forever, I will not mix my Caucasian essence in with their Han-ness: I will not touch a Han Chinese male. This is strictly forbidden, and I know my limits. I want to tell them this. But the eyes keep following me down the street and make me feel like a whore underneath my layers. In their eyes, I am a prostitute looking to corrupt their young Han, like the blondes in those Hollywood movies, you know, the ones who have sex and enjoy it. That is what I am: the teacher whore.

I walk toward the dam that has been built by hand over the course of two months. Huge, two-foot wide bricks of cement have been hauled up to build it, hauled by peasants called in from all over, I suppose. Some are real construction workers, I can see by their muscles. Others are just hired hands, possibly thrown into the job by the government, because the government can tell anyone to do anything here. I watched them building the dam earlier, but now all is quiet. Two women sit on one end, two children run along another end, and there is a bulldozer ready for action tomorrow parked near the road to town. Two workers sleep sitting up, propped up against an old, tiny house of red bricks. My feet squish mud under my shoes. The road has turned to mud after a stretch of concrete. I turn my Walkman up because a child screams "Foreigner!" at me. I pick my way across the muddy part to the rest of the road, dirt and cow shit, but not as much mud. Another child sees me, yells, "Foreigner!" and points.

I walk on, past the two children running along the top of the dam, past a group of three female students who look at

me, past a child who looks at me, past a group of four male
students who look at me, and past two male peasants who look
at me. I look back. I look back into their eyes and they stare,
smile, I stare, scowl, try to get them to read my mind, which
is crying out, "You are being so rude!" but they don't read it
and continue to stare. I look back at the female students who
seem to sense I don't like it when they look at me, and they
look away and at each other and only back at me when I am
past them, which I don't mind so much even though I can feel
their eyes in my back and of course on my shoes: they always
have to check out the shoes.

I turn back, and walk by the shops I went by before, past
the sleeping workers who haven't moved a bit, past three
people chatting in front of their shop, past their looks. I look
at them and frown because of the sun and because I don't want
to look back at them, but feel I should. I am not in control of
this; I have no control over who looks at me and who doesn't.
I cannot do anything except look at them, except I don't want
to because I am tired of that. I feel so tired after a walk because
I feel I have given them my all, I have defended myself with
scowls and frowns and tried so damn hard to get them to read
my mind. That is what makes me exhausted after a walk, not
the walk itself, for my legs could go much longer.

I pick my way back through the muddy part, past the shops
that are in the curve leading up to my village, and turn my
Walkman up again while I hear a "Hello!" and another and
then another, followed by a "Foreigner!" and a final "Hello!"
before I reach my village. The cookie lady with ice cream and
sodas, the peach sellers, the egg people, the restaurant owners,
and the students sauntering about are all there to protect me
with a shell of my own making. This is safety, a safety net that
only occasionally gets torn by children who yell or look at me.
Otherwise, my scowl vanishes and my frown becomes a slight,

very slight smile on my face. I nod to the restaurant man, the photo shop owner, who smile back and yes, here they know my name. Here I am still the teacher whore, but at least I have a name. A country of origin? Many think I am British, but it's better than just being "Western."

With the sun shining faintly above, my muddy shoes traipse through the village road in about two minutes to the back gate to my hotel, to my apartment. I smile at the photocopy man. I turn off my Walkman; I won't hear too many yells now. I walk to the gate which keeps me "safe" in campus, and hear a very faint "Foreigner" said by a child who is accompanied by three adults. I am thankful he said it softly; so I don't turn to glare at him, but keep on walking.

When I turn the key in the lock of my apartment, I can breathe easily. I throw my stuff on the carpet, take my muddy shoes off carefully to be cleaned later, step inside. This is my home. Try to forget the frustration and the anger, knowing that if it were possible for them to have me live in a glass house, to be observed like an alien, they would do this with no second thoughts.

When Miss Luo says goodbye to me after two years, there are no tears wasted. She is only glad I am going without hassle. The driver loads my eight bags into the school car, and I stand waiting in the doorway. Another teacher strolls up to us. When I show my surprise that I will not be riding alone up to Chengdu, Miss Luo is not caught unawares. I am annoyed as usual at the change of plans, and she is too glad this is my last frustration here.

Bags in the trunk, people packed in (two of them ready to be dropped off in town), Luo stands ready to wish me well. I force her to shake my hand and feel her soft, little, bony hand held limply in my strong one for a second. Then we're off, and we've said goodbye. The car drives away from the place I have lived for two years of my life, and I feel close to nothing. Regret, sadness, elatedness, tenseness, and a bit of excitement at seeing my group members the next day, but not much else. The hills of patchwork farms and the oxen pulling coal carts have already begun to disappear. I try to concentrate on nothing specific, on going home, and relieve my muscles in the back seat as the driver and the teacher chat for the full two hours. My headphones can't drown them out, giving me another reason to be glad to leave. I can't wait for silence.

I feel I have survived with the attitude of one who has walked away from a fire, damaged by heat and blackness, but still able to walk and talk and eventually laugh. I know that I would react differently if I were to go there now, as a tourist. But that is one purpose of Peace Corps: merge with a culture as much as you can, as much as they let you, and see how it changes you. The place where I lived for two years is a tiny blip in a massive country on the other side of the universe, but it was my experience. When I go for walks around my neighborhood, communicate easily in my native language without having to barter for a better price, and laugh and joke with my friends, I relish the freedom of those actions. I am happy to be anonymous.

Lisa McCallum was part of China 3 (1996-98). She is a writer and teacher of adult ESL students in the Twin Cities. Her travel essays, short fiction, and poetry have appeared in Travelmag, Tango Diva, inTravel Magazine, Whistling Shade, Loonfeather, The Mid-America Poetry Review, Rive Gauche, *and* Colere.

CYNTHIA BROZE

✦

A Latex Glove

*When so much is needed, and so little available, the
mind latches on to what seems safe and familiar.*

I WISH I HAD A LATEX GLOVE FOR PROTECTION. JUST ONE. BACK
home I took gloves for granted. Here at Eversly-Child
Leprosarium in the Philippines I have to dodge the blood.

I steady the scalpel. I etch a line on the patient's earlobe,
and a drop rolls onto the collection slide. I hand him a folded
scrap of cloth. "Hold this on your ear," I say in my best 1980
Tagalog, though he speaks Cebuano. I vow to improve my
language by next year.

I pour water into a glass; I pumped it out back. I don't trust
that well: the water's reddish, the handle's rusted. No concrete
around the base, just rotting wood to stand on. I pumped ten
minutes for only half a bucket. Covered my legs with splashes
of dirt.

Sweat dripped down my back to my ankles. I had to run
under the trees for a respite of shade. The sun is not just hot-
ter here; it's intense. Seven degrees from the equator is a hand
held close to a light bulb. My skin burns more in ten minutes
than it did in five hours back in Oregon. No umbrellas in

Eversly-Child like the women use in town to keep smooth and creamy. Out here, skin gets dark and thick.

Why isn't the water pump under the trees where it would be cooler? How far back does that palm forest go? Someone found this forgotten spot in the Philippine island of Cebu. They hacked out acres through 100-foot tall coconut palms to conceal a hospital for people no one wanted.

This morning, without warning, a chartreuse coconut had plummeted down from a treetop: large enough to toss through a hoop, with the velocity to fracture a skull. But it didn't break open. An eight-year-old boy heard the sound and flip-flopped out to retrieve it. I don't know where he came from. He whacked the skin, separated the husk with his three-foot bolo knife. He located the brown dots and split the shell between those two dark eyes to crack it open. If the coconut is dry inside, they don't grate it for recipes; they feed it to the pigs. But it was soft. "*Buko*," he said and smiled at the sweet coconut flesh.

Now I coat the slide with purple dye and heat it with a burner made from a kitchen jar filled with kerosene. I add a counterstain. Will the cells be positive? Is he infected? The microscope is the weight of a glass Coke bottle. A single ocular, the stage, and one knob for lens adjustment. No choice of powers, no cord with a plug. I move close to the window to capture a ray of sunlight. No glass in the window, of course. When I return to Oregon, the brag to my colleagues will be: Have you ever used a microscope lit by the sun?

He's waiting for my answer, standing motionless, his fingers clasped in front of his shirt. He's not the layman's textbook picture of leprosy. He could be a next-door neighbor. Twenty-five years old with a cut of muscles across his upper back. He's blue collar; he lifts something for a living. Eighty-pound burlap sacks of rice? I'll bet he loads the sacks onto a truck at the mill, endless bags to fill the need for the staple used at every meal in this country. Even breakfast. Without rice, food is considered a snack, but rice alone can be a meal. He uses a local greeting: "Did you eat yet," instead of the American, "How are you?" Neither country cares about the reply.

His wife is waiting, too. And their three children. And although he didn't mention it, I'm sure he has a long lineage in his town. Maybe his great-great grandma died last year at the age of 101. She birthed her first child, his great-grandmother, when she was fourteen. The trend continued in his family, so he would know the personality of his antique grandmother for many years.

He has no obvious signs of leprosy—just a light patch on his arm that lacks feeling when I touch it with a pin. But that's enough for suspicion. Leprosy is a bacterium that settles into nerves creating loss of sensation.

There they are. The purple spheres. Minuscule champagne bubbles clinging to each other in a gentle S on the slide. The cells took up the dye.

I look around for soap and paper towels, an American habit I can't break. I pour water on my hands and dry them on my skirt. Too hot for jeans. Too barrio for shorts.

"*Oo,*" I say to him, Tagalog for "yes." He understands he has leprosy. The nurse, my assistant, will explain the details: how medicine keeps the disease from advancing; how it is almost considered a cure. And how some people have side effects. They can't take the medicine, so their disease lives on. I leave the lengthy explanation to her. I'm only here to learn. This assistant nurse of mine cares about the man's outcome, too. She's his wife. She works here at Eversly-Child, so he let me use his ear for my first diagnosis.

I nod and shake his hand. He's wiped a finger under his nose and not washed, we all do it. I hope I don't catch his disease. Leprosy concentrates in nasal secretions.

I don't live in Eversly-Child. I live on the island of Mindoro, north of Cebu, in a village called Sablayan. It's more isolated. No leprosy, but fewer supplies. We pump our water out back. We use empty food jars filled with kerosene and rag-wicks to light our evenings. Or candles. Every night I light a thin four-inch candle, glued to a chair with wax, to read under a blue mosquito net, until the wick burns down. The Peace Corps sent me here. I live in a concrete house of fifteen people: parents, children, cousins, and me. The mother in the house is a doctor: she's fifty years old, and I'm twenty-eight.

Doctora studied medicine in Manila, but moved to Sablayan when she was twenty-six. She had throat cancer five years ago from too much smoking; she breathes through a tracheotomy hole in her throat. You cannot see it—I never have—it's always covered with a scarf. Her voice is air-filled and raspy. When she's excited, she has to cover the hole with her finger so enough air flows past her vocal cords.

My first day in Sablayan, Doctora planted a papaya seed. After only six months, it had grown ten feet and sprouted foot-long fruit. Sunset orange inside, fully matured. I never ate papaya in Oregon.

One day she sliced a papaya in half and left the black seeds on top, a party presentation. The seeds looked like heaping mounds of black caviar. "Eat them," she said. "Guests first." I take chances; I ate without question. But she couldn't hold her laughter for one minute of my crunching. "No one eats those," she smiled. I spit them out. A simple joke on the foreigner made her laugh. I smiled.

Sablayan is two miles square; another hacked-out village in a coconut forest. You can't reach the village by roads—there are none. Only boats. It's in the middle of Mindoro, sunrise-pink mountains on the east side, and on the west the South

China Sea. Gradients of turquoise and phosphorescent water illuminate the fish as they idle by. Odors of frying bananas and the pigs that live out back. The air is hot, but blows clean. Even though I sweat more, my hair needs washing only once a week. Not daily as it did back home.

My second day in Sablayan, we walked a mile to the hospital. The building was constructed around an open courtyard of six patient rooms that have a view of the South China Sea. They smelled of burning copra and ocean brine. One nurse stays on duty, a doctor sleeps there, too. No kitchen. A family member must live with each patient and cook meals in the courtyard on piles of wood.

In the first room, a four-year-old boy stood in a squat on a bed. Hands pressed hard against his knees, cheeks puffed, face red and straining. A bizarre mass protruded from his bottom, dancing like the hair of Medusa. "Tapeworms," Doctora said. "I am waiting for medicine. We feed him extra food. He tries to push them out."

"Impressive," I said, the medically-trained equivalent of "Wow!" Toothless women, boiling pots of rice in the courtyard, nodded to Doctora as we left.

We walked to the two-room clinic near our house. Nurse trainees from Manila help Doctora in her clinic. A family of six squeezed into the exam room; coughs echoed against the bare walls. Doctora listened to each chest and mumbled a curt, "Um." I listened and heard bubbling infection. "I get one vial of antibiotics each month," Doctora said to me.

"What if the next family is sick?"

"They wait."

The student nurse sharpened a needle with a file and gave the family their injections. She didn't change the needle. She smiled when I wrinkled my brow. "Doctora has two syringes and two needles," she said. "I only boil and sharpen between families."

I turned to Doctora. "They could get cross infected. That's wrong."

"They don't get sick," Doctora said.

She doesn't examine life with a microscope as I do. She works with what's available in the moment. I need to practice that, to survive in this country of less.

We deliver babies at night by flashlight. Every day I place the batteries in the sun to recharge. They are not single use. Too expensive. Unavailable.

One midnight, frantic banging on the door awakened us. Two women with a baby. Doctora opened the baby's blanket and screeched in her raspy voice. "The hospital. Run." The women ran as she demanded. "They have a bottle of IV fluid there," she said to me.

But I had seen the baby's face—a brief flash of gray. "Why? It's dead."

She gave me a look of yes, stupid, I know. I guess she didn't want to tell them bad news.

Early on, an assistant showed me the other buildings in Eversly-Child. We toured an area where people live after they've tested non-infectious. They call it the negative barrio. Patients can also return to their family homes; they're not prisoners as they were in decades past.

One man tells me how he came here, long ago. "I lived under my family's porch for ten years. Police found me. They pushed me out with a stick. Brought me here. They would not touch me with their hands." Back then they were lepers, forced into the role of pariah, to live apart in leprosariums.

"They don't do that now," I say.

He says that's what they tell him, but he trusts no one outside.

The final building is hiding deep in the trees, long and wooden, like a leftover barrack from the war. This is a scene from the leprosy nightmare I had back home in my comfortable bed, after they told me I'd be coming to this place. Patients are huddled against the wall on metal beds without mattresses; they pull away from me when I approach. Some have bandaged hands and covered faces where bacteria settled, destroying fingers or a nose. That's what leprosy does to bone: it absorbs it.

There's no odor of decay; the skin retracts tightly as bone recedes. I move closer to touch a shoulder or sit for a moment on a bed. They don't really want to see me—visitors are a threat—but I am so different, so blond and fair they nod and allow me to look.

Within weeks of the start of my service, I'd seen tapeworms, dead babies, flattened noses, absorbed bones, and a beauty I'm inadequate to describe. I should not have lamented the lack of a latex glove. But I did.

Cynthia Broze, R.N., MSN, served in the Philippines (1980-82) as a community health and leprosy educator. She is the Clinical Program Coordinator for the Colorectal Cancer Program and the Anorectal Disorders Program at Cedars-Sinai Medical Center. Her book, Nurses of Los Angeles: Uncapping the Mystery, *was published in 2010.*

TERRANCE CLARKE

✦

Zulia Tells a Funny Story

*Humor can convey a darkness too complicated
to express any other way.*

"*Ema Timor susar barak. Teb tebes.*" (The people of Timor suffer greatly. This is true.) Zulia says this, rising and addressing the group. His face is alive in the candlelight. The harsh syllables of his native language, Tetun, bounce off the walls and echo in my ears. This is how most of the stories begin.

"*Nee los tebes,*" echo the men, old and young alike. They sit around the edges of Joâo's small living area on rough-hewn benches or on the dirt floor.

I had two weeks left in training as a part of the fifth Peace Corps Volunteer group in East Timor. We were hosted in the small village community of Balibar. I lived with an older subsistence farmer named Joâo la Costa and his family. During the long evenings, we would sit and tell stories, a practice that had evolved from my practicing language with Joâo.

"*It was the time when the Indonesians were in Timor. I was a young man; I did not have a wife. I did not have a family. It was night, and I was with my friends. I was a little drunk!*" Zulia continues.

"Liar! Drunkard!" yell the older men, who know how much Zulia loves palm wine.

"A little drunk only!" Zulia repeats with fervor.

Zulia lived in the house next to my family's. He was squat and short with a pot belly made entirely of muscle. His dark hair was machete-shaved near his scalp. He had a stretchable, mischievous face with an easy, plump smile. Unlike most of the men in our *aldea*, Zulia had a job in the capital city of Dilli, working with the police to provide security for visiting dignitaries. At home, Zulia usually had one of his three young children held in his oversized arms, but not now.

I had started this evening with a story about a time in America when a police officer had so surprised me that I accidently spit the soda in my mouth all over his uniform. The officer yelled at me, but eventually calmed down. Zulia laughed loudest of all when I did an encore of the spit take, spraying water all over the young boys who huddled on the ground at their elders' feet. Then he grinned, stood, and began to speak.

"I was with two friends. One was small and one very big and fat. We were not allowed to be out in the night. We were frightened when a van pulled up and Indonesian soldiers got out. They yelled, 'Who are you! What are you doing out tonight?'"

In the beginning, there were no stories, just me and João practicing language. Men from our *aldea*, a sharp hilly community of about thirty families, began to join us. They laughed at how badly I spoke, making jokes in words I could not comprehend, but then they would stay and help me with pronunciation. About three weeks in, when I had enough words to sound like a stunned five year old, I told a story about a huge spider I found in my room.

"The spider was so big," I told them, "It yelled at me!" Then I pretended to be a yelling spider.

They loved the yelling spider! We spent that night with my imitating an angry spider and the men howling with laughter. The next night, the story got longer and more ridiculous. Many of the men could do the spider voice better than I could. Near the end, my host father, Joâo, began to talk about a goat that tried to knock him over. His raspy goat voice was perfect. Pretty soon, story nights were the norm, and the crowd began to grow.

"We were scared, and that is true. 'We are just walking home. We live far from here,' we told the soldiers. They did not believe us. They hit us! Hit us! Hit us with their hands and sticks. We would only say we were walking home."

"True! True!" the men in the circle exclaim, pointing and patting the boys on their backs to get them to listen.

"The leader of the Indonesian soldiers got out of the van. 'You all must tell us what you are doing this night,' he said. And we cried! 'Oh god, we are just walking home!' But he did not believe us. 'Put them in the van!' he said." Zulia's imitation of the Indonesian leader is a study in opposites: stiff in movement, snake-sinuous in speech.

Between 1999 and 2001, most of the buildings in East Timor were burned to the ground as the Indonesian occupation force ceded the country to UN-assisted self-rule. As the country burned, the departing soldiers pillaged East Timor, raping and killing as they went. I knew the men of Balibar had lived through terrible things during the twenty-five year occupation. There had been curfews, secret police, torture, and disappearances. As a Peace Corps Volunteer, I had been trained how to handle finding the unspent munitions that often surfaced on their beaches. I had been told who to contact if I found remains or stumbled upon a mass grave. I was not prepared for this.

"Then we were in the van. My little friend is by the back door, then me, then my big fat friend by the driver. The Indonesian

soldier-leader, he is saying, 'We will take you to the camp, and you will not see you family ever, ever.' He is telling us what will happen at the camp. We are driving too fast for night. We were scared, and that is true. My big fat friend, he begins to cry like a little girl. He is shaking. And I am frightened and trying to pray to god for help, but he is shaking too much, and I cannot pray."

Then the laughter begins. I am laughing, too, because Zulia's imitation of trying to pray next to a mountain-sized man who is crying is hilarious. I'm also laughing because I don't know what else to do. Zulia is fully committed to the story now. His hands are in front of his face, and his eyes are dancing.

"'What were you doing tonight!' asks the soldier-leader. 'Oh god, we were just walking home!' Now we are all crying. 'You are all drunken liars! You are not worth the camp!' says the soldier-leader. He puts his foot on my big fat friend and pushes. And my big fat friend pushes me, and I push my little friend. And the back door to the van flies open. We are driving very fast. We fall out into the night. I am yelling, 'Oh god, I will lose the skin on my back!' No! I landed on my little friend. And I am so happy that I have landed on him and not the road."

The room is filled with laughter and cheers now. The men, normally so stoic, are slamming their hands on their knees. João sees the look on my face and begins to shake me by the shoulders pointing at Zulia. Zulia throws his hands up in the air and bends his knees.

"'Oh god!' I am praying, 'Thank you for letting me land on my little friend and not the road!' But then I remember my big fat friend. I look up, and there is my big fat friend, and he is coming down the mountain fast. Bigger! Faster! He hit us! Hit us!"

Zulia lowers his arms now, and the laughter begins to fade. He looks at me, and my host father looks at me. I get it. Zulia and I told the same story: a boy's humorous encounter with the police where no one really got hurt. But it's not the same. We can never be the same. But we can understand.

"*Ema Timor susar barak!*" (The people of Timor suffer greatly.) He ends with this and sits down.

I know that this is true.

Terrance Clarke served in East Timor, 2005-06. He was evacuated when civil unrest led to riots in Dilli. He returned in 2010 to find conditions much improved. He is currently training to get back out into the world and polishing a memoir titled The Very Worst Peace Corps Volunteer in East Timor.

ADRIENNE BENSON SCHERGER

Her American Sister

When it comes to dreams of love and marriage,
history and culture still prevail.

I REMEMBER HER SMILING UP AT ME ONE EVENING. THE LIGHT WAS fading in the sky, and the Dhorpatan hills of Nepal out beyond the village were turning blue in the gathering dark. The stars would be out soon and maybe a moon. She laughed as she swatted the ox with a short stick, urging him into the barn for the night.

"He is my husband," she joked, slapping the black haunches again. "Isn't he handsome?"

She was seventeen, a high-caste girl from a good family. I was barely twenty-two and fresh from a liberal arts college in Oregon. In Peace Corps training, we learned that Nepalese women are demure, that they laugh quietly and keep their eyes downcast. Saraswati was different. She was loud. When she laughed her whole mouth opened, and her eyes crinkled shut. She shouted when she talked. She taught me to curse in Nepalese. She was named for the Goddess of Learning, a Hindu deity who rides a swan and consorts with Brahma. I realized quickly I was the only one who used her name. To her family she was *kanchi*, youngest daughter, and when she married, she'd be *srimati*, wife. Names meant little. Even my own was forgotten. For two years I was "Aasa": a common Nepalese moniker, my real name awkward and hard in their mouths.

Saraswati was older than most of the unmarried girls in Pula, the tiny mountain hamlet high in the Annapurna foothills where we lived, but her twice-failed exams made her dreams of university impossible. So she woke early, casting aside her blankets and dipping her thick hands in the cold red mud that she washed daily over her family's earthen floor. She gathered wood before I even woke up, started the fire, made tea, sifted the rice free of stones. She banged on my door every morning at dawn, "*Aasa, didi!*" she'd yell, "*Chai kanay!*" She'd set a hot metal cup of sweet tea, thick with water buffalo milk, on the stoop outside my door, and dash off again, her flip-flop soles flashing as she ran, her full, dark arms gathering her sheet of black hair back and up in her favorite purple barrette.

Saraswati asked me questions. In the early afternoons when the morning work was finished, and dinner had yet to be started, she huddled on my doorstep, resting her chin on her knees, and hugging her sturdy thighs close to her chest. She was round and full; womanly, and her childlike posture was disconcerting. She wondered why I wasn't married. I told her in America all marriages are love matches and that twenty-two was too young to marry. She laughed, awestruck. Later, she told me her best friend had hanged herself when her parents denied her a love match and instead promised her to an older man who lived in a village two days walk away.

Saraswati took me to the first wedding I attended in the village. The bride was one of my English students, eleven-year-old Ram Maya. When we crowded into the narrow room where Ram Maya was getting dressed, Saraswati took charge.

"She can't get married in a t-shirt! Someone get her a *choli!*"

It was Saraswati who made Ram Maya switch tops with a sullen girl I'd never seen. Ram Maya sobbed the whole time. Dutifully she lifted her braids so her sister could button the tight *choli*, the sari blouse, up her back. She stood ramrod straight while her crimson sari was wrapped around her, the *pallu* draped over her head. She didn't try to stop the tears. When it was time to lead her out to the ceremony where she'd meet her husband for the first time, Ram Maya filed past me. She was so close I could feel her ragged breath on my arm.

Saraswati held my hand the next day when we went back to the see the *janti*, the procession that would lead Ram Maya forever out of Pula and into her husband's village. Ram Maya was shrieking when we got there. Her family grasped at her hands and pulled her to where her husband waited. Ram Maya's feet clawed at the earth beneath her. Saraswati whispered; "Brides are supposed to do that. It would offend her parents if she wasn't sad to leave them." But her grip tightened around my arm.

I taught in Pula for two years. The months I spent in the village were contrasted with my trips into Kathmandu where I drank beer, smoked cigarettes, and flirted shamelessly with the male Peace Corps Volunteers in from their far-flung sites. Saraswati had no idea of my other life. In Pula I never spoke of Kathmandu, of dancing all night long in smoky discos. My behavior would have shocked her. I never told her I wondered if I'd ever fall in love, that I yearned for marriage as strongly as she dreaded it.

I laughed when Saraswati told me that if she didn't like the man her parents promised her to, she would run away to India. I high-fived her when she swore she'd hit any husband who beat her. Who was I to remind her of her fate? We both knew we would be spun away from here, inevitably and intractably. We both knew that our intersection was a blink in the vast breadth of our lives. I was her American sister, she my Nepalese *behini*, but only for an instant.

I was ready to leave Pula after two years. My future tugged at me, home beckoned. Saraswati and I both cried on my final afternoon. But when I strode down the dirt path out of the village that last time, I didn't look back. My volunteer years there had filled me with confidence and courage; if I could make a life in Pula, I could do anything I wanted. The world sparkled before me like a shell, opening wide.

It's been thirteen years since I last saw Saraswati. In the meantime I married and had two sons, made a life in three different cities. Years ago I received a letter from her older brother. He wrote that Saraswati had married just after I left. She moved to a village to the West, a place nestled in the curve of those same Dhorpatan hills that I used to watch darkening from my door in Pula. I was glad had I missed her wedding, missed her stumbling through her *janti*, missed her tears.

Sometimes I dream about Pula. I see the sunlight slanting on the poinsettia flowers, the mud brown houses, and the students lined up outside the village school where I taught. In my dreams, I never see Saraswati as she was; a girl folded up on my doorstep; a girl rising with the roosters to help her mother; a young woman terrified of her inescapable future. But sometimes, just before I wake, I see Pula floating away below me, my dream panning out like a movie, and I hear a familiar whoop from a hilltop in the distance. When I look, when I try to find her, all I can see is a shadow hovering there, arms outstretched, face tipped towards the sky. Not Saraswati at all, not her. Just a bird-girl, wings cocked to catch the updrafts, soaring away above the mountains, her song like laughter, captured in the breeze.

Adrienne Benson Scherger served in Nepal from 1992-94. She is a freelance writer and mother of two young sons. She is currently working on her first book, a memoir of an African girlhood titled I Never Had a Birdcage Hairdo. *Her story is the winner of the Jason and Lucy Greer Foundation for the Arts Prize.*

PART FIVE

Sustainable Peace

JERR BOSCHEE

✦

And the Light in Their Eyes Would Begin to Die

Namaste all over again.

JANUARY 1995: NARWANA

The village remains, but its boundaries have exploded. Dozens of shops bustle down the road toward the school. A model town grows to the north. Motorcycles shoulder through the streets, and television antennas leap from every other rooftop.

But...

In the older part of town, the lanes still wander quietly, then disappear. Women sit comfortably outdoors on *charpois*, surrounded by their children. Solitary pigs snort past them toward unseen destinations. Cows pick their way across broken cobblestones. Occasional students race homeward.

As the day wanes, the sky reaches down, all reds and golds and orange, inches above my head. Chants from the temple drift across the rooftops, and spices scent the air from hundreds of kitchens. Families gather...and a warm glow slips over my memories.

I lived here for two years. I came of age here. From 1968 to 1970 I served as a Peace Corps Volunteer teaching English

as a Second Language to sixth and seventh grade boys. I was
the first Caucasian to live in the village since the bloody mas-
sacres of Hindus and Muslims that birthed the nations of India
and Pakistan in 1947. Me. A naïve, twenty-three-year-old kid
from suburban Minneapolis.

August 1968: Narwana

The Peace Corps jeep dropped me in Narwana shortly after
noon one stifling August day, off-loaded my sea trunk, and
disappeared in a swirl of sand and heat. One hundred miles
northwest of Delhi, halfway to the border of West Pakistan.

Alone.

And then, emerging from the shade trees on the school
grounds, came a slight, middle-aged man—Baldev—who
would become my friend and mentor. A teacher and community elder, a Brahmin. He offered me chai, then offered me his
home. And the adventure of a lifetime began.

The next morning, as I walked with Baldev toward the
school where I'd be teaching, hundreds of townspeople fell in
behind me. For days, whenever I started to speak, everybody
leaned forward to hear what I'd say. School ended in early
afternoon because of the triple-digit heat, and one morning
a traveling yogi asked me to feel his wrist and verify for a
school assembly that he could stop his heartbeat, then serenely
allowed groups of husky students to strain at opposite ends of
a bulky rope wrapped around his neck.

And the boys...

They were eleven, then, and twelve, learning English for
the first time. I taught them on dirt plots, in sheds without
walls, in my home. Scruffy little kids with brown uniforms,
sparkling eyes and ear-splitting grins.

I chattered with them in broken Hindi and broken English,
sent them scurrying on errands, brought them books. They
called me "Mr. Bosch," and one of them, the smallpox

freckled son of an untouchable, teased me unmercifully about "Many-apples," Minnesota.

I quickly fell in love with them and yearned to unveil the world beyond their village. I wanted to give them hope... because hope, in village India, in the 1960s, scarcely existed. Young men entering their teens would inevitably realize that the poverty bearing down on their parents would have no mercy on the next generation: And the light in their eyes would begin to die.

So I opened a library in my home, pinned huge maps to the walls, filled my lesson plans with stories about the greater world, took more than fifty of the boys on a three-day trip to Delhi. They'd never been out of the village before.

I coaxed an optometrist from a nearby city to visit the school and do eye exams for more than four hundred students, then raised money from my father's Lion's Club in Minnesota to buy glasses for more than a hundred—and watched all but three discard them within months because glasses were a sign of weakness.

And then, near the end of my tour, I chose ten boys to join me on a month-long trip through southern and western India, and I asked my friend Surya for help. I needed to visit the parents, to ask their permission, and I wanted Surya to be my interpreter because I didn't have the language skills I needed to tell them what I hoped for their sons, why I wanted to take them so far from their families.

I can still see those one-room homes, none of them lit by more than a kerosene lamp. Dirt floors and hardly any furniture, yet always the offer of food and drink. I can still see the hopeful eyes of the parents, the boys sitting quietly nearby. And I can still feel the mother gripping my arm as I prepared to leave, whispering words I will never forget: "He is your son now, Mr. Bosch."

We rented a train car and lived in it for a month: Fifty-three students, five Peace Corps Volunteers, five Indian teachers, three cooks and 1,000 pounds of flour. The first leg of the journey went from Delhi to Madras, forty-eight hours straight south, with coal dust billowing through the open windows, cooks leaping onto the platform at each stop to boil tea and cook *chapatis,* vendors poking their heads through the windows crying "Chai-chai-chai! Coffee-coffee-coffee! Soda-soda-soda!"

We took the boys into the ocean at Madras, into the tropical forests of Kerala, into the Bombay metropolis, into the desert caves of Rajasthan, and into the Taj Mahal, the soul of India.

We took them home.

And then we left.

January 1995: Narwana

For twenty-five years, I dreamed of returning. Literally, at least once a month. Sometimes in color, sometimes in black and white, sometimes with my parents, sometimes my children.

Finally, my oldest daughter, Sarah, turned twenty-one, and I turned fifty. So we decided to take three weeks together, just the two of us. A week in Nepal, a week in Thailand, and a week in India.

I'd lost track of the boys, but hoped to find a few of them again. I needed to know what happened after I left. I needed to know if I'd made any difference in their lives. I needed to know if they'd purchased glasses for their children.

On New Year's Day 1995, Sarah and I arrived in the village, and Surya took us immediately to his home for a welcoming party. When I first met him in 1968, he was twenty-three, my age, finishing college and dreaming about graduate school. Along with Baldev, he became my lifeline. A year later I wrote about him to my father. I knew Dad had a close friend and business associate who'd been born in India and had become a successful businessman in Arizona. Dad and Mr. Ohri decided to pay for Surya's graduate school tuition, room and board. When I embraced him again in 1995, Surya had become Dr. S.P. Gupta, a college professor with an educated, professionally employed wife and two college-bound children.

More than thirty members of Surya's extended family had gathered to greet us. The chai and cakes were ready, in abundance, and the memories started to flow. Time disappeared.

Suddenly, two of my former students were at the door!

We hugged and started talking excitedly, trying to cover twenty-five years in half an hour. And before long we found ourselves walking toward the school at the other end of town, moving slowly through the heart of the village, discovering the motorcycles and the television antennas along the way. Crowds began to follow, just as they had during my earliest days so long ago, and another former student roared up to us on a Kawasaki. My daughter walked quietly beside me, taking it all in.

As we neared the village center, I looked to the right, expecting to see the school across an open field, but shops and homes had filled the horizon. More people joined us, and when we reached the edge of town I quickened my step. The school began to appear. First the grounds, then the outlines of the buildings themselves. With each step, my past came rushing toward me: And then I stopped.

They were waiting for me at the front gate, garlands ready...

My former students...

Twenty-eight of them...

I blinked, then blinked again. I couldn't see. My companions urged me onward, and I stumbled to life, kept walking, Sarah beside me. The "boys" were lined up to greet me, one at a time. As I approached the first man, he slipped a floral garland over my head and another over Sarah's, then looked at me with hands raised and palms together.

"Namaste," he said. "Welcome."

Each of the twenty-eight men did the same, and as they greeted me and told me their names, I could see their youthful faces peering at me through weathered skin and memory.

For years I'd wondered: Did my two years make a difference? Kaku Ram, unbidden, told me they did. Molar Ram appeared in the morning mist the next day, with his children. Dharm Pal took me to his father. And Baldev smiled and told me they'd been telling stories about me for twenty-five years.

That evening, at a celebratory dinner, the "boys" gave me an engraved sculpture. It sits on the mantelpiece in my living room.

Ashok Kumar committed suicide…

But ten are shopkeepers, two are teachers, three are bankes…

And Krishan Dev, the untouchable's son, outranks them all. He's the district magistrate.

Jerr Boschee served in India (India 54) from 1968-70. In 2003, he and Chris Klose founded Peace Corps Encore! (now known as Encore! Service Corps International) to send former Peace Corps Volunteers back into service on short-term assignments that match their professional expertise with specific social needs. He has been an advisor to social entrepreneurs in the United States and elsewhere for more than thirty years, delivering lectures in more than forty states and a dozen countries, and has long been recognized as one of the founders of the social enterprise movement worldwide. He is currently Professor of the Practice of Social Enterprise at Carnegie Mellon University and Board chair for an international NGO that encourages teenage social entrepreneurs in more than twenty countries

Acknowledgements

THE HEART OF PEACE CORPS AT 50 BEATS IN THESE STORIES from Asia and the Pacific: *Even the Smallest Crab Has Teeth.* And so I would first like to thank the contributors whose work appears in this volume, the last of the four in the set of 50 Years of Amazing Peace Corps Stories. I want thank them especially for introducing me, and all others who enter here, to the people they met and came to know during their time of service. They have pushed wider the boundaries of my world—how it has changed and stayed the same—and broadened the context of my own time as a Volunteer in India.

I would like to thank Chris Richardson and his PushIQ team for creating a website portal back in 2007 through which contributors could safely pass their stories. Chris has brought his artistic talent not only to the project's website, www. peacecorpsat50.org, but also to the creation of all four covers in this collection.

Working behind the scenes as a Spirit Guide through the thicket that is the publishing world, Susan Brady holds the modest title of "production director." In fact, without her help and instruction, these books would have been something much less. Her presence on this project gave Travelers' Tales/Solas House the reassurance it needed that the books we proposed would meet their high publishing standards. I cannot thank her enough.

Thanks also to Howie Severson whose interior layout makes this and all the other books in this series easy on the eyes and a pleasure to read. His professionalism eliminated any worries that the layout would be less than elegant and clear.

As the stories in this book suggest, the recollections of each Volunteer rise from unique perceptions, told in the first person singular. But no Volunteer takes on a country and assignment singularly. A shared purpose with fellow Volunteers, especially those from the same training group, lends the experience lightness and possibility. The members of India 45—in particular my site mate Maggie Harding—gave my efforts an anchor and helped engrave the experience on my self. I thank them all.

Likewise, I never felt alone in the singular process of editing this one book of four because of the work of Aaron Barlow—an invaluable second set of eyes on this manuscript—Pat and Bernie Alter, and Jay Chen on the other three. Ten hands are so much better than two.

Finally, I thank Kate Browne who has watched over me as I have watched over this project since its first glimmer. I am a most fortunate person to have had such companions on a journey that that began in 1967, one which fills me still with wonder.

Story Acknowledgments

Acknowledgements

"The Mosquito Bar" by Michael Schmicker published with permission from the author. Copyright © 2011 by Michael Schmicker.

"At the Foot of Mount Yasur" by Usha Alexander published with permission from the author. Copyright © 2011 by Usha Alexander.

"Handsin's Story" by Havard Bauer published with permission from the author. Copyright © 2011 by Havard Bauer.

"The Boarding House" by Farrar Atkinson published with permission from the author. Copyright © 2011 by Farrar Atkinson.

"Parmesan and Politics" by Michael Levy published with permission from the author. Copyright © 2011 by Michael Levy.

"The Week of the Jackal" by Marsha Martin West published with permission from the author. Copyright © 2011 by Marsha Martin West.

"A Different Kind of House Guest" by Lili Yocom published with permission from the author. Copyright © 2011 by Lili Yocom.

"The River at My Door" by Lela Lentz published with permission from the author. Copyright © 2011 by Lela Lentz.

"Foreigner! Forever" by Lisa McCallum published with permission from the author. Copyright © 2011 by Lisa McCallum.

"A Latex Glove" by Cynthia Broze published with permission from the author. Copyright © 2011 by Cynthia Broze.

"Zulia Tells a Funny Story" by Terrance Clarke published with permission from the author. Copyright © 2011 by Terrance Clarke.

"Her American Sister" by Adrienne Benson Scherger published with permission from the author. Copyright © 2011 Adrienne Benson Scherger.

"And the Light in Their Eyes Would Begin to Die" by Jerr Boschee published with permission from the author. Copyright © 2011 by Jerr Boschee.

Special thanks to
The Jason and Lucy Greer Foundation
for the Arts for their generous support of
the Peace Corps@50 Project.

About the Editor

JANE ALBRITTON, AWARD-WINNING JOURNALIST AND TEACHER, signed up for Peace Corps training not because she thought she might save the world, but because she was a Texan who had been a Girl Scout. She felt confident that as someone who viewed both talking and camping as excellent pastimes, she would be good at working with others to solve problems and be O.K. living without modern amenities. Indeed, as an Applied Nutrition Volunteer in rural India (1967-1969), she found that her native inclination to strike up a conversation with anyone about anything at all—kitchen gardens, cures for lice, sari cloth, train schedules—as well as the outdoor skills she had learned as a Scout served her well.

After returning to Dallas, she earned a master's degree in English, taught freshmen composition at Southern Methodist University, and served as the writing specialist for the SMU School of Law. She also created Tiger Enterprises, a company for writing, editing, and instruction. Fifteen years later, she followed her partner Kate Browne, professor of anthropology, to Colorado State University in Fort Collins, Colorado. There she has taught in the Department of Journalism and Technical Communication, and it was there she met Peace Corps pioneers Maury Albertson, professor emeritus of engineering, and his longtime associate and friend Pauline Birky-Kreutzer. Both are now gone, but they staked a claim on the origins of the Peace Corps that remains firmly fixed in the collective memory of Northern Colorado.

In 2007, having recently passed 60 and noting that the 50th anniversary of the Peace Corps would soon arrive, she decided the time was right to collect stories from Returned Volunteers and with them create four books of stories from the four regions where Volunteers have served. With an amazing team of collaborators and supporters, she has now completed the second big volunteer project of her life. It, too, is good.

When not writing, editing, teaching, or herding Peace Corps stories into print, she writes about travel, art, and food. Her stories have appeared in *the Northern Colorado Business Report, Edible Front Range Magazine, American Way Magazine, Southwest Art,* and *Travelers' Tales: Hawaii.* And when not working, she can be found riding her horse Paniolo in the foothills of the Rockies or working out the fingering for a blues melody on her guitar. She is profoundly grateful for the life she has been given and for the opportunity to celebrate what she sees as her country's best initiative for peace.

Jane Albritton lives in Fort Collins, Colorado.